D1098127

JACOBSEN
of CARLSBERG

JACOBSEN
of CARLSBERG

Brewer and Philanthropist

BY

Kristof Glamann

TRANSLATED BY
GEOFFREY FRENCH

GYLDENDAL

Jacobsen of Carlsberg

© 1991, 2011 Kristof Glamann og Gyldendal A/S

Translated from the Danish: *BRYGGEREN*,

J.C. Jacobsen på Carlsberg (Gyldendal, 1990)

by Geoffrey French

Special edition 2011

This book is composed and printed in Garamond by

GB-sats, Copenhagen

Printed by Ednasprint

Printed in Slovenia 2011

ISBN 978-87-00-79978-4

To Kirsten

Table of Contents

J. C. Jacobsen's "Roman" friends were a circle of artists whom he met in Rome when he visited Italy along with his son Carl in the summer of 1862. From one of them, the Norwegian-Danish sculptor Olav Glosimodt, the Brewer commissioned in 1877 a relief in ivory of which a limited number of copies were made and used as gifts for a chosen few. The copy in the Carlsberg Museum is reproduced here in less than actual size.

The block of stone

The family was in an uproar. The stern, unbending father had forced his son to break off his engagement. „When I see how Carl looks I could burst out crying," wrote a niece who was staying with the Jacobsens at Carlsberg, „and Emilie, poor creature, is sitting there brokenhearted at the parsonage [she was daughter of the rural dean of Karlebo] and may not see him, may not come to Copenhagen, but is barbarously condemned to be sunk in despair without being able to relieve her feelings by telling her troubles to someone of her own age." The niece had recently become engaged herself and was naturally on the side of the young people. „All the members of the family are the very images of sorrow," she wrote in a letter to her fiancé in Jutland, „except for Uncle," and then added for emphasis: „that block of stone."

That block of stone is what this book is about.

The father got his way, but it was not easy. How he did it will be related later, as will the consequences this brought, which were vast. In fact the young lady's invective was not badly chosen. For J.C. Jacobsen was quite immovable once he had made his mind up on a matter. There was no getting round him. There still is none. Why is a question to which I shall come back. But first one or two words about this book and my own involvement in it.

I have Jacobsen around me every day. Quite literally. Hewn in marble or cast in bronze, he is a part of my surroundings. He steals unobtrusively from his niche in the Carlsberg Foundation boardroom, and when I go up the staircase of the Foundation building he stands on the landing leading to the abode of the Royal Danish Academy of Sciences and Letters. I meet him in the main hallway of the administration building at the breweries, and encounter him again in full figure before the entrance to the Carlsberg Laboratory on Old Carlsberg Road. When business takes me to the Foundation's museum at Fredriksborg Castle, he receives me at the entrance. His bust features in the portrait gallery of Copenhagen Town Hall as a reminder of one of the city's great sons. He held the rank of captain in the civic guard, a title which he prized highly. His close friend Frants Djørup, a physician, once asked him why he clung to what he, Djørup, felt to be a somewhat droll – indeed antiquated – title. Jacobsen replied gravely: „I want to make it clear that I am a citizen, sprung from the class of citizens." We should take him seriously. Our having recently passed the two hundredth anniversary of the French Revolution may be all the more reason for elucidating what a man of Jacobsen's time read into the concept of citizenship. Le citoyen Jacobsen.

I live at the top of Valby Hill, cheek by jowl with the life's work of J.C. Jacobsen. Brewer Jacobsen came out to Bjerregaarden in 1846 and bought land on which to build his modern brewery, which he had decided after much pondering to locate outside the city close by the railway which was under construction through the grounds of the estate. He named the brewery after his son Carl, and the bjerg (hill) was where it was situated: hence „Carlsberg". Like all brewers Jacobsen kept horses, both for the brewery and for riding. He rode himself, and made use of the entire terrain extending down to the open sea. They were broad acres in those days. From his terrace he could see the lighthouse at Stevns Klint. More parcelling of the Bjerregaarden estate occurred later on, when the West Cemetery was laid out, but that is a different matter – except perhaps for the fact that this is the resting place of another „block of stone", one of the few of the Captain's contemporaries who ventured to cross swords with him, Professor Emil Chr. Hansen, head of the physiology department of the Carlsberg Laboratory. The Brewer himself was laid to rest in the crypt of the nearby Jesus Church, where his son established a chapel for the family.

The brewery itself remains there still, as does the Brewer's own mansion and garden grounds. Recently we took the old plant out of its „mothballs" and put it in order. It is one of the best-preserved early industrial plants in Denmark, unusual by virtue of its location, surrounded as it is by modern high-technology installations with an inbuilt potential. The Carlsberg Breweries are one of Denmark's great workplaces, and to stroll around the site is somewhat akin to leafing through a history book. It is scarcely coincidence that the first great account of Danish industrial architecture, Industrial Buildings, published by Jørgen Sestoft in 1979, devotes so much attention to it.

The milieu has become a part of me. It has fallen to me along with others to manage the heritage handed down to us by Jacobsen and his son, and this has been my life for a fair number of years. As I have indicated, history is still a living part of the business culture of Carlsberg even if not, of course, one which engages our attention from day to day. The breweries are world-wide in scope and their horizons are future-orientated. The Foundation's work, too, is of the here and now and tomorrow. Nevertheless, amidst all the rush of business I have paused now and then among the monuments of the past and asked myself: Jacob Christian Jacobsen, you who started all this, who were you really? He used to sign himself not with his first name but simply Jacobsen – even when writing to his wife and son, as was the custom of the time – or J.C. Jacobsen. Who was the man concealed behind the strong, stylised features and the Roman toga hewn from stone?

Several times before I have made some attempt to answer this question, but each time have had to put my studies aside because of pressure of other affairs. I state this without any undertones of regret. Most of the book has been written in two rounds. The first was in the summer of 1987, following upon a scrutiny of the correspondence between Nanna Rygaard and Jens Brask, very kindly placed at my disposal by Mrs Grethe Stig Iuul. This set me off, but I was interrupted by an invitation, which took me quite aback, to move into the Brewer's own residence, which had become vacant on the death of the astronomer Bengt Strömgren. After much cogitation I decided to decline the honour with thanks, but then I had to collect my thoughts a little. To have been faced with the opportunity of having Jacobsen drawn so intimately into my own life brought after-effects resembling what doctors call post-operative shock. The second round of writing came to pass during the summer of 1989, when everything suddenly fell into place to make a number of successive weeks available for writing.

Now I have completed an opus which was written wholly con amore. No one set me the task: no external cause forced me to it. It is purely and simply the result of an obsession. Call it the riddle of the

Sphinx.

Jacobsen was reserved by nature, and he himself felt this. He kept no diaries and was devoid of any urge to confide and confess in the grand style. But there are other roads one may travel. He was a splendid letter-writer, lucid and usually brief. He wrote his letters himself in a hand which Johanne Luise Heiberg, the grande dame of the Danish theatre, flatteringly called the „most attractive" hand she knew. And the postal authorities in little Copenhagen were certainly acquainted with it. When Jacobsen decided to assist Holger Drachmann, the poet, he insisted on anonymity and got a friend to deliver the letters au main. The letters are an important source for anyone seeking a deeper insight into the Brewer's life.

It has been vital for me to draw a picture of J.C. Jacobsen in which his conceptual world and fundamental ideas come to life. I wanted to get to know his personality and qualities of character, and I wanted also to offer a candid view of his marriage and other family relationships without descending to mere sensation-mongering. The literature of reminiscence does anything but contribute to our knowledge of the relationship between J.C. and Laura. The accounts of friends dwell most especially on the pleasant hours spent in the family's company. They do not penetrate into the private sphere and would doubtless regard any attempt to do so as unseemly. Some of the „official" works border on the hagiographic, while others maintain a considerable distance from the principal character. It is this distance that I want to reduce.

„You know that for choice it is my habit to let my feelings express themselves in deeds," he wrote to his son on one occasion. When it comes to the point, his deeds are the most tangible evidences we have. They are the warp of the tapestry from which the portrait of him is to be woven. This is the background against which his own utterances and those of others have to be evaluated. This is what I have tried to do, and I have felt it important also to view Jacobsen and his work in its wider setting at both the national Danish and the European level.

It goes without saying that my biography of Jacobsen bears the marks of my profession. I have deliberately projected J.C. Jacobsen into the retina of our own day. My object has been to reflect his life and work into our own experiences, not only my personal ones in the business concern which he established and the Foundation which he instituted but also into the updated sum of the knowledge possessed by historians today of the three quarters of a century spanned by his work.

Viewed thus, there are aspects of him which are inextricably rooted in his own time, while others appear very close to us and indeed can almost be injected into the present-day debate as contributions to it. Finally, his life and personality contain elements which to my eye are woven of the same timeless stuff that is to be found in novels of drama and romance. These are not the least fascinating aspects. Reality does not fall short of fiction in this family chronicle.

Two epochs of opposing temper collide in the 19th century. Jacobsen is marked by both of them. On the one hand he was drawn to a former age then vanishing, characterised by local markets, empirical production and the ties of guild and government. Pulling him in the opposite direction was a new kind of entrepreneurial spirit, waxing vigorous in the winds of economic liberalisation. It was rooted in new techniques and knowledge, new organisational forms; it acted in the broad markets created by urbanisation and the expansion of the transport system; it did not feel bound to a particular calling but sought to wrest a livelihood wherever chance might offer. Investments were valued in proportion to their yield. The majority of entrepreneurs in the new age were not trained to a craft but to business. Few of them were engineers or technicians.

Carl Jacobsen has left us a description of his father's encounter with one of the representatives of the new age, one of J.C. Jacobsen's competitors, a stock exchange magnate and, in Jacobsen's words, a „moneyed plebeian" who, while not himself a trained brewer, had founded a brewery in order to make money. Carlsberg had just reduced the price of its beer, and this competitor came along with a view to discussing a common pricing policy. He argued that at the lower price the brewery could not pay. It would be better to put one's money into bonds, an idea which Jacobsen found pricelessly amusing. The poor man had built a brewery but would now rather put his money into the funds: how contemptible!

J.C. Jacobsen was and remained a brewer. He chose to dwell at his workplace alongside his fellow-workers all his life: this was the master-and-man tradition from the days of the guilds. In relation to his employees he was an old-fashioned patriarch. *L'oeil du maître* watched over everything, assisted by a works manager.

And he was likewise old-fashioned in his scepticism vis-à-vis the many new joint stock companies which saw the light of day in the 19th century. He believed that they were run for the short-term profit of the shareholders, which led to the milking of the companies and a deterioration of their products. This outlook was undoubtedly a factor which contributed to the testamentary dispositions he made placing his breweries in the hands of a foundation, the Carlsberg Foundation, with the additional stipulation that they were never to be merged with any other breweries.

On the latter point posterity has not complied. There have been two amalgamations with others. The first was in 1902-03, when Ottilia and Carl Jacobsen made over the New Carlsberg breweries to the already-existing Foundation and simultaneously established the New Carlsberg Foundation alongside it. This donation paved the way for the subsequent fusion of the two Carlsberg brewery establishments. The second occasion was in 1970, when Carlsberg and The United Breweries/Tuborg came together in a joint stock company with the Foundation as principal shareholder. This event resulted from the desire for a strengthened position abroad in the light of the emergence of new European markets.

Another consideration that made the foundation an attractive model was Jacobsen's implicit faith in product development based on research. This mode of thinking, which is wholly accepted today, was unusual in the last century. There are very few examples, if any, of a 19th century entrepreneur's opening a true research laboratory, as Jacobsen did in 1875, charged with the task of studying the basic processes of production. The laboratory was incorporated into the just-established Carlsberg Foundation the following year and got off to a flying start that gave it an international status.

Its theoretical advances were such as allowed of being turned immediately into results that were tangible. For example, in 1883 Carlsberg was the first brewery in the world to be able to base its production on pure cultivated yeast. This was a reform that removed one of the most important obstacles which had stood in the way of quality control of beer production. Such control could now be instituted on a large scale.

It was Jacobsen's ambition to be a paragon of his craft and its leading figure. Internationally he wanted to be one of the élite. His horizon was European. Every year he went travelling. When summer came knocking at the door he would set off with the regularity of a migrating bird, constantly on the lookout for new ideas and new technology. Impulses from abroad would be tested and adapted to those at home. In the 1870s and 1880s the innovative tide flowed in the opposite direction. The name of Carlsberg became known far and wide, thanks especially to its research. Little Valby got its name into the microbiological world atlas. Jacobsen finished up as Altmeister in the coterie of Europe's leading brewers. Many of them became his personal friends. They met at congresses and exhibitions, wrote for trade journals, made study visits to one another and exchanged staff. This very capacity of his for capturing and manipulating the impulses of the age, coupled with the will to adapt himself and react resolutely to its challenges, form the key to the understanding of J.C. Jacobsen's success. This was displayed not only in the 1840s, when he shook off the straitjacket of the city and took the plunge with a novel product to which by careful nursing and brilliant marketing he gave a profile that distinguished it clearly from the brands of other producers.

In 1867 he again showed what resources he was able to draw on. Catastrophe in the form of fire had devastated the brewery, but during the course of the summer he managed not only to rebuild the plant and thus maintain deliveries uninterrupted but also to incorporate advanced technology and plan for the development of new products.

Perhaps Jacobsen faced his greatest and most critical challenge in the 1880s. This decade was a watershed in many respects, as we now know. Fast-growing urban populations with high purchasing power all over the world – in Western Europe and the United States – stimulated and encouraged the marketing of standardised, mass-produced foodstuffs. In the case of breweries, for example, the selling of brewery-bottled beer contrasted with the old system whereby the beer was sold by the cask to beer-bottlers, who then handled the actual retail sales to the public.

From this period of revolutionary change emerged a few large enterprises many of which still exist today. From the cost standpoint they enjoyed the advantages of large scale. They served a market which was no longer local but regional and national, with a new distribution system built into it and sales in which advertising became a very important factor. Carl Jacobsen had much feeling for this new style. J.C., on the other hand, found it difficult to adjust himself without at the same time straining his principles. His exertions during the 1880s, however, were marked by great tenacity of purpose and intense energy. His position as market leader was threatened at one point, not least by competition from his son, but he recaptured and enlarged his share. It was during these years, moreover, that he laid down a long-term strategy for the Carlsberg Breweries which showed itself fruitful even after his death.

This vigorous effort followed in the wake of a period when his patronage had developed to cover a very broad front and when he assumed large fixed financial obligations, towards the Foundation for example, and towards the Frederiksborg Museum. The word „patron" was one which he did not bandy about. Civic sense covers it better. In England it was called „public spirit", and that was an expression he took to. Wealth laid him under obligation, and he acknowledged a debt to science and research. Furthermore he felt a desire to strengthen the national self-esteem after Denmark's defeat at the hands of Prussia and Austria in the war of 1864. The museum in the rebuilt castle of Frederiksborg was to be a house of cultural and national history with a didactic purpose.

His distrust of his son had been smouldering for a long time. It went right back to the 1860s. It accelerated in the early 1880s and it underlay the decision embodied in Jacobsen's will in 1882 to make over his breweries to the Carlsberg Foundation after his death. Matters came to an open breach between father and son, followed by a bitter struggle which took a heavy toll on him. „A black shadow hangs over the evening of my life," he wrote to Frants Djørup, his physician friend. His great need for achievement remained undiminished, and he pressed on with new initiatives on more or less every front: „Jacobsen never rests, always building and scheming, knowing nothing of Sundays and holidays." So runs a description of him by one of his colleagues in these later years. Self-activity was now and always the medicine which the Brewer was accustomed to prescribe for himself when under strain.

One spring afternoon in 1882 Carl sent some of his men over to his father's residence with two cartloads of furniture, paintings, books etc., all of them gifts which he had received over the years but now wished to keep no longer. The men been instructed to leave the articles in the entrance hall or, if they were not allowed to do so, then to put everything on the lawn outside, perhaps unharnessing the horses quickly and leaving the carts behind. „Then my father can keep those as well."

His father was not at home. Everything was delivered peacefully, but in the evening J.C. Jacobsen went to visit Emil Chr. Hansen in the laboratory. He talked for a long time, talked and talked. It was one of the rare occasions when Jacobsen tried to open his heart to an outsider, an employee into the bargain. He deplored the high-pressure brewery operations of his son. „Then came a sigh," noted Hansen in his diary, „and I felt sympathy for the old man."

The block of stone was beginning to crack.

„Jack Puddle"

A couple of years prior to his death, J.C. Jacobsen gave a lecture to the Danish Technical Association entitled „The Brewing Industry's Progress during the Past Fifty Years". It was both a retrospect and a professional testament. He also had the lecture, which was printed in the Association's journal, translated into French and sent it to Louis Pasteur in Paris, who read it with great interest, underlined some of the passages and kept it among his papers. Today it lies in the Bibliothèque Nationale in Paris. The scope of the lecture was European, with its emphasis on the Nordic region and Central Europe, while England, whose advances had taken place mainly during an earlier period, was omitted from the account. The half-century had revolutionised the brewing industry. In fact, in Jacobsen's view, there was no other branch of industry which had experienced anything like it.

At the beginning of the century, beer manufacturing everywhere in Europe was in a state of profound crisis. It was in the trough of the wave. In the Middle Ages and during the Renaissance, beer had commanded much esteem. It was regarded as the wine of the Nordic countries and stood in high favour everywhere. Even at princely tables beer was enjoyed. However, increasing luxury caused wine to acquire a more important place in consumption at the expense of beer. The growing indulgence in distilled spirits worked in the same direction. Beer gradually lost significance as a wine-like drink and became reduced to an ever simpler and thinner soft beverage for quenching the thirst. Its diminished value and importance brought a corresponding loss of care in its manufacture. This linkage between changes in consumption patterns and production reveals itself in many parts of Europe, including Denmark, which had been one of the typical beer-drinking regions from the dawn of time.

In his lecture to the Technical Association, Jacobsen laid the blame for the poor state of beer manufacturing in Denmark in the late 18th and early 19th centuries on the „abominable guild and rotation systems". In this he was referring to a scheme imposed in Copenhagen by the municipal authorities and the government in concert with the brewers' guild in 1739 after several earlier attempts. It lasted until the abolition of the brewers' guild and the liberalisation of the economy in 1805.

„Rotation" was what we would today call a quota system or sales cartel. The sales office was located in the guild premises, where it received and kept account of orders for beer from customers, households, bottlers or innkeepers, and shared out the brewing of beer between the various brewery establishments in turn, on a rota system. The scheme, which also went by the name of „the roster", or „brewing by roster", meant that the customer had to put up with receiving his beer from whichever brewery had its name at the top of the sales office roster board for the next week. Prices and discounts were fixed and resulted from agreements reached between guild, municipal authorities and government. The cartel covered mainly the then-current types of brown ale – all beer in the pre-industrial age was top-fermented beer. These current types had in fact been the object of price regulation by the authorities since the Middle Ages for the very reason that they formed an item of daily fare.

Towards the end of the 18th century, attacks on rotation and the guild became increasingly clamorous, and after press freedom was introduced the public did not mince words. In verse and prose the Copenhagen rota brewer was jeered at under the scurrilous nickname of „Jokum Pøl" (which may be roughly translated as „Jack Puddle") and pilloried alongside „Finkeljokum" (Fusel-Oil Jack), i.e. the distiller and the fluid he produced. This was the setting in which the patriotic beer-drinker stepped forth and declaimed in favour of brewery reform, with wholesome beer for the nourishment of the city's young people. Good beer would also safeguard the old from rheumatic attacks and pains, and would also be the best weapon for combating the increasing alcoholism of the age. The argument is not new. Earlier on in the century we come across it in London, where William Hogarth, among others, illustrated the theme in his well-known and oft-reproduced prints depicting the depraved, hopeless squalor of Gin Lane contrasted with the flourishing, happy life of Beer Street. J.C. Jacobsen in fact used the theme himself a century later in his account of the brewery industry's progress during his own day.

In the end the bottom was successfully knocked out of the old rota-brewing barrel, while the guild system was tottering towards collapse as well. The carpenters' strike in Copenhagen in the summer of 1794 gave occasion for the establishment of the Copenhagen guild commission, in which a majority of members favoured abolition of the guilds, and at the end of 1801 the government set up a commission to investigate the brewers' situation. The brewers' guild was the only one of the city's 54 trade and craft guilds in which there was rotation of the business. In this commission too there was a majority in favour of abolition of the guild system, which was carried into effect by an ordinance of 30 August 1805. In the course of the commission's work the low technical level of the Copenhagen breweries came under the searchlight, and at the instance of Crown Prince Frederik new concessions and new brewing permits were made conditional on the applicants' undertaking to introduce technical improvements. A special technical commission was established in order to examine what productive improvements were feasible both in new breweries and older ones as well. This commission consisted of Professors Ludvig Manthey and H.C. Ørsted (the celebrated physicist and the discoverer of electro-magnetism), along with a judge, C.G. Rafn, and an alderman, G.J. Lange.

The commission issued its report in July 1807. It strongly recommended reducing the number of small and inadequate breweries and concentrating production in fewer and larger establishments. The example of England was cited, where a revolution in brewery technology during the 18th century had turned familiar conceptions upside down. The English breweries were one of the leading sectors in the industrialisation of the island kingdom, and English beer, mainly porter, was exported in growing quantities to many parts. It could also be obtained in Copenhagen, where its excellent quality had caused the public to rediscover the possibilities of beer. The perspective was not to be mistaken. „At large breweries one can and must have large reservoirs in order always to have a stock of mature beer in storage, so that there would never be fear of a shortage of beer in the city," said the report, „[and] in wartime the fleet could swiftly be provisioned with fresh beer and households supplied at all times." The supply situation was in fact a topical and vital problem during the

Napoleonic Wars. The commission continued with these quite prophetic words: „The cause for which we speak here will one day find acceptance on its own, without the government's assistance, because it is so incontrovertibly right; but certainly many decades will pass, many men will go to their graves before their time and much money go out of the country, before people in Denmark, where such enterprises are not part of the daily order, may perhaps see it introduced only through the bitter law of necessity."

During the British bombardment of Copenhagen one month later the breweries' guild house in Skindergade was hit and burnt to the ground. This great building was one of the sights of the city and was frequently used by the citizenry for dancing schools and festivities. During the celebrated assembly of the Estates of the Realm in the autumn of 1660 which preceded the introduction of absolute rule, the citizenry had used the guild house as their meeting place. Every day there were innkeepers and beer-bottlers, journeymen brewers, porters, messengers, maidservants and labourers hurrying up and down the stairs on their way to or from the rotation offices, the testing rooms (where the quality of the beer was tested) and the roster boards on which the orders were written down. As the visible monument to the palmy days of the brewery guild, the house vanished simultaneously with the guild and its sales cartel.

Nørregade, Copenhagen's brewery street par excellence, with a large concentration of licensed brewery establishments, was also badly damaged by the bombardment. And although the catastrophe of 1807 meant that some of the rebuilt establishments did not apply for new brewing licences, even after the war Copenhagen was dominated by a large number of small and excessively ill-equipped breweries, despite the fact that the industry had been liberalised and the guild abolished. The economic depression which followed in the wake of the national bankruptcy of 1814 did nothing to encourage reform. Moreover the breweries of the capital were still protected by a 15-kilometre prohibited zone, which the 1805 ordinance had retained, within which no new breweries could be established. Beer-making was still dominated by the relatively weak, top-fermented beers. This product did not differ essentially from privately-brewed household beer and was highly variable in quality and very perishable. What the beer lacked in quality and strength the consumer tried to make up by drinking it along with aquavit, the Danish distilled spirit. The recipe was the old one known to readers of the comedy „Jeppe på Bjerget", by Ludvig Holberg, 18th century poet, history professor and philosopher. It was called beer-and-aquavit, and the mixture was indulged in at the village shoemaker's place. The aquavit was poured into the beer so as to „prime the pan", as with German beer.

Beer and aquavit were closely associated products. In the smaller provincial towns they were produced under the same roof in fact. The distilleries had to use two products of the breweries, beer and yeast, for pitching, without which it was impossible to induce a powerful fermentation in the aquavit mash. The residue from distilling, viz. the draff or lees, was in demand for livestock rearing in the country and for stall-feeding in the towns. Pre-industrial agriculture included few fodder crops but an abundant cultivation of corn, and the straw from the latter was given to the beasts. When soaked in draff it was swallowed more easily. In addition, aquavit cows gave more milk. According to the celebrated physician Emil Hornemann, a pioneer in the field of health and nutritional hygiene, something like half of Copenhagen's milk supply around the middle of the 19th century was dependent on the cows stalled in the lofts of brewers and distillers. In a sense this was rationally-organised cattle-keeping, specialising in milk production and based on the waste products of beer and aquavit manufacturing. Cows in calf, mostly of the sturdy Holstein breed, were purchased from the cattle dealers, hoisted up to the cattle-floor – usually the first storey – of the brewery or distillery, and kept there as long as they yielded plentiful milk, i.e. about 6-9 months, after which they went either for sale or for slaughter along with the calves they had produced. This furnished a copious supply of calves' brains, to which urban cooks exerted their ingenuity to impart whatever variety the recipe book would allow. Another surplus product of the „milk factory" was manure, which was either spread on the plots of the towns or sold to the farmers of the surrounding region. This closed the circle. Expressed in today's terminology it was a vicious circle of underdevelopment, with unhygienic installations, products to match, and the constant risk of disease in an environment where poverty and alcoholism were always lurking in the wings.

Many of the city's merchant establishments also had distilleries. Along with the so-called fattening stall, the distillery was located in the rearmost yard, where the mucked-out stall manure was collected together to form a lake of brown liquid. In many places the distilleries' intoxicated animals were packed so tightly in the narrow stalls that they could scarcely lie down. The dung and rotting manure in the yard were highly likely to pollute an environment that was already under severe strain. Emil Hornemann estimated in his 1847 study „On Cleanliness in Copenhagen" that around this time, when the city's inhabitants numbered a little over 126,000, there were still about 1500 cows and nearly 3000 horses within the city ramparts, quartered in stalls in the yards and requiring an annual night-soil removal of 24,000 cartloads (each load comprising 4 barrels). A macabre statistic.

Copenhagen did have one large brewery, the King's Brew-House. Brewing had taken place in and around Copenhagen Castle since time immemorial. This multi-storeyed red brewery building, still to be seen, was erected at the extreme corner of Slotsholmen overlooking Frederiksholms Kanal, between the years 1616 and 1618 in the reign of Christian IV, an enthusiastic builder. It lay in natural proximity to the arsenal and victualling yard, and in its own day was a fully modern establishment capable of meeting the requirements of the court, the fleet and the trading companies. Because of its efficiency and high-quality product it was superior to most of the city's small breweries and therefore a thorn in the flesh of the brewers' guild, until the guild succeeded in bringing it under its own control in conjunction with the introduction of rota-brewing in 1739. The Brew-House was ravaged by a serious fire in 1767, and it was decided to rebuild it but at the same time to start from the bottom upwards with an entirely new brewery on the other side of the canal, leaving the old Christian IV premises to be used as a store. The new brewery, called the Langebro Brew-House, which was destroyed by fire in 1960, was expanded at varying tempi and can best be described as an industrial installation from the pre-industrial age. After the abolition of the guild it was converted to a partnership consisting originally of 90 partners. Its shares became negotiable instruments, and the original condition of being a shareholder – viz. that the individual concerned should himself be a brewer or proprietor of a brewery establishment in Copenhagen – became forgotten. The beer types from the King's Brew-House differed from the ordinary ones in the city and included a range of strong beers, for example.

The King's Brew-House, whose production for a while during the era of Napoleon's Continental System attained the volume of a medium-sized London brewery, was one of the Danish breweries which soon began to evince interest in the brewing revolution which had been taking place in England during the second half of the 18th century and to which the great brewery commission had referred. Several of the commission's members had drawn particular attention to the success of the English porter breweries, and one of them, Carl Pontoppidan, businessman, alderman and writer on political economy, emphasised the renown of beer in England, in contrast to Denmark, where it was wine, tea and coffee that were the objects of snobbery: „A large ox steak with trimmings together with good strong London porter is still the finest Sunday repast in the true Englishman's family, and the English squire still holds it an honour to treat his guests to his own October-brewed ale. This is why, for the Englishman, his beer is such an important trade both at home and abroad."

Large-scale production made porter cheap compared with ale and encouraged more careful measurement, e.g. of wort strength, at the various stages of brewery. The instruments used – the thermometer and saccharometer – were modest enough but well adapted to sharpen the sense of precision and care in the preparation. They gave the inspiration to economise in the use of brewing raw materials; in this way, in a long-term perspective, the new English brewery came to form the bridge between the empirical handicraft stage and the modern epoch of quantity and quality control.

England was the master. It is thus very characteristic of J.C. Jacobsen that throughout his life he cherished the greatest admiration and respect for the English brewery and its quality products. The Germans too went to England to learn, even brewers from Bavaria, most of whose breweries in the 1830s were still small and managed on handicraft lines. An establishment such as Hofbrauhaus in Munich had an annual production similar to that of a small London brewery. Mechanical power began to penetrate the South German and Austrian

"*As well as the other magnificent objects which have arrived at the house there is a plaster bust of Uncle modelled by [H. V.] Bissen, which is first-rate; however, it is intended to have it carved in marble,*" wrote Nanna in her Christmas letter of 1865 from Carlsberg to her sweetheart in Jutland. The bust shows Jacobsen with the full beard which he adopted during his travels in France that year. Several copies of the bust exist, some of them executed by V. Bissen. The one shown here is in the New Carlsberg Glyptothèque.

Onsdag Morgen.

Da jeg følte mig lidt træt i Aftes, gik
jeg i Seng Kl. 11. og faaer derfor først idag
besvaret Skrivelse. Nu skal jeg paa Sorten
for at besørge nogle tilbagestaaende
Correcturinger og forsøge paa at træffes
Maren, som jeg ikke talte med, Men havde
Tid til at sige. I hvert Fald vil jeg gjøre
mig færdig til i Aften og afrejse Snappen
i Morgen tidlig med Gøteborg for at
være i Kjøbenhavn paa Søndag Eftermiddag
Kl. 5. —

At jeg befinder mig fuldkommen vel,
kan du skjønne af disse Linier. Jeg haaber
ogsaa at Opholdet paa Landet i disse dage
har gjort dig godt og styrket din Søvaften.
Hils alle Rummer og Omgivelser og vær
selv hjærtligst hilset fra din Fanginen

J. C. Jacobsen

Hahns Bastion with the steps down the rampart slope to Teglgaardstræde. To the right of the steps is the entrance to J. C. Jacobsen's Bavarian beer cellar, which was originally one of the exit ports through the rampart of the fortifications. Undated.

◀ *The "most attractive" handwriting Mrs Heiberg knew. Jacobsen's writing remained constant throughout his life. This is the postscript to his letter to his wife sent from Stockholm on 3 September 1886.*

The Brolæggerstræde establishment. Drawing by Alfred Larsen, 1896. ▶

breweries from the mid-1830s onwards. Two young sons of brewing families, Anton Dreher, of Schwekat, near Vienna, and Gabriel Sedlmayr the Younger, of Munich, after several study tours including a visit to England, set about introducing an improved method of working using steam power.

It was from abroad that the inspiration came, and it was export beer that paved the way with the public for new products: this was so in Denmark as well. First came porter, then Bavarian beer. The porter era turned out to be relatively brief. In England porter retained its leading position until about 1830, when ale regained some ground, partly because the English ale brewers at last succeeded in devising a temperate form of fermentation capable of being applied on a large scale. In Denmark the brewing of porter never became big business as it did in Sweden at the Carnegie breweries in Gothenburg and Stockholm; but still, porter was introduced in several breweries at the beginning of the 19th century, and Danish porter or bitter beer figures in King's Brew-House price lists in 1811, 1815 and 1819.

The long storage requirements of the new beer types imposed new exigencies on the Danish breweries, especially with regard to obtaining storage cellars. A large brewery such as the King's Brew-House could cope with these demands, but the smaller ones could not, at any rate not for the moment. However, stored beer was not a matter of cellars alone: it involved the tying-up of large amounts of capital as well. The King's Brew-House audit for 1830 made mention of an excessively large stock of 16 rix-dollar and 12 rix-dollar brown ale. The capital thus tied up was not employed profitably enough, said the auditors. The management replied that the these stocks consisted of porter and added: „As far as we can perceive, the assets of the Brew-House are most particularly destined to the brewing of beer and holding stocks thereof, and although of recent times the traffic in bonds has been more lucrative than that in beer, nevertheless we do not consider ourselves competent to convert the Brew-House's stock of beer into bonds or other interest-bearing securities, for it is scarcely the object of the Brew-House to act as rentiers or as speculators in the funds."

This reply reflects a dilemma between the short- and the long-term views of investment, two mutually opposed approaches which often came into conflict with one another during the subsequent decades while Denmark was moving away from the handicraft style of beer-making in favour of large-scale industrialised production. We meet it as a constant theme in J.C. Jacobsen's life and work. There is a striking kinship in the choice of words, in fact. One of the directors of the Brew-House (or „administrators", as they were entitled) was called Chresten Jacobsen Nørkjær. He had retired from the Brew-House management in 1829, but was responsible for the accumulation of beer at which the auditors' remarks were directed. He could easily have fathered the answer cited, but that is speculation. What is not speculation, however, is that he did father J.C. Jacobsen and was the first generation of the Jacobsen brewing dynasty.

The first generation

Towards the end of the 18th century Danish society started to become more mobile. The agrarian reforms opened the way for the scattering of farms away from the old villages and the old common field system, along with a switch from copyholding to freeholding. The abolition of the adscription system in 1788 also encouraged mobility. The adscription ordinances, which re-established the militia, had imposed a residence obligation upon farm labourers. They had to remain in the manor of their birth until their 40th year; also, soldiers who had completed their service commitment had been obliged to settle in their conscription district. Time-expired soldiers and men unfit for service were now to be freed forthwith, while those conscripted were to be released from adscription by 1800 at the latest. Peasants were to remain in their county of birth from birth until their 36th year unless in possession of the county prefect's permission to leave, in the form of a „county passport" or „free passport". The wider radius of movement provided new scope for social mobility. The towns, especially the capital, now became magnets drawing young people to them. The call of far-off places proved compelling.

Chresten Jacobsen was a copyholder's son. He was born in 1773 of adscripted parents, the 35 year-old Jacob Jensen and his 40 year-old wife Gertrud Clemensdatter, on the copyhold farm of Nørkjær in the manor of Gjettrup, Dronninglund parish, in Vendsyssel. Chresten was the only child. In 1793 he was registered for military service, the entry stating him to be Jacob Jensen's son Chresten, 19 years of age, 68 1/2 inches tall, with the additional remark „Old man's son". This indicated a family responsibility to which regard should be paid in the event of call-up. He was considered to be a reservist. Two years later Chresten's mother died, and four years after that his father followed her to the grave. The main register for the 1799 call-up records that Chresten did not report in; a certificate stated that he was ill, and it is also noted that his father was buried on 6 February.

Chresten Jacobsen did not wish to take over the freehold of Nørkjær, and he decided to set his course for Copenhagen. He managed to keep clear of military service for the time being by obtaining a county passport, for which a relative stood surety, in the following year. Chresten and a couple of cousins (sons of an uncle who had occupied the copyhold farm of Vestergaard in Asaa) went off together on the great adventure to the capital. It was the year 1800. Conditions in the country were harsh and straitened, and there was no future for young people of their class.

The winter of 1799-1800 was one of Denmark's very severe ones, with no fewer than 115 days of iceboat navigation across the Great Belt. It began to freeze on 19 November and persistent frost continued right through to 7 April. In March the cold increased, with sharp easterly winds. The late spring brought blizzards, sleet and rain. Huge heaps of snow kept the ground wet, so much so that on clayey land the plough could not be put to the soil until the end of May, and in many places not until mid-June. The winter ate into fodder reserves, cattle died of hunger, the spring seeds were sown too late, all summer it was rainy and cold, the famished cattle were unable to recover their strength because there was insufficient grazing. The autumn, which began in many places as early as September, brought the difficulty of autumn rains occurring earlier than usual. The half-matured seed stood sprouting in the stooks and was brought into the house half spoilt. The winter seed was damaged as well, as the following year's poor harvest of rye and wheat testified. Prices rose.

It was not merely the weather that was out of joint but the times as well. The world was at war, with France and England locked in a life and death struggle from which the Danish-Norwegian monarchy did not manage to stay aloof, although it did endeavour to play the customary neutral role as long as possible. At the end of July 1800 the frigate „Freya", Captain Krabbe commanding, was making passage through the English Channel as convoy escort for six merchant vessels when a British squadron closed her and demanded to search the convoy, which Krabbe, acting in accordance with his instructions, refused to permit. After an hour's fight the Danish convoy was captured and taken to an English port.

This episode impelled the neutral powers to adopt an uncompromising stand and had high political consequences. Denmark-Norway entered into the so-called League of Armed Neutrality along with Russia, i.e. a form of offensive neutrality which in reality came to signify war with Britain. This was in December 1800. It was clear that Britain for its part would react to the League offensively – but which partner would she strike at first? Czar Paul of Russia had no doubts. „I am the one whose ice breaks up last," he declared without regret to the Danish envoy. „If the English come to the Sound with a fleet in April, I shall be unable to get there in time."

Britain resolved to strike at Denmark-Norway first and force the monarchy out of the League of Armed Neutrality. In January 1801 all Danish ships in British harbours – 149 of them altogether – were seized, and on 12 March the British North Sea fleet put to sea. Nine days later it anchored in the fairway north of Kronborg. Fishermen from Hornbæk hurried to Copenhagen with the news that the British had been ashore for drinking water but without making any commotion.

The mood in the capital was courageous, at least in the clubs and among the beaux-esprits. The poet Adam Oehlenschläger has left a vivid description in his memoirs: „The sense of an ancient glorious heroism at sea had quite taken possession of the nation, especially Copenhagen. All the petty vices of the age – envy, avarice, arrogance, vanity, backbiting – had skulked inside the taverns like cowardly knaves. But now fraternity, goodwill, mutual help and support burgeoned everywhere. Strangers who had never seen each other before shook hands enthusiastically when they met on the street. An indescribable cheerfulness disseminated itself over the entire city." Just let the English wait! The Copenhagen citizenry swelled with patriotic sentiment.

Unfortunately the city's military preparedness did not match the psychological. Much of the Danish fleet – the fourth largest in Europe – lay unrigged in the naval dockyard. The government had feared that to equip the fleet would be provocative. Now time had run out. A hastily equipped and inadequately manned defensive force now had to do battle with a military super-power, and although the resistance did surprise the British, the outcome of the Battle of Copenhagen on 2 April was the fact of defeat. Denmark had to renounce the neutrality principle which the country had defended throughout the 18th century.

Denmark had not been at war for something like eighty years, and Copenhagen had not experienced war at first hand in any serious sense since being besieged by the Swedes in 1659. Now Copenhagen had gone through the fire, and its own seamen, artisans and workmen, the rock on which the fleet was founded, had offered up their lives and physique. Everyone in the city had seen with his own eyes what happened. The battle had been watched by thousands of spectators, every one of whom could tell of the brave deeds of individual commanders and their men.

From the latter sprang legends, especially in family histories. Thus, for a long time afterwards it was said in the uncle's family in Vendsyssel that the cousin Jacob Pedersen along with Chresten Jacobsen himself had taken part aboard one of the fleet's defensive vessels, and there was also a story to the effect that another of the cousins had been wounded in the leg by a bullet which remained there for the rest of his life.

At any rate the two cousins became brewery workers, Jacob a yard labourer for a brewer named Andreas Tronier in Brolæggerstræde and Chresten a workhand at the King's Brew-House, where he figures in the books from April to November 1801. His testimonial from this job states that he had served faithfully and well. His cousin Jacob was promoted a year later to brewery hand, married in 1803 and then set up as an independent petty tradesman, but decided in 1809 to return to his native tract, where he purchased Asaa watermill and the appurtenant miller's yard and land for 6000 rix-dollars; two years later he had already paid off this sum in full and received the deeds of the property. It could be profitable to betake oneself to the capital if one's luck was running.

Chresten Jacobsen stayed on in Copenhagen. In 1808 his military service situation was resolved at last. The chancellery wrote to the militia call-up board for Hjørring county advising that Chresten Jacobsen's name could be deleted from the county register when he established that he was entered in one of the registers under the first Zealand district and had appeared before the call-up board appointed under the recent public notice of 6 November 1807 to draft recruits for militia service.

In 1807 Denmark was at war again, and this time it lasted for seven years. Britain launched a lightning attack on Copenhagen to ensure that the Danish fleet did not fall into Napoleon's hands. The French Emperor had initiated a grandiose manoeuvre with a view to isolating Britain from mainland Europe, the so-called Continental System, which Frederik VI had joined enthusiastically in the hope that Britain's economy could be devastated by this means. The hour of vengance never struck, however. Totally unprepared for war, Denmark was overpowered yet again. The British surrounded the capital from both land and sea without meeting any resistance. The Zealand militia regiments were shattered in a battle at Køge – afterwards dubbed the „battle of the wooden shoes" because of the utterly unmilitary equipment of the peasant-soldiery. Copenhagen was then subjected to three nights of bombardment, after which the civilian population pressed the commandant to sue for an armistice. Under the terms of the capitulation of 7 September, confiscation by the British of the entire Danish fleet along with all its supplies had to be accepted. The treatment meted out to Copenhagen in 1807 was unheard-of in those days and there was an outcry all over Europe, which was not of any particular help to Denmark, however.

After the capitulation the government hastily attempted to reorganise the army and navy, including the militia. Chresten Jacobsen managed to avoid being called up under the terms of the public notice of 6 November. A new letter from the chancellery superseding the previous one said that „reservist" Chresten Jacobsen Nørkjær was exempted from appearing before the call-up board and from militia service altogether provided he remained in the Copenhagen civic artillery corps until he reached the age at which militiamen were exempted from further war service.

This meant that Chresten Jacobsen's military status was settled at last. The militia, which had been the terror of many young peasant lads for generations and caused many of them to flee abroad, was replaced by the Copenhagen civic guard. And the outlook was becoming brighter from the career standpoint too. The copyholder's son was on his way to admission into the ranks of official citizenship. He had made a success of himself in the capital. He had become a journeyman brewer at the Gyldenfeldt brewery, in premises at the present Brolæggerstræde 9. He himself lived in the corner house at Knabrostræde-Brolæggerstræde. Now he could also think about setting up a home. On 27 September 1810 he received a royal licence to marry Caroline Frederikke Schelbeck at home without previous publication of banns, after which they were married on 24 October by the parson of the Church of the Holy Trinity.

Chresten's wife was 14 years younger than he, daughter of a journeyman silk-weaver and one of a large family consisting of two brothers and five sisters. One brother appears in the Copenhagen Directory as a tea dealer from 1814 onwards, later on also bearing the title of lieutenant in the civic artillery corps. The home in Knabrostræde accommodated two other families as well, Jon Grelsen Berg, a master painter, and Christian Falkenberg, a royal footman. Chresten's dwellings was on the first floor and consisted of two rooms, a spare room and a kitchen. In 1815 the Jacobsens moved from no. 9 to no. 13 in the same street, all adequately in keeping with the station of tradespeople and shopkeepers.

The couple's only child, a boy, was born on 2 September 1811, and was christened on 11 October at the Church of the Holy Spirit. He was given the name of Jacob Christian Jacobsen. The shift to a fixed surname was in accordance with bourgeois custom. The parents acted as godparents themselves along with the midwife, a Mrs Hansen. The father's occupation is entered in the church register as „tenant brewer". A tenant brewer, as the name implies, was a one who rented a brewery from the owner of a licensed brewery establishment. A considerable number of Copenhagen's breweries were run by tenant brewers or journeymen brewers at this time. Presumably in Chresten Jacobsen's case the Gyldenfeldt brewery was the one in question. In 1817, when the Copenhagen police court pressed him for the trade licence which had to be taken out by a tenant brewer, it addressed him by the title of „tenant brewer" at that brewery. He submitted his tenancy agreement to the municipal authorities along with his drill certificate and patent as a member of the civic artillery corps. Now he had official citizenship.

The next step in Chresten Jacobsen Nørkjær's career followed in August 1823, when he purchased a 1500 rix-dollar share in the King's

Brew-House and immediately thereafter became a member of the shareholders' committee, consisting of seven members. The other representatives were Didrik Beckmann (cashier of the Sea Assurance Company), Fr. Hammerich (chief war commissary), N. Keilgaard (assistant supercargo), M. Skibsted (alderman and chancellery official), P. Stephansen (bookkeeper of a life annuity company), and Captain L.P. Wall (warden of the shipmasters' guild). In the following year the shareholders' committee proposed a change in the company's articles to regularise the long-prevailing situation whereby a large proportion of the Brew-House shareholders were not brewers but people who simply regarded the ownership of shares as a source of income.

The big leap forward came three years later with the acquisition of the brewery premises at Brolæggerstræde no. 5 along with the property at Knabrostræde 13, where the couple were living as tenants. The two properties had belonged to the brewer and master joiner Christian Velschow. The premises were put up for auction in January 1825 but without being sold. Three auctions had to be held before they went. This happened on 20 February, after it had become known that the Fire Insurance Company was willing to let an 18,000 rix-dollar first mortgage remain outstanding on the property and that a brewer's widow named Rindom would allow a second mortgage of 2600 rix-dollars to remain outstanding on payment of 1200 silver rix-dollars cash. The highest bidder was Captain Weinreich on behalf of Chresten Jacobsen Nørkjær. The hammer fell at 23,240 rix-dollars. On the same day Jacobsen secured the Knabrostræde property for 9,555 rix-dollars by a bid from master carpenter Kofoed. Here the Fire Insurance Office allowed a first mortgage of 6000 silver rix-dollars to stand and the widow Rindom a second mortgage of 1400 rix-dollars on payment of 600 rix-dollars by the Easter removal date. The costs involved in the purchase were over 2000 rix-dollars, which Jacobsen settled in cash.

Immediately after issue of the title deed Chresten Jacobsen applied for and was granted a new trade licence, this time as a fully-fledged brewer, along with the licence for the brewery itself, which he immediately set about enlarging and improving. The reconstruction work was executed by master builder Thomas Blom. The rearmost outhouse was raised by one storey and the back-building by two. A white-malt kiln was erected in the outhouse, where the bottom floor, which had previously been fitted up as a cowhouse, was cleared. The kiln had a barrel-vaulted ceiling. It was two storeys high and could be fired from three furnaces. Smoke and hot air were led through pipes to avoid imparting a smokey flavour to the malt, and this gave independence in the choice of fuel. After the expansion, the back-building had grown to five storeys high. On the ground floor he replaced the old 14-barrel copper with a larger one of 20 barrels capacity. A new cowhouse was fitted up in a part of the gatehouse to the house on Knabrostræde.

The rebuilding was completed in January 1827. After a survey the chief fire officer and city clerk of works approved the new establishment, and in the following month Jacobsen requested a revaluation by the Copenhagen Fire Insurance Company. Master builder Blom and master carpenter Kofoed acted as valuers. They fixed the valuation at the low figure of 34,500 silver rix-dollars, viz. the same amount as at a valuation made in 1821, despite the alterations made.

The purchase and the rebuilding programme tell clearly of the financial resources at Chresten Jacobsen's disposal. To acquire the house and brewery premises he paid out a total of 13,492 rix-dollars in cash. To finance the rebuilding he borrowed 4000 rix-dollars in notes from the Rigsbank in October 1826, giving specie bonds as security; but the following year he had already repaid half of the loan. The rest was cleared off in the course of a couple of years. Two short-term loans of 1000 rix-dollars each were taken and discharged in 1831 and 1832 respectively. Finally there is a list of minor outstanding debts from this period in which Chr. Pedersen, a tenant farmer of Karslundegaard in Køge, is one of the creditors. This was where Jacobsen used to buy part of his barley.

After 25 years in the capital the lad from Vendsyssel had become a man of substance, and a busy and energetic one too. At the same time as he was establishing himself in his own brewery he was elected, in October 1826, to the board of the King's Brew-House along with Colonel C. Malling and Jens Hostrup Schultz, a university book publisher. The directors' emoluments consisted of 1% of the annual surplus. When the King's Brew-House decided in 1828 to add another building to its plant at Langebro, the general meeting appointed Jacobsen to negotiate terms with the master tradesmen on behalf of the firm. On the expiry of his three-year period on the board in 1829 he joined the shareholders' committee of the company for the second time.

In an account book surviving from Jacobsen's time as a tenant brewer in the Gyldenfeldt establishment there is an entry under the date 7 February 1825: „Had myself enrolled in the Society for the Dissemination of Natural Science. Paid subscription in silver rix-dollars, 10 rdl." This is one of many evidences of his alert interest in assimilating new knowledge and new skills, especially those bearing on the brewing processes. During a visit to England, the Danish physicist H.C.Ørsted had formed a plan for a great „patriotic" enterprise that would disseminate knowledge of natural science and so enable tradesmen, farmers and industrial workers, both managers and men, to fit themselves for their occupations and open their eyes to the usefulness of natural sciences and also, therefore, to the beauty and expediency of nature. This plan was realised the following year by the establishment of the Society for the Dissemination of Natural Science, which Ørsted headed until his death in 1851 and to which he devoted much of his time. The Technical University of Denmark, founded in 1829, also worked to the same end.

Chresten Jacobsen was among those who listened to the series of popular science lectures which were launched at these institutions. He urged his colleagues to accompany him, but not all brewers were motivated, and some of them, to Jacobsen's irritation, soon left the lecture hall with the remark that they had no intention of sitting at a school desk again. Some of the lecturers could also have difficulty in striking the right note. The organic chemist W.C. Zeise earned a reputation for being rather dry and tedious, and about as impenetrable as one of his text books, of which it was said that one read them with the same sensation as if driving a sledge over sand. A greater attraction was G. Forchhammer, the chemist and mineralogist, whose popular and semi-popular dissertations held particular appeal for the farmer. The biggest draw was H.C. Ørsted himself.

Chresten Jacobsen recommended his 17 year-old son to follow the

Ørsted lectures in chemistry, sowing a seed in his son's mind which quickly sprouted and developed into a lifelong commitment to science and its applied aspects. J.C. also followed Forchhammer's and Zeise's lectures and spoke of them often when he looked back over his career.

H.C. Ørsted had a special interest in the fermentation industries and the brewing business dating back at least as far as his earlier-mentioned membership of the technical commission of 1806-07 to consider improvements in the fitting out of Copenhagen breweries. In 1820 he revised a book entitled „Brief Instructions in the Art of Distilling Aquavit", by C.A. Brøndum, whose aquavit was the finest of its day and who was another of the energetic practical men of those years, striving to progress in technology and production processes in collaboration with research. In 1822 the Royal Danish Agricultural Society invited Brøndum to write „Instructions for producing Wine from Apples" and later on a paper on the brewing of beer. The latter was published in 1828 under the title „The Principles of Beer Brewery" and was dedicated to the Society for the Dissemination of Natural Science with a foreword by H.C. Ørsted. Two brewers in particular had helped Brøndum with this treatise, viz. Chresten Jacobsen and C. Høyer. The two of them knew each other already from the King's Brew-House, where Høyer had been administrator from 1818 to 1824, when pressure of business at his own firm forced him to relinquish this activity, though he was still elected to the shareholders' committee in 1826.

Among the small but significant improvements during these years was the increasing use of the thermometer for measuring wort temperature and other temperatures in the brewery. Looking back over the progress in brewing in his own time, J.C. Jacobsen believed that his father was the first to introduce the use of the thermometer in Danish breweries, though actually we must modify this and state that he was among the first to have his eyes opened to the step forward represented by the thermometer. A couple of the submissions to the technical commission of 1807 show that in fact the thermometer was in use at a number of places, and even as early as the end of the previous century a dissertation by Molbech recommended the use of the thermometer in breweries. To a question raised by the King's Brew-House auditors on the accounts for the 1828/29 season on the presence of five recently-obtained thermometers, the management replied: „Thermometers are an item of equipment which are frequently moved now here, now there, since one has need of them; however, they could certainly be entered in the inventory." However that may be, interest in a more „scientifically" based technique was awakening, and the model at the beginning of the century was English.

The expectations placed by the foremost leaders of the industry in the possibilities of natural science were not falsified. Indeed the fermentation industries furnish one of the 19th century's neatest examples of the interplay between theory and practice, and also of fruitful interaction between countries. Danish conditions must once more be viewed in a broader context. Some of the greatest names in the natural sciences are to be found in this chapter. In his retrospect, J.C. Jacobsen declares that the first great step towards the understanding of an important aspect of beer brewery was taken in 1833 when the Frenchmen Anselme Payens and Jean-François Persoz discovered diastase, or the diastatic ferment developed by the sprouting of the barley. It had previously been thought that the conversion of the barley's starch to sugar and dextrine occurred essentially during the malting, and that the mashing merely broke down material already formed. Now it was realised that the malting only served to prepare the process which in essentials takes place during the mashing, when the enzymes formed during sprouting bring about the conversion of the starch, partly into sugar and partly into dextrine. The correct management of the mash must therefore be one of the main features of the well-run brewery.

In 1836 Carl I.N. Balling, who was professor in chemistry at the technical university in Prague, began trials with the saccharometer with a view to determining more accurately the ratio between specific gravity and concentration in cane sugar solutions. His broadly conceived and widely-ranging work was of fundamental value for beer fermentation and led to the working out of a theory of attenuation which was more complete both theoretically and practically than the similar doctrine developed by the Englishman Richardson in the 18th century. Here Balling introduced the coefficients which have since been named after him. His major work was published in four volumes in 1845 and for thirty years was referred to by brewers the world over. The weakest section was the one dealing with the fermentation process itself, where Balling described the different hypotheses but had to conclude, as was true, that „we possess a very imperfect knowledge of the forces active in alcoholic fermentation".

While chemistry and physics had put brewers to some extent in a position where they could partially understand and manage malting and mashing, these sciences led them „completely astray", as J.C. Jacobsen put it, with regard to fermentation. It was quite true that three researchers, the Frenchman Cagniard-Latour and the Germans Schwann and Kützing, working independently of each other, had in 1837 already deduced from microscopic study of fermenting fluids that the sediment which had hitherto been regarded as chemical precipitates was actually a living plant which had formed itself in the fluid, and that this plant was the cause of fermentation. The Dutchman Antony van Leeuwenhoek, who lived in the late 17th and early 18th centuries and who discovered the microscope, had in fact seen and sketched the tiny spherical bodies in the beer sediment, though without being able, with the primitive instruments at his disposal, to explain their true nature. All through the 18th century there were many researchers using improved microscopes to study the small „infusoria" which were found everywhere in nature, but not until the 19th century did it occur to anyone that the yeast might be a living organism rather than an inanimate chemical growth, an „excrement" of the fermenting fluid. But it proved very difficult to get the new theory accepted. The most eminent chemists of the day, led by Justus Liebig, rejected the idea as nonsense. Along with a colleague Liebig composed a satirical paper in which these „vitalistic" researchers, as they were dubbed, were mocked and derided, and shortly afterwards, in 1839, Liebig published his purely chemical theory of fermentation, which explained fermentation not as a living process but as a chemical agitation of a substance, a „ferment". The agitation of the ferment was transferred to the sugar in the fluid, which was thus broken down into alcohol and carbonic acid. The small spherical bodies at the bottom of the fluid were a product of this decomposition. Liebig's authority was great in the scientific world of the day. The defeat of the „vitalists" meant in fact that many years were to pass before doubts were again entertained and a crucial step forward taken in fathoming this stage of the brewery process.

When Chresten Jacobsen acquired the brewery premises, he and his family moved into the large ground-floor apartment of four rooms, one of which was a parlour with three bay windows overlooking the street, and a kitchen. It had formerly been the home of the Velschow family, a residence very appropriate to the station of an independent brewer with domestic staff and other employees. When the family moved in the son was just under 15 years of age and completing his schooling at Hr Bisserup's School, a private establishment in Copenhagen. Jacob Christian was confirmed at the Church of the Holy Spirit on 8 October 1826, after which his father took his further education in hand, firstly in brewery and secondly in the things of the mind and spirit such as politics, literature, art and science. The boy had shown much ability at school and had been rewarded for his results. His favourite subjects were mathematics, ancient history and German literature. There was also a practical subject in which he scored top marks, drawing, which was a discipline which he later pursued with ardour. The drawing board was the indispensable item of equipment in his study. It was here that most of the multitude of buildings which he erected first saw the light of day in the form of sketches and constructional drawings.

Chresten Jacobsen's health was beginning to fail by the beginning of the 1830s, and his son had to take over more and more of the running of the brewery. To the latter's chagrin he had to give up his studies in chemistry and other brewery subjects. This pained him greatly, but family discipline was strong. The father insisted on his son's taking over day-to-day responsibility, and Jacob Christian had to follow his muses in his spare time, which became more and more sparse.

Chresten Jacobsen was vitally involved in the great issues of his day. He was a full-blooded romantic, Oehlenschläger being his favourite author, and on religious questions his touchstones were rationalism and the worship of nature. The parson Christian Bastholm was one of his idols. Bastholm tried to turn the Christian life into a direction where importance was attached to the doctrine of duty and to the priestly function as a useful element in the life of civic society – accordingly parsons in the countryside, in his opinion, ought to be educated in physics, zoology, agriculture, gardening and veterinary science, so as to make an impact among the intelligent, enquiring classes of the peasantry. Politically Jacobsen sympathised with rebellion against tyranny. When his son told him of the fall of Warsaw in 1831 as a piece of ordinary political news to be read about in the newspapers, he flared up and took J.C. heavily to task for not feeling more deeply about the tragic outcome of the Poles' heroic rising against the superior strength of the brutal czarist hegemony in Russia.

Many years later, when the historian Johannes Steenstrup was collecting material for his essay on Carl Jacobsen and his Father, he asked Doctor Frants Djørup to give him his impression of the grandfather, whom Djørup had encountered as a young student. Djørup remembered him as a tall man with a strong ruddy face, persevering and energetic. He admired his decisiveness and tenacity. An ordinary peasant upbringing had been his starting point; all else was self-taught and self-created. Djørup summed up his description of Chresten Jacobsen thus: „In my view he was an extraordinarily gifted man, perhaps even more gifted than his son." These are surprisingly strong words from one of J.C. Jacobsen's very closest friends and admirers.

Authors of business histories sometimes view the life of a firm in the perspective of the generations, saying that first generations create, second generations consolidate, and third generations dissipate. This cliché model cannot be applied to the case of the Jacobsens. But there are grounds for regarding Chresten Jacobsen Nørkjær as the first generation. He did not merely make his mark in an entirely new profession and create a solid foundation on which the next generation could build. Through example and upbringing he also implanted in his son interests and attitudes which would determine the direction of his life and career.

Inside the ramparts

Chresten Jacobsen, then almost 62 years of age, died on 13 February 1835. His son thereupon assumed total responsibility for the brewery on his mother's behalf, acting as tenant brewer from 1837. When his mother died in 1844 the brewery establishment became the son's own. On 24 October 1839 Jacob Christian was married at the Church of the Holy Spirit to Laura Cathrine Holst, of Thisted, 20 years of age and the daughter of Lars Hillemann Holst, a merchant, and his wife Helene Cathrine Steenstrup. The couple had a son in September of the following year but he died ten days after the birth. On 2 March 1842 Laura was delivered of another son, Carl, who survived as the only child of the marriage. Thus the single-child tradition was carried forward to the third generation.

During Chresten Jacobsen's time, his own or his wife's relatives, close and distant, used to stay at the family home in Brolæggerstræde when they visited Copenhagen. Chresten's family would find young girls for domestic work from among their relatives and friends in Jutland. It was in this way that Laura had been brought into the house as a 15 year-old, accompanied to the capital by one of the relatives of the old brewer. A whole new circle of young people, most of them related to Laura, was introduced into the Jacobsen home along with her.

Jacob Christian was a shy and reticent boy when very young. If strangers visited the home he would try to slip away. His only friend and confidant was his schoolmate „Little Møller", whose real name was Lauritz Ridder Møller, son of the precentor and organist of the Cathedral choir. They stuck together, went travelling together, in Italy for example, and they both married in the same year. Lauritz was associated all his life with the publisher C.A. Reitzel's bookshop, first as an apprentice and assistant, later on as bookkeeper and partner. He lived in Fiolstræde. The friendship between the bookkeeper's and the brewer's families was continued by the two only children, Carl Jacobsen and Sophus Møller.

Family tradition has it that one day the recently-arrived little Laura went with Mrs. Jacobsen to the church square in front of the Church of the Holy Spirit, which at that time was used by the families living in the vicinity as a clothes-drying yard. While they were hanging out the washing, Laura happened to spot two of her cousins, Frants Djørup and Japetus Steenstrup, on the street outside. The joy at the reunion was great, and it was followed by an invitation to pay a visit to the house in Brolæggerstræde. In this way a connection began which turned into a lifelong friendship.

Frants Djørup was studying medicine. He lived at the university college of Regensen, then afterwards at Valkendorfs College, and he introduced Jacob Christian to many of his college friends. His two cousins Peter and Jacob Stilling, for example, were members of the circle. The former of these abandoned theology, compelled by „reasons of common sense", in favour of the philosophy of religion, while the latter became a parson. There was also Rasmus Nielsen, who had shared a school desk with Djørup at Viborg and subsequently became professor of philosophy at Copenhagen University and an influential philosopher, whom many students got to know through attending the compulsory course of propaedeutics known as filosofikum. Japetus Steenstrup was a student from the town of Aalborg. His father, Johannes Vogelius Steenstrup, was a parson and a cousin of Laura's mother. Japetus was for a while the mentor of his younger brothers, one of whom, Mathias, graduated in theology in 1845; by marrying the daughter of a well-to-do landowner he became financially independent and so was able to pursue liberal humanistic and scientific studies. An older brother who also became part of the circle was Michael Vogelius Steenstrup, a jurist who eventually became borough judge and clerk of Frederikshavn. Japetus himself became professor of zoology at Copenhagen University. As such he played a very prominent role in his profession and at the university, and also in the Royal Danish Academy of Sciences and Letters. He was a dynamic personality and in time became J.C. Jacobsen's closest scientific adviser. Laura Holst had a third cousin as well, Frantz Jacobsen, a student of theology from Aalborg, who was one of the circle of friends. He was greatly interested in natural science though he finished up as a parson on the island of Samsø.

The impression which J.C. gave the students was of the silent brewer. However, they soon discovered that behind the closed facade lurked many interests and much knowledge – and also, when at last he found his tongue and joined in the discussion, a remarkable logic. The year before his death, J.C. Jacobsen wrote to his friend Frants Djørup and thanked him for more than 50 years of friendship. It was an occasion for acknowledging his debt to the youthful circle. It is an autobiographical confession, one of the few from his pen. As such it deserves to be cited. It runs:

„My acquaintance with you in the days of my immature youth has exerted a great and fruitful influence on the direction my mind has taken, partly by introducing me to a circle of young students and thus to a large degree contributing to my education, but still more by the daily impress of your whole personality. The elements which my natural aptitudes and my upbringing at home had produced were thus subjected to a multi-faceted development which they would not have enjoyed otherwise. Without this influence I should neither have become a useful and capable citizen representative, deputy to the estates, or member of the parliament; but most important of all, however, is the personal influence on my character and mode of thought. Without it I might very well have become a capable brewer, but very likely a self-seeker cocooned in materialistic philosophies of life, and I should not be able to look back over something like 75 years of life with the degree of satisfaction which on the whole I can feel now.“

One spring day in 1836 when J.C. Jacobsen and Frants Djørup were out for a walk together, J.C. invited Djørup to take a glass of wine at the cellar of a wine merchant named Waagepetersen in Store Strand-stræde. The wine turned out to be just an excuse. What Jacobsen really wanted was to taste a bottle of imported Bavarian beer, which the „Schleswig-Holsteiners“ (an élite of officials dominating the Foreign Ministry at that time) were fond of drinking. Djørup was not particularly enthusiastic, but Jacobsen tasted the beer over and over again, examined its colour and clarity, tasted it once more and pronounced it to be a remarkable type of beer which invited further investigation. It invited him. Later on that year he travelled to Hamburg to study the beer at closer quarters. Like many other innovations, the new beer came to Denmark via the twin duchies of Schleswig-Holstein, but its real homeland was South Germany, as the name implies. A reform of beer brewing emanated from here which attained far greater significance on the Continent than English porter had had.

The Bavarian method was characterised by storage of the beer in deep, ice-cold cellars, either natural or artificial. As long ago as the 16th century, a decree of the electoral prince had prohibited all brewing during the period from 23 April to 29 September, which had compelled the brewers to brew their beer at such strength and to handle it with such scrupulous care during storage that it was able to retain its freshness throughout the summer and part way into the autumn. The ban remained in force right up to the middle of the 19th century. Moreover, the mashing process used in Bavaria was the so-called „thick mashing", which differed from the „infusion" method and included repeated boiling as one of its features. Finally, the fermentation was effected at very low temperatures („bottom fermentation", as it was known) and continued with a slow secondary fermentation during several months of storage in the cold cellars aforementioned. At this stage the beer assumed a more vinous character, becoming rich in carbonic acid, unusually clear and very resistant to acidification. This in turn meant that it was unnecessary to add to the beer the large quantities of hops that were used elsewhere to prevent its from becoming sour. However, until the 1830s most of the Bavarian breweries were small despite the high quality of their product and were run on handicraft lines. The chemist E.A. Scharling, who had been a deputy for Zeise at the Technical University, emphasised this in a lecture he gave to the Industrial Association. It was based on a study tour he had made in Bavaria in 1845. He believed that some of the difference in taste was attributable to the Bavarian brewers' method of preparing their barrels. In order to prevent the carbonic acid in the beer from penetrating the pores of the wood, they lined the insides of the barrels once a year with a layer of resin, a treatment which despite thorough airing afterwards gave to the barrels a piquant tang that was characteristic of the Bavarian beer.

It is interesting too that Scharling concludes his impressions of his tour by saying that with some exceptions the Bavarian brewery establishments were still far behind the better English ones and only in one respect substantially better than the majority of Copenhagen breweries, viz. in having more suitable fermentation and storage facilities. Brewery in Bavaria was subject to government regulation for the protection of both public and producer, a regulation which in Scharling's eyes was somewhat reminiscent of the roster-brewing system in Copenhagen. Prices were fixed by the authorities; the quality of the beer was checked as well and brewing was authorised by licence; the peasantry were not allowed to brew beer but could distil spirits; publicans were allowed to contract for supplies with only one brewer each season; beer was dutiable and all the firms were small. Not all the beer was bottom-fermented; much of it was weak, top-fermented beer, brewed chiefly at the royal breweries and other similar breweries licensed for the purpose. The strong beer types, the celebrated „Bock Bier" and „Salvator Bier", were bottom-fermented types which were exported and well known beyond the German frontiers, and these too were reserved for selected breweries licensed for this particular form of brewing. The beer was also called „spring beer" after the season of the year when it was brewed.

With regard to the yeast, Scharling noted that the Bavarian brewers helped one another with it. The very dissimilar courses that could be taken by the fermentation process meant that it was frequently necessary to obtain yeast from a neighbouring brewery, and likewise that when there was a surplus of yeast it would be sold to colleagues in distress. For it did not always happen that a sufficient quantity of yeast was formed during brewing to enable production to proceed to the next stage. In this respect, therefore, there was a lively traffic between the Bavarian breweries.

There were two kinds of storage cellar: natural and artificially-constructed. The natural cellars in Austria and Norway – the true „Felsen" cellars („Felsen" meaning a rock or mountain) – were constructed in the mountains. In Budapest, where the Austro-Hungarian brewer Anton Dreher had one of his large breweries, the cellars were dug underground into the limestone, and in the course of time several kilometres of passageways to the storage cellars were established.

They are still there. During the Second World War resistance members and refugees hid in them. In the midst of the system of excavations, astonishingly, one stumbles across a chapel which was built by the brewer directly below his elegant residence. To this underground place he could descend with his family and, surrounded by his slumbering stocks of beer, offer thanks by candlelight to his God and Creator for his good fortune. A Missa Cervisia – a beer mass.

Bavaria itself was less well supplied with natural cellars. Munich was particularly short of them, and here a system of brickwork chambers had been constructed, covered by artificial ramparts or mounds. At the same time special ice-cellars had been built for storing the ice which was sawn or hewn out during the winter. Ice was an article of trade and quite indispensable to the Bavarian beer breweries in the vicinity of the town. Until cooling machinery made its appearance, ice retained its leading position as a method of cooling. It was cheaper than producing cold artificially, and the trade in ice could in fact be practised over long and even inter-continental distances. Thus, throughout the 19th century and up to the beginning of the 20th, ice was carried by ship from North America to the East, from Boston to Hong Kong for example, where the old ice warehouses by the harbour were still standing until a few years ago as a monument to the former ice trade. Bies Brewery in Hobro is a good Danish example of a 19th century provincial brewery with a very rational production line beginning next to the fiord, where the ice was cut in winter, with the ice-cellar lying close by the water, then the storage cellars, fermenting cellar, malt house, brew-house and appurtenant departments, a retail outlet up on the town street with the brewer's residence on the first floor, and the stabling and wash-house in the yard.

Jacobsen tried his hand at the Bavarian beer. He was not the only one to do so. Trials were being conducted elsewhere as well, in Odense for example, where Bavarian beer from the brewery of Consul Thomas Charles Grut and his partner, Carl Wilhelm Høyer, on Nørregade, was advertised in 1836-37. The King's Brew-House in Copenhagen sent out bottled samples of Bavarian beer to a small group of selected customers in February 1838, informing them that sales would commence on 1 May of that year. In its covering letter the Brew-House spoke of the growing imports of Bavarian beer into Copenhagen. The Brew-House had now engaged a brewer from Bavaria, J.G. Pflanger, of Uttenhof, near Offenheim. He had brewed a batch – the first – and familiarised the Brew-House with the special method of manufacture. J.C. Jacobsen, who had inherited his father's shares in the Brew-House (and did not sell them until 1839), was among those present at the pitching of the yeast at the Brew-House; one of the points he noted was that the German brewmaster added a bottle of champagne „to give it strength".

He had his own experiments in full swing at Brolæggerstræde. He set up a test plant in the cellar using a small apparatus consisting of his mother's wash copper and a couple of small malt vats with a capacity of 1-1 1/2 barrels. He began with top-fermented lager beer and after lengthy experimentation managed to achieve complete bottom-fermentation. Traces of the tests can be detected in his account book. There are repeated purchases of yeast along with champagne and colouring; douceurs are paid to the journeyman cooper for his assistance in the wash-cellar; finally, in April 1838 and again in June 1839, he inserts advertisements for Bavarian beer. He leases cellar space outside the brewery, and he studies the German technical literature avidly. In 1837 he obtains a work just published in Leipzig by C.H. Dorsch on the enlargement of existing breweries with special reference to the establishment of good storage cellars in an urban environment. He also studied the chemical principles of beer-making as expounded by Professor S.F. Hermbstädt of Berlin. But he was disappointed in Hermbstädt, who taught him only that there are such things as false prophets.

Concerning the beer which he advertised in April 1838 Jacobsen remarked in an entry made earlier in the month: „This venture has worried me for some time, not for its importance in a pecuniary sense, but because I regarded it as a touchstone of my competence, of which I have not entertained the highest opinion since my unsuccessful effort last year."

In subsequent years too he went on with these small test brews, advertised, bought bottles for his new beer and so forth, becoming convinced little by little that the sale of imported Bavarian beer was about to pioneer a change of taste in Copenhagen that would open a market abundant with opportunities in which Danish-produced Bavarian beer could participate. There was the prospect of a really profitable business, but it necessitated production on a large scale, and it was now clear to Jacobsen that he must go to Bavaria to study the Bavarian method at first hand.

Jacobsen's first visit to Bavaria took place in April 1844 as part of a tour he made with Lauritz Ridder Møller. He had suggested to his friend that they should spend a week hiking in Switzerland, but when it came to the pinch it transpired that „Little Møller" was nervous at the idea of going up into the mountains. He was a bookworm and was happiest in the numerous antique shops and bookshops which he visited on the way down through Europe. Jacobsen therefore had to walk the mountains alone while Møller trotted about in safety in the valley below, accompanied by a guide. „His intolerable, pedantic caution and fear of catching a cold" set limits to Møller's development as an outdoor man.

The trip lasted from 16 April to 8 June. The two friends celebrated Frants Djørup's birthday in Liebfraumilch at the Restaurant Ott, which the painter Fr. Storch, who was one of the small Danish artist colony in Munich, had recommended to them. „Little Møller's" meticulously kept diary also tells of their first encounter – no further along the road than Stettin, in fact – with „Bayerische Bockbier", and of Jacobsen's interest in the Bavarian method of tarring the beer-casks, with which he made acquaintance in the town of Hof. There were other things that attracted his notice too. One was a pretty Viennese. The friends made their longest stop in Munich – a week altogether – but their itinerary also included other important brewery towns such as Prague, Dresden and Vienna.

The final goal was Venice, Queen of the Adriatic. The city-state's lost wealth and advanced state of decay impressed Jacobsen. To him it was a town of tyranny and death in spite of all its art treasures. In fact he considered it salutary that the once-splendid palaces now stood dressed in rags and tatters as cautionary reminders of torture and abuse of power. He left the city with some relief, irritated on departure from the Hotel l'Europe at having caught the cashier charging, in the Venetian manner, an exorbitant price for cigars when making out the bill. Out of sheer annoyance he forgot to enjoy the sail outwards

The oldest Carlsberg building with the original bridge over the newly-laid railway line. Water-colour 1847 by the copper engraver and black-and-white artist H. G. F. Holm ("Poor Holm").

Nanna Erasmine Rygaard. Little Nanna as a mature adult and wife.

through the lagoon. „Not until we reached the open sea did my good humour return, and now I felt myself as inexpressibly at ease as a fish in water. A fresh wind was blowing straight towards us, mild and yet not warm, such as we do not have at home." The sea was a little rough during the passage to Trieste, too, and „Little Møller" retreated hastily below with his qualms.

That same summer Jacobsen obtained permission to establish a storage cellar in Hahns Bastion, in the fortress ramparts around Copenhagen. It was situated opposite Teglgaardsstræde. Up to this time he had managed by renting cellars in various places from one Hansen, a grocer, and Aagaard, a wine merchant: now he built two vaults in the ramparts connected to an ice room. Each vault was capable of holding about 700 barrels of beer. Next, he travelled to Munich for a second time in October-November 1845 and obtained from Gabriel Sedlmayr, of Zum Späten brewery, a quantity of bottom yeast which he succeeded in keeping fresh on the journey back to Copenhagen. He had had a tin to hold two quarts of yeast made for the purpose. It fitted into his hatbox, and at every stopping-place of diligence or train he hastened to the nearest water-point to cool the yeast down. This difficult mode of transport was a resounding success. During the winter of 1845-46 Jacobsen used the bottom yeast from Gabriel Sedlmayr's brewery to brew about 300 barrels of Bavarian beer, which was received with enthusiasm by the public – so much so, in fact, that Jacobsen found himself mentioned in the satirical weekly „Corsaren" (The Corsair). The reason was that the National Liberal paper „Fædrelandet" (The Fatherland) had printed a list of candidates nominated for the impending elections to the Stænderforsamling, the assembly of the Estates. The name at the top was Jacobsen, and „Corsaren" declared its concurrence with „Fædrelandet"'s choice on the assumption that it was „the Jacobsen who brews the excellent Bavarian beer; for anyone who can brew such beer can surely also be a deputy, not a doubt of it". A fine advertisement.

The beer found a ready sale, and Jacobsen now realised that a market had opened for him. At last he had found a product that met his requirements. Neither the brewery in Brolæggerstræde nor the cellars under the ramparts would suffice. On his mother's death he inherited not only the Brolæggerstræde plant but also a cash fortune of 11,000 rix-dollars. This gave him a starting capital in hand which would let him build a Bavarian beer brewery from scratch while simultaneously carrying on with the former business.

The founding of Carlsberg

Two conditions had to be met to enable a new Bavarian beermaking establishment to be set up: space for digging and lining deep storage cellars, and an abundance of fresh water. Jacobsen combed the vicinity of the city systematically to find a locality where both requirements could be satisfied. He pondered first whether to look for a site out towards the harbour, but dropped the idea because the ground water was too high and would render the installation of cellars impossible. He considered the „Kildevæld" district on Strandvejen, but in the end he chose Valby Hill, which offered fresh air and sufficient depth of soil for digging, and which was also situated to the westward, the direction in which the Water Board's soundings pointed.

The unhealthy drinking water of the capital had come under the spotlight of publicity. The physician Heinrich Callisen had strongly criticised the city's spring- and pump-water as long ago as 1807. Since then the situation had become worse. Tainting was becoming more widespread. Not infrequently rotten fish would come up with the pump-water. When an eel became stuck in the innards of the pump, the sanitary engineer would have to be sent for. The writer Vilhelm Bergsøe relates that the pump in the School of Civic Virtue at Christianshavn supplied much good material for the study of natural history, especially of the lower animal species such as mosquito larvae and other small fry. With any luck a leech, a newt or a tadpole might pop up. The water from the lakes could be semi-tepid in the summertime. Its nickname then was „eel soup". The water conduits were often rotten. A.G. Sommer, who made an investigation of Copenhagen's drinking water around the middle of the century, cited an example of a conduit which led straight through a latrine pit. Emil Hornemann, writing in 1847, drew attention to the connection between disease, especially epidemics in the city, and the deplorable water supply.

These criticisms eventually brought some action. A series of test drillings were put in hand with a view to finding new sources of pure water. These began at Taastrup-Valby, about 17 kilometres from

Copenhagen, where a flow of about 12,000 barrels of water a day was found at a depth of about 14 metres. J.C. Jacobsen kept himself informed of the results of these drillings. He was particularly interested in the fact that water had been found in 1846 during excavation of the great cutting through Valby Hill when the railway was being built. At the end of that summer the water was still gushing down towards the dip of the permanent way east of the newly-erected railway bridge.

One cold spring day Jacobsen had dragged his friend Frants Djørup out on a visit to the railway workings. Jacobsen questioned the workers, tested the ground and could not be torn away, while poor Djørup hung about, miserable with cold. The water engineer, Jens Sørensen, measured the source and thought there was an abundance of water in the hill. Next Jacobsen asked the chemist Professor C.T. Barfoed, who lectured at the Agricultural College and with whom Jacobsen was acquainted from both the Royal Agricultural Society and the Society for the Dissemination of Natural Science, to examine the water. It turned out to be very pure. That decided the matter. There still remained the question of a permit to establish a brewery outside the city ramparts but close enough to the town to be within the 15-kilometre limit, which had been retained since ancient times and was reserved as the Copenhagen brewers' market. Jacobsen contended that the brewers of the city would not suffer any injury to their sales, since the Bavarian beer which he wanted to manufacture could not be a threat, either in price or quality, to the simpler and cheaper types of beer which the city breweries must necessarily make because of the nature of their plant and equipment. Neither would there be any loss to the public revenue; the excise duty on rising sales of lager beer would more than offset the loss of customs revenue on that proportion of imports which would in future be replaced by Danish production. Finally he argued that the location of his plant would also accord with the desire of the military to keep the ground in front of the Copenhagen fortifications clear of buildings. He underlined the need for fresh and clean air. In addition he enclosed a copy of brewmaster C.H. Dorsch's book on the difficulties of constructing storage cellars in towns and cited the fact that even in Bavaria, new breweries were now being built outside the towns or in the areas around them.

The application was approved. It had been recommended by the chairmen of the Copenhagen brewers, J.N. Bjerre and K.G. Groth, as well as by the city council, of which Jacobsen himself was a member, and the corporation. The Ministry of Industry and Trade, also recommended it. The licence was issued on 25 November 1846. Three days later Jacobsen purchased from G. Bloch, wholesale merchant, a plot of „Bjerregaarden" land situated between the railway and „Bakkegaarden", for 7000 rix-dollars. He then took a loan of 45,000 rix-dollars from the merchant house of J.P. Suhr & Son. This house, which dominated the iron and coal trades, also played an important role in the money and credit operations of the business world. The banking era had not yet arrived. The house had connections with the leading banking firms of Hamburg and London. J.P. Suhr & Son also had investments of their own in the rolling mill at Frederiksværk.

The day after the acquisition of the Bjerregaarden land Jacobsen began a series of drillings with a view to charting the nature of the soil and the location of the water-bearing strata. The latter would be the cause of much anguish for him.

The beginning was promising enough. At the western end of the site a well was dug in a sandy area, and this filled with water to within a couple of feet of the surface. The accession of water was so great that the well could not be sunk deeper than about 13 feet, and the water engineer believed that this would be sufficient to meet the estimated water consumption. Jacobsen then drew up his plan for the brewery and its projected storage capacity of 5,000 barrels of beer. He made use of his notes from Munich and had the front elevations revised by Conrad Stilling, an architect whose previous work included the planning of the Tivoli Gardens in Copenhagen after the original draft by Georg Carstensen in 1843 as well as the Hippodrome, the Copenhagen Folk Theatre, in 1846. A few days after the new year Jacobsen had the main outlines of the layout ready and so was able to make a start on the excavation work. He engaged something like 100 men who had just been discharged on completion of the railway works. The laying of the floors in the storage cellars commenced at the beginning of April, but pile foundations had to be laid for the substructure of the brewery, which was discovered to stand on shifting sand.

With masonry and carpentry operations well under way, Jacobsen set off for Munich again at the end of May in order to note various details from Gabriel Sedlmayr's brewery. He also wanted to engage a Bavarian brewmaster. He was unsuccessful in this, however. He did not consider any of the candidates he interviewed to be qualified. A fortnight later he was back at the Valby building site, where he was able to hold topping-out ceremonies for both the brewery and the storage cellars on 15 August. Jacobsen christened his establishment by pouring wine over the chimney located at the centre of the plant, and gave it the name „Carlsberg". The brewery was then fitted out with inventories of equipment and came into production at the beginning of November.

The first brewing was carried out on 10 November 1847. It was a clear success, as were those that followed. Jacobsen had brought only one of his former employees over from Brolæggerstræde, his maltster N. Westrup; the rest of his men were from outside, most of them having no experience of brewery work at all. Apart from a couple of casks spoilt through lack of supervision, all operations proceeded without problems throughout the winter.

What did the original Carlsberg look like? The brewery itself was a building about 175 feet long and 45 wide. It contained three cellars: the fermenting cellar, where the main fermentation process was conducted; the winter cellar, as it was called, where the beer that was to be sold during the winter season was stored; and the malt cellar, where the steeping and germination of the barley took place. On the ground floor was the actual brew-house with its coppers, mash tun and draining vat, so called, into which the wort from the mash tun was drained. Next came the chill room with its cooling surfaces on which the wort was cooled down before the fermentation process began. Finally there was the engine room, where a steam engine supplied motive power to the beer-, wort- and water-pumps, to the malt screen, which sifted out rootlets from the malt, and to the malt crusher. The ground floor had halls and rooms for employees as well. The mezzanine floor held the granary, the malting floor, the kiln (where the ready-germinated malt was dried for further storage and use), and finally the hop room. The lofts above the entire building were used for air-drying the sprouted malt before it went to the kiln. In the loft was also located a large water tank from which the brewhouse, fermenting cellar and steam boiler were supplied with water directed via a system of pipes and stopcocks.

In the storage cellar itself alongside the brewery building was stored the beer which was to be sold during the summer. It consisted of four separate vaults, each of them 52 feet long and 16 wide. They lay at a depth of 28 feet and were furnished with ice containers and a front cellar alongside. Above the cellarage was a two-storey building used for holding stocks of storage barrels, as workshops and so on. The 4 newly-built storage cellars at Carlsberg were supplemented by the 2 old ones, which were still in use in the ramparts of the city fortress.

Finally there were a building containing stabling and barn spaces, and a wash-house where barrels and casks were swilled out and cleaned. There was also a waggon shed.

This was how it looked to begin with, but it was not very long before new buildings were being added. Throughout Jacobsen's lifetime Carlsberg was a permanent building site, so to speak, the establishment as such never being left in peace.

Marketing was conducted from the old office in Brolæggerstræde. Carlsberg's Bavarian beer was snapped up by the public. Before the season was over 2700 barrels had been sold. There were periods when people demanded the beer in vain. In his first real season with Bavarian beer, viz. 1845-46 – like all brewers Jacobsen used the old harvest year as his accounting year, i.e. 1 October to 30 September, and in fact the firm still does so – Jacobsen had brewed in the city the modest total of 300 barrels already cited. The volume for the next season, 1846-47, rose to 1805 barrels. Then production began at Carlsberg, with the result that the figure for 1847-48 rose to 2700 barrels, for the following season to 3366 barrels and for 1849-50 to 4773 barrels.

In other words, Jacobsen's expectations with regard to the market were well on the way to being fulfilled. But there was one fly in the ointment: water was short. The well turned out to be situated in a water-bearing sandy layer of limited extent. By the middle of December 1847, only a month after production started, the well had to be deepened, an operation repeated twice in the new year. The bottom of the sand layer had then been reached. This was directly contrary to all calculations and a situation that quite frankly threatened the business. Jacobsen set about getting water up from the railway trench with syringes, hand-pumps and hoses, but it was clayey and had to stand for about 12 hours in containers or surface coolers to settle before it could be used in the malt house. In frosty weather the trench froze up and then there was no water at all. A well was hastily dug right at the foot of the hill, about 500 feet away from the building – but there was no time to install pressure pumps and lead piping up to the brewery, so it was a matter of having to carry the water to the brew-house in transport barrels by horse-drawn vehicles. When the ground thawed, this form of transport had to stop. The waggon wheels sank into the wet earth and stuck fast.

The equanimity which was normally one of Jacobsen's characteristics was rudely shattered. He was „badly shaken", to use his own words. In the evening when he was walking back to the city – for he still lived in Brolæggerstræde – he followed the tracks of the newly-built railway. The railway management had given him permission to use this route. His head was spinning with his thoughts. He had played for high stakes, borrowed to the hilt, and the market was there, open and waiting for him. But had he, despite every conceivable careful preparation, nevertheless chosen wrongly in locating his new enterprise in Valby? He knew that his doings were being watched by everyone, for he was one of the city's notabilities. It was heartbreaking. The train came rushing towards him, its eye glaring. For a moment, he is reported to have said in later days, he even contemplated putting an end to it all.

But the timber in Jacobsen held firm. When the winter was over he opened a new well in the inner yard to help out. Pumping equipment and piping were now brought down to the well at the foot of the hill and water from there and from the newly-established well was led up to the brewery. This eased matters. His spirits rose, and he summoned courage to devise further improvements, which were soon in operation. Intense pressure of work had made inroads on his vitality, however. One evening in the spring he took a severe chill. He refused to take notice of it, but it developed into a violent attack of rheumatic fever which confined him to his sickbed for six weeks. This illness brought Jacobsen to the realisation that he could not go on without expert assistance. That autumn, therefore, he took counsel with Professor Barfoed, on whose recommendation he then appointed E. Gottlieb, a graduate in pharmacology, as inspector at Carlsberg.

Brewing proceeded satisfactorily during the 1849-50 season, but much water had to be pumped by hand from the garden well (well no. 3), which was the most productive. It was irksome and expensive, and so Jacobsen installed a small steam engine, manufactured by Lunde, to drive a double-acting water pump. A new engine house was erected in the spring as an extension of the wash house in which the beer barrels were swilled out and cleaned, also a process requiring water. In 1854 the steam engine was moved down to the garden. The water level in the well had fallen to the point where the pump had difficulty in drawing the water up the hill to the wash house and brewery.

By the middle 1850s production at Carlsberg had risen beyond the projected 5000 barrels, and water supply was still the brewery's Achilles heel. Jacobsen had consulted Professor G. Forchhammer, who was in charge of the test drillings being made on behalf of the Copenhagen Water Board, including the drilling at Taastrup-Valby mentioned earlier. Here it had been possible to carry out an „artesian" drilling, i.e. a drilling which struck such quantities of water that they gushed up through the drilling pipe of themselves and spilled out over the ground. However, for geological reasons Forchhammer had rejected the feasibility of an artesian drilling on the Carlsberg land. But Jacobsen still clung to the idea. He believed that the Water Board's drillings indicated that on the other side of Valby Hill too there might be water-bearing strata deeper down, right down at the edge of the Saltholm limestone. He therefore drilled further via the garden well, and at a depth of 58 feet, or 23 feet below sea level, he struck a layer of gravel containing considerably more water than the overlying layer. He therefore commenced excavation of a large new well in August 1858.

During the second half of the 1850s the need for water became still more acute. Production at Carlsberg almost quadrupled, reaching more than 20,000 barrels during the 1860-61 season. Once more the wells had to be deepened and new and more powerful pumping equipment installed. The excavation of new, deep storage cellars reduced the ground-water level, other industrial establishments in the vicinity were also making inroads on the water reservoirs, and when the first cooling machines were installed in 1878/79 a further strain was put on the water supply. Efforts were made to relieve this by implementing strict economy, with re-use of the cooling water from the cooling installations; and the drilling continued, deeper and deeper. Then at last, in the 1880s, the drilling reached right down and established a well in the Saltholm limestone, thus accomplishing what Forchhammer had sworn was impossible at the Carlsberg plant.

In 1855, when Jacobsen had secured an abundance of water for a while, he was able to consider expanding his brew-house installation. In accordance with his established custom, he decided to make a lengthy study tour before getting down to it. He had been in Munich, Nuremberg and Dresden during the summer of 1851 in the course of a holiday trip with his wife Laura and son Carl that included visits to the museums of Switzerland and North Italy, where they took in Milan. He had noticed that there were not many changes in brewery technology going on, apart from the fact that Gabriel Sedlmayr was beginning to mash by steam and was engaged in erecting a large new brewery outside Munich. The time was ripe for another journey of orientation, and this time Jacobsen set off on his own.

Growth and expansion

The tour took place in July and August 1855. It took J.C. Jacobsen to Dresden, Prague, Vienna, Munich, Stuttgart and Karlsruhe, „where I gathered together a mass of interesting information which put me in a position to draw up a definite plan, which I began to put down on paper one Sunday afternoon in a public park at Kannstadt".

For a brief moment he wondered whether to return home, but since he was anxious to visit the World Exhibition in Paris and see the Crystal Palace in London he carried on. The visit to France was Jacobsen's first. From his earliest years he had been interested in the history of the French nation, and like so many of his generation he was deeply fascinated by the figure of Napoleon. He had read about Napoleon and studied him „both in success and failure". „I have admired his greatness in both cases, a greatness the like of which the world has not seen since the glorious days of Rome." The Napoleonic cult received a massive boost during the Second Empire, which was inaugurated in 1852 by Louis Napoleon's self-appointed raising to the imperial purple under the name of Napoleon III. One of the new régime's triumphs was the staging of the World Exhibition in Paris in 1855, which attracted visitors from every country in the world.

Jacobsen's mind was open and receptive. He arrived in Strasbourg from Karlsruhe in the evening. „My first step on to French soil made a wonderful impression on me, the cause of which I do not rightly know how to explain. Perhaps it had something to do with my mood, which was elated by the favourable outcome of my travels in Germany, during which I came more or less to an understanding of my future line of action." He was struck by the contrast between the tedium of the German towns, especially Karlsruhe, and the liveliness of Strasbourg. „I had to bite my lip to stop myself walking down the street smiling."

His spirits rose higher still when he reached Paris. His appetite for the city was enormous. „When I am in Paris it is like getting a new novel; I have no peace until I get to the end of it, but it is not easy to get to the end of Paris, for every time one turns over the page wanting to peep at another scene, one is captured by the contents and advances only a little way." He devours everything: the Tuileries, the Place de la Concorde, the Louvre from all sides within and without, the boulevards, the Théâtre Français and the grand opera, the first Napoleon on the column of Vendôme, the towers of Notre Dame, the Panthéon, the Luxembourg gardens, the botanical gardens, the zoo.

On the way to the Café Danemark to read the Danish newspapers he past tense the Palais Royal quarter. This ancient part of the city is „a fairy tale", „I know of nothing more true", and his description of his promenade through the quarter burns with enthusiasm.

„The clamour of motley humanity, the merry shouts of children at play, the splash of fountains and the soaring peal of music, the waiters' sing-song cries – all these captivate and stun the ear, as the passing show of varied life, the massive, handsome buildings surrounding the garden with its statues, flowers and lawns, likewise assail and overwhelm the eye. And when the thousands upon thousands of gas-jets are lit and their gleam is multiplied by the numberless shops resplendent with gold, silver and precious stones, one may well be tempted to pinch oneself to make sure it is not a dream. One feature which magnifies unbelievably the magical effect of the sea of light produced by the innumerable gas-jets – one little shop selling sweets and candied fruits, for example, boasts no fewer than 108 of them – is the immense use made of mirror glass on all walls, side-windows and even on the pillars outside. It is accordingly impossible to tell whether what you see is in front or behind, whether it is on the one side or the other of the street or arcade. Thinking you have brushed against someone's arm you begin to say 'Pardon, m'sieu',' – but then you see that what you touched was nothing but your own reflection in the mirror. When at last you leave this enchanted garden and walk up the Rue Vivienne, for example, the surroundings, while less lavish, still glitter hardly less brightly with a similar superabundance of mirror glass and gas-jets both inside and outside the buildings, so that the street very much resembles the Corso in Rome on Moccoli evening; and as to the noise – well, that is even louder. Lemonade hawkers, newsvendors and heaven knows what else deafen the ear with their

incessant cries, to which are added the sounds of the countless vehicles and the constant long drawn-out warning cry of 'He-e-eh!'
from the drivers of every possible type and dimension of conveyance,
from the huge 20-foot long two-wheeled carts and the big double-
decker omnibuses to the light fiacres or the other lighter cabriolets
with a fine, whip-cracking, mounted jockey as driver."

The Palace of Industries itself, on the other hand, was something of a
disappointment, apart from the second section, „which is as long as
Frederiksberg Allé" (one of Copenhagen's longest thoroughfares)
and where he found interesting items among the machinery and
building articles.

He tackled the museums as well. In the Louvre he found his
particular favourites, the Italian masters, to be better represented than
elsewhere. He lingered over the Napoleonic relics: the Emperor's
grey coat, the small three-cornered hat, the threadbare patched hat
from St Helena and – gem of gems! – the banner of the Guard, the
one of which the Emperor took his farewell in 1814, kissing it with the
wish that the kiss might resound through posterity. „His wish has
been fulfilled," wrote Jacobsen in his letter home from his travels.

The historical picture gallery at Versailles he found unforgettable, a
succession of vast and splendid halls „wherein the whole of France's
history can be read, so to speak, in paintings and illustrated works".
Again it was Napoleon and his generals who seized his interest. Their
mighty exploits were depicted on gigantic canvases or in marble by
artists such as David, Gérard and the then much-esteemed painter of
battle scenes, Horace Vernet. Jacobsen considered it an excellent way
of writing history. It made an impression on people. „Louis Philippe,
who created this gallery, deserves gratitude for having done so."

It detracted nothing from the perfection of Versailles that the
celebrated fountains were playing on the day Jacobsen visited the
palace. At the great Neptune basin the stroke of five was the signal for
everything to start. Hundreds of jets of water flew heavenwards while
at that very moment the sun broke through the light cloud cover and
played on the gushing water in all the colours of the rainbow. The
crowd of spectators murmured, but there was no shout of acclama-
tion, „in which I should certainly have joined".

Jacobsen was bowled over by the pomp and circumstance of the Napoleonic renaissance. He left France convinced that the country possessed all the conditions for becoming once more „la grande Nation" of which Napoleon I had spoken. The lively, intelligent spirit of the French, their industriousness and incessant activity, coupled with their ambition and strong national sentiment, would secure for them a new place in Europe's culture and history. The visit made him a convinced francophile for the rest of his life. The historical picture gallery of the palace of Versailles, along with its gardens, made an abode in his soul, residing there until one day they became a reality at home in Denmark.

Neither was Jacobsen disappointed when he crossed the Channel and visited the Crystal Palace, which had been built to house the Great Exhibition in London in 1851. After the Exhibition closed the Palace had been dismantled and tranferred from its place in Hyde Park to Sydenham, where it was used as a panopticon or museum, with objets d'art, zoological and ethnographical tableaux, botanical gardens and so on. He sent his son a letter including a description of the collections. The grand scale of the construction was what struck him most. „It is not merely the biggest human work that I have seen in the scope of a single glance, but it is also the most complete." This eighth wonder of the world was prefabricated entirely in cast-iron components and panes of glass – 293,655 pieces in all – manufactured in advance. The idea was fathered by Joseph Paxton, a practical man with no distinguished examination certificates, gardener and handyman to the Duke of Devonshire. It was quite simply a gigantic greenhouse. And it had another virtue in Jacobsen's eyes: it was not financed by the government but from private funds. Nine men had set the enterprise in motion, relying on their countrymen's assistance, an expectation in which they had not been disappointed. „In this respect the English are greater, far greater, than the French and all the other nations of Europe."

From London, Jacobsen's itinerary took him through Belgium, where he saw a brewery utilising cylindrical boilers for boiling the wort. Next he travelled to Cologne, whence he made an excursion to the quarries at Neuwied, which were used as beer cellars for summer beer because some of the ice formed in the cold quarry in winter remained unthawed and kept the temperature down.

At the end of August Jacobsen was home again at Carlsberg, where he set to work at once on his new plan. What this involved, briefly, was a substantial expansion of production. A new winter and spring cellar was built, with ice-cellars above ground on the Bardili model, which he had seen in Stuttgart. The principle was quite simple in itself, viz. to place the stock of natural ice above the storage cellar so that the heavier cold air would sink down into the cellar. The difficulty lay in establishing a completely impervious cover between the overlying ice and the storage room, but this was successfully overcome. The system was introduced in the subsequent period when new storage cellars were built at Carlsberg.

Next the old winter cellar was fitted out as a fermenting cellar. Twenty small fermenting vats (two to each brew) were installed, and also a cooling apparatus for wort, and this new fermenting cellar went into operation on 21 January 1856.

Radical changes were made in the brew-house as well. As has been noted, the brew-house fitted out in 1847 was designed for a maximum annual production of 5000 barrels of beer. It consisted of a so-called „pre-heater", i.e. a copper in which the water for the doughing in was heated up, plus a „boiling copper", which was an open copper with furnace for the boiling of minor quantities of mash and for the subsequent boiling of wort and hops; and finally there was a wooden mash tun, fitted with a sieve bottom. The mash was stirred manually, as a rule by at least four men. They used a wooden instrument resembling an oar and known in technical terminology as a „mash rower". The small steam engine which Jacobsen had purchased from Lunde drove a pump which transferred the mash and wort from tun to copper. No other mechanical power was employed in this first installation.

Mechanical capacity was increased when a 10 h.p. steam engine of Baumgarten and Burmeister's manufacture was installed in 1857. Another important new step was taken when hand mashing was replaced by mechanical mashing. Jacobsen had seen a mash machine (also by Bardili) at work in Stuttgart and decided to introduce this technology at his own establishment. The old mash tun was taken out and replaced by a new machine whose rake-shaped arms revolved on an axle in the middle of the tun. By January 1856 the teething troubles had been overcome. It was now possible to make two brews a day at Carlsberg, one during the day and one overnight, and this shift-working arrangement was instituted at the brewery on 12 January 1856.

Jacobsen had already enlarged the copper capacity a year after the establishment opened. A new open copper was obtained in which the heating surface was 5-6 times bigger. An important further step was taken with the procurement of a closed copper (over an open furnace) on the Belgian model in the summer of 1857. This too was part of the plan. It was brought into operation in December. Another closed copper was added two years later, so that there was now a double brewing plant, which in the winters of 1859 and 1860 was able to accomplish four brewings every 24 hours during the 2-3 months' high season of winter brewing.

The establishment of a larger malt house also featured in Jacobsen's plan of 1855. In the spring of 1856 a new malt house was erected, provisionally with three malting spaces. Next followed the installation of two double kilns, one of which was immediately equipped with floors while the other had them fitted in the autumn of 1858.

The area of the site was enlarged. On 11 December 1856 Jacobsen purchased about 5 1/2 acres of „Bakkegaarden" land adjoining Carlsberg for the sum of 10,000 rix-dollars, then began building four new storage cellars during the following summer. Other installations included the erection of a hoist and an „Archimedes screw" for malt transport. These were driven by the steam engine.

The new plan put Carlsberg in a position to multiply its production during the second half of the 1850s. Production reached over 15,000 barrels annually, surpassing the 25,000 mark in the early 1860s. In other words, sales of the recently-launched lager beer continued to be spectacular.

Jacobsen embarked on the construction of four new storage cellars in the summer of 1860. They were ready the following year. The old cold cellars in Hahns Bastion were filled for the last time in March 1860 and then abandoned, which immediately reduced storage capacity by about 1400 barrels of beer, although 300 barrels were regained

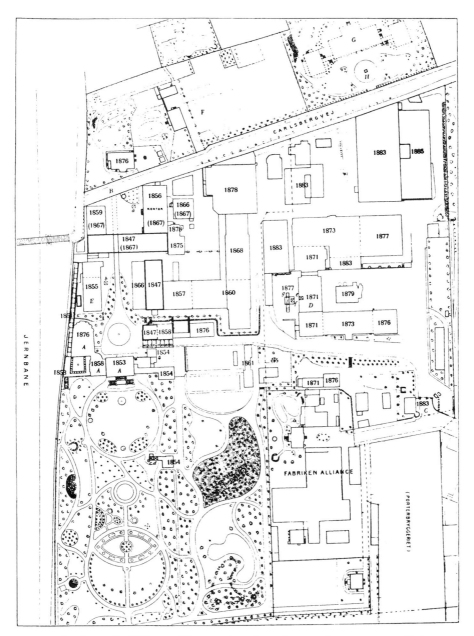

Ground plan of Old Carlsberg showing the various stages of the ex-
pansion of the breweries. The small squares with crosses show the wells
and their location. At bottom right alongside the garden grounds is the
Alliance bottling factory. Carlsberg Road (Carlsbergvej) is today called
Old Carlsberg Road (Gl. Carlsbergvej).

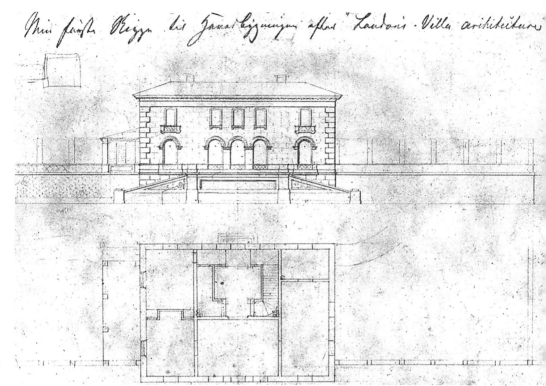

J. C. Jacobsen's first sketch of his residence at Carlsberg. Jacobsen cites as his model the "Encyclopaedia of Cottage, Farm and Villa Architecture" (1833, enlarged 2nd ed. 1842), by the Englishman J. C. Loudon, but only part of his conception is drawn from this work: the facade of the house is Italian-inspired.

by using larger barrels in the older cellars at Carlsberg.

Jacobsen maintained his prices for Bavarian beer from its launching in 1847 until 1859/60, when he reduced the price from 12 rix-dollars a barrel to 10. He followed this up a year later, in the 1861/62 season, with a further reduction of 1 rix-dollar, to 9 rix-dollars per barrel.

The background to this vigorous expansion and the tempo at which it was driven forward, and to the price reductions of the early 1860s, is formed by the buoyant business conditions prevailing in Denmark, including the capital, during the decades around the middle of the century. These conditions are best seen in perspective if we go back in time a little.

Apart from a few good years after the end (for Denmark) of the Napoleonic Wars in 1814, the postwar period as a whole was characterised by crisis and a restructuring of the Danish economy. The national bankruptcy of 1814 also left its mark. Copenhagen suffered especially. The loss of Norway, which Denmark had had to cede under the peace treaty, hit the capital particularly hard. The competition from English industrial goods made itself felt in the city's business life. The transit trade in overseas goods, which had flourished under the shelter of neutrality during the so-called „golden age", shrank drastically after the war. More and more of the Danish export trade deserted the merchant houses of the capital in favour of provincial merchants – a shift not unconnected with efforts to open up new markets for Danish agricultural produce to the westward in England and to the southward in Germany and the Netherlands following the loss of the market in South Norway, formerly reserved for Denmark under legislation passed in the 18th century.

The trend of events is also reflected in the demographic figures, for example in the ratio between country and town and between the capital and the provincial towns. The Copenhagen growth rate was a mere 0.5% during the first four decades of the 19th century, while that of the provincial towns was 1.1% and of the rural population 0.9%.

Business conditions changed in the 1840s. The boom came first in agriculture, which was Denmark's leading occupation. The corn trade in particular expanded, but the years up to the middle 1860s were chiefly marked by progress on a broad front in which urban occupations, including those of Copenhagen, also participated. Again we can turn to the population figures as an indicator. From 1840 to 1870 the towns' share of the total population of Denmark rose from 21% to 25%.

Copenhagen with its suburban parishes had an annual population growth of 1.6% during this period. From the beginning of the 1850s onwards new building gathered momentum in the capital, with a building boom in the second half of the decade. The former geographical limits were burst by the early enlargement of the city outside the ramparts. Industrialisation of the capital was accelerated by the introduction of the steam engine for motive power in craft trades and industries. Even around the middle 1850s Copenhagen had a considerable number of horse gins, but in the longer term horse gins, or horse walks as they were otherwise known, could not solve industry's power problem.

The brewery trade was aware of these developments. The growing urban population signified growing demand, and a rising standard of living fostered a demand for more finished products; this opened the way for production in larger establishments, where the steam engine came just at the right moment as a new power source for the breweries, as also did the steam copper as an important instrument in the brew-house. According to the industrial census of 1855, Copenhagen in that year still had 26 small breweries and one large brewery, the King's Brew-House. Carlsberg was not counted because it was situated outside the city boundaries and was not covered by the census. A law passed on 9 December 1851 lifted the former ban on the establishment of breweries within 15 kilometres of the capital and on the selling of beer to the town by breweries in the country. In other words, the road trodden by Jacobsen in 1847 was now open to everybody, and it is therefore not surprising to find that by 1865 the number of breweries with steam engines in the Copenhagen district had grown to seven. As well as Carlsberg and the King's Brew-House, these were Aldersro, Rabeshave, H. Tvede, Svanholm and Vogelius. Three of these – viz. Carlsberg, Svanholm and Aldersro – were Bavarian beer breweries, the others ale breweries. Whereas in 1854 Bavarian beer accounted for only 6% of beer production in the Copenhagen area, the proportion had risen to just under 30% by 1871. During the intervening period beer production overall had just about doubled, while production of the new Bavarian beer, which had chimed in excellently with the urban public's taste, increased almost tenfold.

The business climate for investment in a new venture of the Carlsberg character was favourable. Neither legislation nor the government offered resistance. Although the general trade law signalling the victory of economic liberalism in Denmark was not passed until the Freedom of Trade Act of 29 December 1857 (to come into force in the new year of 1862), conditions in the brewery industry, as in many others in fact, had changed decades earlier. The ordinance of 30 August 1805 had opened brewery as a free occupation, subject only to citizenship and licence, it being left to the practitioners of the trade themselves to decide which types of beer they wanted to brew and at what prices. The only requirement was for the police to set twice a year a certain stock of grain and malt per brewery for reasons of security of the city's supplies, and supervise quality. Breweries were not allowed to sell beer from taprooms, and the old 15-kilometre limit around Copenhagen remained in force until 1851, when it was abolished for the provincial towns as well. At the same time the special malt excise duty, which Jacobsen had had to pay on deliveries of Bavarian beer to the capital, was abolished.

The government's policy on dues and imposts in this field reflected also a desire to get away from the absolutist state's predilection for regulation and consumption taxes. Bavarian beer-making achieved its breakthrough during one of the few periods in Danish history – probably the only one – when beer was not taxed. The taxes on the grinding of corn disappeared with the abolition of excise duty. It is true that the possibility of imposing a specific purchase tax on beer was mooted around 1857 with a view to compensating for the revenue lost by the abolition of the Sound Tolls, but the idea was abandoned out of regard for the needs of the common man. Beer was a necessary article for the working class. But a new customs duty was imposed on imported beer, which further benefited the home-produced beer types. Not until 1891 was real taxation of beer introduced in Denmark.

These favourable conditions explain the very substantial earnings of Carlsberg. One or two figures tell the story. As early as 1849/50,

Jacobsen was able to amortise over 19,500 rix-dollars on the Carlsberg brewery and the Hahns Bastion rampart cellar opposite Teglgaards-stræde, plus another 4000 rix-dollars on the property in Brolægger-stræde, while his assets grew from about 61,000 to over 100,000 rix-dollars in the same period.

Jacobsen's leading position and his product's character as a proprietary article (in today's terminology we should call it „premium beer") is apparent also from his pricing policy. Obviously such a lucrative growth market as that for Bavarian beer would attract others, but the advent of the first competitor, the Svanholm brewery, on to the market in 1853 made no difference to the price. The new firm followed Carlsberg.

In 1858 there was a suggestion from one of the shareholders, N. Wolff, that the King's Brew-House should go into the Bavarian beer market. He calculated the net profit of doing so at 5 rix-dollars per barrel, or just under half of the sale price from brewery to beer-bottler. The entry of a third Bavarian beer brewery might admittedly trigger a price fall and so reduce the high profit level, but Wolff did not consider the risk to be great „as long as just two Bavarian breweries dominate sales". The Brew-House shareholders did not adopt the proposal, however, though there were others who did feel attracted.

Carlsberg's price reduction in December 1859 followed hard on the heels of the announcement of plans by the merchant George Owen to form a joint stock company – it was established on 4 January 1860 – for the purpose of building a Bavarian beer brewery on land at Aldersro. The further reduction of 1 rix-dollar per barrel in February 1862 was timed to coincide with the expansion of the Svanholm brewery in that year.

It has already been related that Owen felt disturbed by Jacobsen's price reduction and appealed to him in vain for an agreement; the price of Bavarian beer was amazingly stable for all that, and Carlsberg was the price leader. When Jacobsen, after the fire at his brewery in 1867, wanted to increase his earnings and raised the price of his beer from 9 to 10 rix-dollars, the other Bavarian beer breweries followed suit, and this price level held until 1881. Under the pressure of competition from the numerous new producers who appeared on the scene during the intervening years, Jacobsen then reduced the price to 9 rix-dollars per barrel, or 18 kroner after the changeover to the new currency system in Denmark.

Jacobsen started off at Carlsberg with a labour force of between 10 and 12 men. This grew to between 20 and 28 men during the second half of the 1850s. In the first half of the next decade there was a further increase to 35 men. Productivity as a function of volume of output and size of workforce exhibited an annual rate of increase of 5.1% up to 1865, while growth in output was 12.6% and growth of the workforce 7.1% per year. The reason for the improvement of productivity was a more intensive use of labour and fixed capital. Thus, in the early stages brewing went on for only 6 months of the year, whereas in 1865 this had been extended to 9 months. The switch to mechanical mashing enabled two brewings a day to be made, as has been noted; and when the doubled brewing plant was brought into operation, four brewings a day became possible.

The training and disciplining of the labour force went hand in hand with this more intensive use of the new plant. J.C. Jacobsen's overriding concern to improve his product and to be able to offer a continuous supply of high-quality beer spurred him to practise an employment procedure and a wage system which sought to motivate his employees to stay with him by offering them opportunities of advancement and training. The established labour force fell into three groups according to the work function. The first group was employed on heavy outside work, the second on the actual brewing, while the third and best paid comprised the draymen who did the selling and the work leaders of foreman category. All these were paid monthly. In addition Carlsberg employed a small number of casual labourers, but these comprised only about 10% of the total workforce at this period. They were men employed to excavate storage cellars, cut ice, dig wells and work in the grounds – the latter including the laying out of the large garden adjoining the brewer's planned residence. Jacobsen started the levelling and planting of the garden in 1851, groups of conifers featuring prominently in the layout.

There was a great difference between established employees and casual labourers: the latter's wages were about half those of the trained workers.

As was remarked earlier, except for Westrup, the maltster, who had come with Jacobsen from Brolæggerstræde to Valby, the labour force of 1847 was newly recruited and in the majority of cases had no previous knowledge of brewery work. Importance was attached to getting young workers of strong physique, from the provinces for choice, and – after conscription was brought in – with their military service behind them, since it provided some guarantee of discipline. Many of the operations in brewery work were rough, heavy drudgery, especially in the malt house and in racking and handling the big vats and barrels. This harsh toil exacted its price, notably in the form of back injuries such as slipped disc, often known in those days as sciatica.

The code of labour discipline was set out in the rules with which employees were presented on being engaged. Later on in the century, for example in the code promulgated in 1871, the new employee was required to append his signature to the rules. He was now established or „tenured", a status possibly suggestive of a master-and-servant relationship, but it also invested the appointment with a certain individualistic stamp. Regardless of signature, the rules were legitimate in the eyes of the authorities. They were considered to be oral agreements between two parties and therefore binding.

The most important element in the actual conditions of tenure was the underlining of the employer's right to direct and distribute the work. Next followed a series of rules designed to ensure the proper handling of machinery, raw materials and finished products, auxiliary materials, tools and so on; for example, the duty engineer was held responsible for the water level and pressure in the steam boilers. Finally came a set of rules for securing good order such as bans on smoking and the use of naked flame as required by the fire regulations, visiting times in the employees' day-room and other rooms, order and cleanliness in the latter, and so forth. The rules concluded by specifying the disciplinary measures which could be invoked, which took the form of a system of fines. Disobedience or insubordination towards owner or manager were grounds for dismissal, as were breaches of the fire regulations or the ban on accepting tips. The latter was aimed at the draymen of the sales force. Their position vis-à-vis the brewery was that of agent. They had a permanent circle of customers, and when Carlsberg beer was in demand they were wont to take an excess price which went into their own pockets, and they also favoured customers who bribed them.

Working hours were long, as they were elsewhere in Denmark. They varied at Carlsberg according to the nature of the work; but the rules mention a normal work-period of 11 hours between 6 a.m. and 7 p.m. with breaks totalling two hours (i.e. 11 hours net and 13 gross). Saturdays were worked and most of Sunday up to 4 p.m.

Unmarried employees lived at the brewery. Many of the married ones, who comprised fewer than half the established employees in the early days, settled in nearby Valby. Until 1861 unmarried employees received their board. Laura Jacobsen administered this system, inasmuch as she drew up the bills of fare. Her surviving kitchen day-book with recipes shows us a daily diet adapted to meet the high-calorie requirement of a hardworking team of men, with potato, porridge and dried cod dishes dominating the menu and typifying the age with such items as the inevitable Saturday øllebrød (a dish made of bread and ale) accompanying the herring and potatoes. Employees generally were allowed free beer from day to day ad libitum. This was limited to four quarts a day in 1860 and then reduced to half that amount later on in the century.

Laura's dietary notes also show festive meals, e.g. on Michaelmas Day, which was both interest-settlement day and skiftedag, i.e. the day on which servants used to change jobs. It was celebrated with rice porridge, a roast and beetroot for dinner, which was normally taken between 12 midday and 1 p.m. but between 12 and 2 p.m. on a festive occasion such as this; also on this day there would be a variety of open sandwiches at the afternoon mealtime, known as Vesperkost, between 4 and 4.30 p.m., with cakes and punch as well. Laura reckoned 5-6 measures of rice per man for the rice porridge; in her own household she managed with 3 measures per family member.

Martinmas was another festive day at Carlsberg, being also the anniversary of the brewery's opening. On this occasion roast pork and punch would be served. And Christmas Eve was the festival when family and employees ate together – just as master and men had shared a table and broken bread together in the guild days. The menu comprised rice porridge, roast goose, five apple-batter cakes per person and punch.

The provision of meals was abolished in 1861. The system had had its day: the labour force now included a larger number of married men taking responsibility for their own board and lodging. However, accommodation continued to be provided at Carlsberg for the unmarried. The management compensated for the loss of free meals by adding 10 rix-dollars a month to wages. Board and lodging were a languishing phenomenon in the craft trades generally: by the beginning of the century, over 40% of craft journeymen in Copenhagen lived in their own accommodation. From now on brewery employees must bring their own food and drink. They employed women to make morning coffee and bread at 8-8.30. Pork butchers' men from Valby came up to Carlsberg to take orders. They came running up with deliveries several times a day at eating times, and that was when the employees settled accounts with them.

Eating times were signalled by the ringing of bells. At the Jacobsens' family home mealtimes were announced in original fashion by the blowing of a bugle. The domestic staff, consisting of Lars the coachman, the housekeeper, the cook and the maidservant, took their meals downstairs, while the brewer and his family assembled upstairs in the dining room.

When Laura died, Carl Jacobsen took over the Brewer's former residence but allowed the rooms to remain as "Rooms of Remembrance" and used only the Old Carlsberg main building for receptions and the like. A series of photographs show the rooms as they were at this period. Here is "Grandpapa's Room", or the Captain's study, with its view over the brewery.

"Grandmama's Room", with Laura's bust on the corner cupboard. On the walls are engravings after the Italian masters whom J. C. admired. The window faces out into the conservatory.

The dining salon at Old Carlsberg photographed facing the east gallery.
Bissen's bust of Jacobsen is positioned between the pillars.

The "garden room" in the Old Carlsberg main building.

Through Nanna's eyes

Nanna Rygaard, aged 18, arrived at Carlsberg one spring day in 1863. She came from Eveldrup, near Hobro, where she had lived in the house of the rural dean and taught at the infants' school. Erhard Kogsbølle and the manservant met her at Valby station, and together they walked along by the railway lines to the brewery. Nanna was to be Laura Jacobsen's companion. She would have the status of a member of the family. Her mother was a cousin of Laura and the widow of Mads Rygaard, a merchant of Holstebro, who had died in 1854 leaving a family of eight children.

Aunt Laura, who knew Nanna from her visits to the family in Jutland, had always enjoyed the young girl's confidence. Laura was younger than her cousin and, in Nanna's own words, „loves me like a mother". It was Laura's idea that Nanna should come to Copenhagen to live with her in the family home. In accordance with family tradition there was the unspoken idea that Nanna might make a suitable daughter-in-law. If so, however, matters turned out otherwise.

When she arrived, Nanna was already head over heels in love. Her suitor was Jens Brask, a lawyer 13 years older than herself who worked first in Mariager, then in Holstebro. The couple had become engaged earlier in the year in great secrecy. Nanna knew exactly when she had fallen in love with her Jens. It was one morning at Christmas time in 1861, when they were dressing the Christmas tree together at the home of a gentleman farmer named Lindahl, a close friend of J.C. Jacobsen. Not even the Christmas snow was wanting in the romance; Jens had arrived from Randers during a tremendous snowstorm. Nanna was a ready victim of the infatuation with students prevalent in those days. Students „possess more refinement and are better read than both merchants and farmers – and – good heavens, I almost forgot an entire class, the pharmacists, but of course they are neither fish, flesh nor fowl". So she set her cap at her lawyer, and now he had pledged himself to her.

However Jens Brask, who still did not have a permanent job, wanted their relationship to remain secret for the time being, but Nanna wanted to put her cards on the table for both her mother and her aunt. She wrote to Carlsberg about it before setting off and received a letter of good wishes in reply. On the other hand her „serious-minded uncle" shook his head and regarded her as a child, but „of course I have my own free will in this respect, and on this matter they would never, whomever I chose, place any restraint on my freedom," she assured her beloved as she set off for the capital.

Her sojourn at Carlsberg was to last three years, a long time to wait for a young girl eager to be married and who characterised herself as „a woman with a good deal of sensuality as well". Despite the proclamation of free will, it turned out that the family did interfere, as was the wont of families in those days, if not in the choice of partner then at any rate in the question of the length of the engagement. Laura did not want to lose Nanna; the mother felt that her daughter owed the family at Carlsberg some consideration; then there was housekeeping to be learnt as well; and J.C., who appreciated comely women with personality, was fond of her. The „Little One" livened up Carlsberg with her humour and temperament; she used a degree of licence in speaking to Jacobsen.

Nanna was by no means blind to the fact that in this opulent home there were rocks on which the unwary might strike. She was likewise aware that there were others who envied her the entré she had into this wealthy family with the young son and sole heir in the house. She was especially nervous of Aunt Faye, Laura's elder sister, a widow who lived in the Brolæggerstræde property but had a room permanently at her disposal at Carlsberg, where she often stayed to keep her sister company. Nicoline Faye was not a lady of the gentler sort. Nanna consoled herself with the thought that Aunt Laura was on her side, for „she is tolerant and affectionate and not nearly as particular as Aunt Nicoline".

It therefore came as a big surprise to her that Laura simply did not live up to all these expectations. On the contrary, Nanna found her irritable, „delicate" in health – and unhappy. She quickly realised that there were deep tensions inside the four walls, pulling the family towards a showdown. On the broader national plane too the clouds were gathering: a war was on the way.

Letter-writing was a problem at first. Letters were the lifeline between the two lovers. They exchanged letters every week, chatted with each other, opened their hearts to each other, prepared themselves for each other – which irritated Laura, who was by no means in the frame of mind for all this billing and cooing. Nanna had to write her letters clandestinely, mostly at night. Things went on like this through the summer, then the letters became the subject of serious debate in the family. Laura declared that letter-writing had nowadays passed quite beyond reasonable limits. It had simply become a vogue among young people. „In contrast I can tell you that Uncle only wrote to me once a fortnight and sometimes not even that. He did not want any definite rule about it." The debate continued at the house of Kogsbølle, the manager. Two short letters a week was his advice to young people in love. However, the outcome was that Nanna was able to go over to writing during the day: in other words, the letters had become legalised. But the theme was not thereby exhausted. Now Carl joined in, remarking that Nanna ought to make rough drafts of her letters: „One ought not to waste one's own and other people's time on something not fully thought out." If one wrote as one spoke, „so much nonsense would come into it – for one is always speaking badly, either without any point or without any conclusion". And that was his opinion.

Nanna stuck to her guns – fortunately. Precisely because of her spontaneous nature and wide-awake faculties her surviving letters furnish snapshots of life at Carlsberg with the brewer and his family which are refreshingly different from carefully considered, neatly posed representations. They are small glimpses caught by a very young girl very much in love, and have all the advantages and drawbacks inherent in such a source.

On her arrival Nanna was installed in a room on the first floor above the vestibule to the main building. It was an excellent observation post, which she retained until the last few months before her departure, when she exchanged rooms with Aunt Faye, who was annoyed by the wind.

„Saturday morning! Now I can carry on, having finished all my domestic chores. Aunt has gone to town and the gentlemen are looking after themselves. Carl is not well, by the way ... I am sitting up here by my own window ... Well, Uncle has just crossed the courtyard on his way to the brewery – now I ought to use my time for singing do-re-mi-fa-so-la. If he is low-spirited, then certainly I should rather spare his ears [Nanna was taking singing lessons from Rung, the excellent, gentle, amiable Rung, recommended to her by Lindahl] But that is Carl I can hear, yes! So he has just come up. He is calling down the speaking tube for his tea – yes, well, we shall let him drink it, and I shall stay sitting up here a little longer."

Such is the style – authentic spoken language. Some samples of letter-writing:

„I am in a good mood, you know! Can you not see it from my handwriting? It is so *geläufig,* as the Germans say. It breaks all the rules of copybook writing and goes wandering all over the lines, like my thoughts. 'It should be straight as an arrow,' were Aunt Richter's words at school. But don't I understand myself at all? I am not writing what I want to write! And now the green sun-curtains have blown over the writing while it was still wet. 'That was not nice,' as Uncle repeats after me. These words are like Hans Christian Andersen's fairy tales: there is something serious hidden behind them."

Or from one of Carl's carousals with his friends:

„So now the young bloods are singing 'Life's rebirth in Nordic Lands', but Jerndorff the tenor is what they lack ... Their singing is getting hoarser and hoarser down there – I think they are near their peak – however, they never really go beyond the stage of aesthetic beauty – Now I am tired, so goodnight, my beloved, for this evening."

Carl's carousals could in fact end up with outdoor serenading at two in the morning. First outside J.C.'s and Laura's windows. Next a little Swedish ditty outside Nanna's window „which woke me up very pleasantly".

More song:

„Carl is singing, so it is thundering through the house – this evening he is going out, to someone you know, the widow Ramus, where they will play a comedy by Erik Bøgh. Like Orpheus, he says: 'I do it, but I do it reluctantly.' Private theatricals are his bane."

Nanna is ill:

„I am lying here all cosy in my nice room. The doors to the stairs are open, and I can hear from below the music from Faust, which Peter Meyer is producing down there."

On one occasion the cat is away so the mouse will play, and Nanna sits in Jacobsen's room to write:

„Uncle and Aunt have gone to town to see Puggaard the merchant's collection of paintings, the parlourmaid is out, the housekeeper has gone along with her, and Lars the coachman is enthroned on the box of the new carriage, which is his pride and joy. Here I sit at Uncle's desk, the sun is shining in, and the mass of flowers in the greenhouse proclaim that summer is here. Roses, hyacinths, violets and myriads of flowers with Latin names spread their fragrance around. It is very nice and so peaceful today – but I should have nothing against finding myself suddenly transported to Mariager."

The morning mood. Monday mornings were devoted to hot water and tea towels, silver-polishing cloths and wash-leathers:

„I am sitting in the room leading out to the garden and I can hear increasing sounds of movement on the first floor. So there we have Aunt Faye. 'Good morning, good morning'; 'Would you kindly move yourself, Miss?' The floor of the room to the garden has to be polished. Oh dear, there is Jensen the housekeeper. And here comes Aunt Faye ready for a morning gossip."

Breakfast at Carlsberg, 10.30 a.m.:

„Oh, there goes the breakfast call, shall I go down? If only I knew whether Uncle is dressed yet – for to go down and spend my time waiting for him is something I do not want to do."

Nanna was supposed to be taught housekeeping. In her eyes Aunt Laura was an incomparably methodical and orderly lady as far as that went. Spring cleaning took 2 to 3 weeks, one room at a time, under Laura's personal command. The preserving season was a big affair, and so was the Christmas baking.

„So here I am straight back again. Aunt is in the cellar giving out the strawberries. We have such masses of them that allotting them between all the relatives and friends is positively a study in itself. Today a whole throng of the hands from the brewery are getting shares, and we ourselves are eating strawberries morning, noon and night."

Or the portentous issue of the wine cellar:

„When I came down, Aunt was in the wine cellar. Some rooting out had to be done to make space for 2 ankers of Lachrimae Christi which had arrived from Italy and now had to be bottled. Kogsbølle did the bottling, and I had to help Aunt and then cut up labels afterwards."

This was in June 1863. J.C. Jacobsen had been in Italy the previous year and acquired a taste for this celebrated wine, which he now wished to introduce to his table.

If Nanna only would, then she could: that was Laura's verdict. „I am pretty busy these days, and especially just now because Aunt is going to Elsinore for the bathing"- this was in August 1865 and the preserving season again. „Aunt has not lifted a finger this year – but it is quite pleasant to see to it all myself in peace and quiet." Aunt Faye the mischief maker, on the other hand, thought that Nanna was better at playing the fine lady. Perhaps Nanna was not altogether in disagreement with this. „Of course the life here is more agreeable than I had before. Here I am really like the daughter of the house, on whom the demands made are few and small … And the busy social life suits me better than in Eveldrup."

Reading aloud for Laura, whose sight was impaired, was one of the daily duties. „Just now we are reading Barfoed's 'In Dalecarlia', a journey he made last year. He is an ultra-Grundtvigian, which is reflected both in his language and in the observations in his book. This has recently given rise to several grave conversations between us – Aunt and me." Nanna herself had to confess that she found it difficult to follow or feel interested in a sermon from beginning to end. On Easter Sunday in the fateful year of 1864 (when Prussian and Austrian armies invaded and swiftly defeated Denmark) she went to Vartov. „The singing was lovely, but the sermon was smug and pharisaical – like the parable of the Pharisee and the publican."

The rest of the repertoire for reading aloud? Some Dickens: „David Copperfield", „Nicholas Nickleby", „Bleak House". Bjørnstjerne Bjørnson's „A Cheery Lad", Ploug's „Queen Matilda".

They ploughed through the newspapers during the critical winter and spring months of 1864, when everyone's nerves were at full stretch:

„By the way, there is such a mass of newspaper reading that it takes a stupendous time to read it – I have to read it all aloud of course – if I sometimes take some of it for myself, I have to put up with so much sarcasm because Aunt has only got a half, and then we have a complaint over her unhappy existence in the world. Once upon a time I believed I read aloud so well, but even this is not right – now my reading is tiresomely theatrical – When something like that happens I am so vexed, but the worst of it is that she only has to look at me kindly 2 minutes afterwards and I have forgotten the whole affair. And that is bad for me. It is Foolish Good Nature."

In October of the same year Laura and J.C. celebrated their silver wedding with a very quiet party. Only a few were invited. Laura was suffering from a cold. „She always makes a terrible fuss," commented Nanna. J.C.'s gift to her was a „wonderfully elegant writing desk and a ditto sewing table in walnut".

Excursions were part of the rhythm of the household. The summer was welcomed, and the custom of going for picnics in high summer had been continued from the days at the old brewery. Dyrehaven (a pleasure park near Copenhagen) was the preferred venue, while Ved-bæk, Esrom, Fredensborg and Frederiksborg were more peripheral destinations. The family said farewell to the woods in the autumn. „On Sunday we all had an outing to Dyrehaven along with the Linds. Uncle rode the Arab beside the carriage." Carl and Sophus went by train to Klampenborg.

The Arab filly was J.C. Jacobsen's pride and joy. General Heger-mann-Lindencrone had been in Algiers buying horses for stud. He bought „Leila" for the brewer at the same time, a small, light and lithe grey horse which became the whole household's favourite. Jacobsen took her out for a ride every evening. He did not forget her when he was away travelling. There were greetings to her in his letters: „I hope that you will make use of the fine spring days to drive out frequently with friends and acquaintances," he wrote home to Laura in May 1865 from Antwerp, „and that Carl will be able to accompany you on 'Leila'."

Danish Constitution Day at Dyrehaven in 1864 was a strenuous outing. J.C. and Laura Jacobsen drove with the Linds to Frederiks-dal, while the young people drank coffee in the gardens at Klampen-borg and had supper at Fortunen. There were no seats to be had on the train home, so they walked to Charlottenlund, went from there to the Old Square by omnibus and thence to Valby on foot, arriving home at half past one in the morning, dog-tired.

Outings stimulated Jacobsen. So did entertaining. There were persons in whose company he felt rejuvenated. He needed them because his own temperament, as he admitted, was ponderous. He needed the help of others „to give the spirit that resilience by which the slumbering or less developed faculties are roused to activity". Only then did life attain its complete and harmonious development as opposed to the one-sided sort. He was alive to the fact that the ideal was scarcely to be realised in full, but to strive towards it was worth while. For the same reason the sea was the element which Jacobsen admired and appreciated most highly among all the noble phenomena of nature. His fascination with the sea is very characteristic of him. The sea is self-activating, is imbued with inner life, speaks aloud, bellowing at times till it stupefies, and is mighty in action. It is never at rest. The sea is always doing something. It can be compared to a productive system self-sufficient in energy and inexhaustible in resourcefulness.

In one of Jacobsen's many letters to his son during the latter's sojourn abroad we find an account of a particularly successful picnic. This was in July 1868. The weather that summer was the most glorious in living memory. J.C. compared it to spring in Rome in 1862 – the absolute topmost point in the barometer of his memory – on which Carl was well informed, since he had himself been with his father on that occasion.

Lind the bookseller and family were again invited, this time along with brewer Vogelius and his family. They went to Hillerød and from there drove around the prettiest parts of the woods at Grib, then along Lake Esrom back to Frederiksborg; „and there, in the glow of the sunset – like Rome again – we gazed at the beautiful castle from the venerable castle gardens and from Jæger Hill". He added: „It was an Olympian day!" And like a child who has enjoyed an exciting turn on the switchback and immediately demands another, Jacobsen is in full swing planning a da capo, this time to be the outing par excellence, with the young people in the carriage to be selected from his son's circle of acquaintances: Michael Lunn and his lively Norwegian inamorata, and Lunn's sister – whom Jacobsen called „my pearl" – and her fiancé, a student named Backe. However, he does remember to cross his fingers: „If I can spare the time for it." He did not: the everyday round called.

Hardly surprisingly, it was pater familias who decided the excursions. At the dinner table on the last day of July 1863, a Friday, Jacobsen suddenly proposed a trip to Stockholm:

„We have just finished eating, so I have not had time to talk to Aunt about it," Nanna records in haste. „Nothing much has ever before been said about travelling by Uncle or Carl, so the journey simply was not debated before or after the suggestion was made – so I still do not know if anything will come of it. Aunt was obviously very pleasurably surprised that she was to go too."

The tour has an improvised look about it. Carl had arrived the evening before from a walking tour around Zealand. The departure for Sweden was to take place on Monday, but it was postponed for two days and they set off on Wednesday – J.C. and Laura, Carl and Nanna. First they visited the places nearby: Kullen, Malmø, Kristianstad and Lund. Then they took the southern railway to Elmhult – the track did not go any further – and thence by stagecoach to Jönköping and on by train again to Stockholm. They stayed there for a week and made visits to Uppsala and Old Uppsala. They drank mead from the great drinking horn, as was the custom. Nanna availed herself of the opportunity to look through the book of names from the great Scandinavian student congress of 1852, but did not find the name she was seeking – her sweetheart's. Falun, Dannemora and Gävle were also included in the programme of excursions; in the vicinity of Stockholm there were Gripsholm and Haga, and in the city itself, Riddarholm Church, the royal palace and other places. From Stockholm they took the train again to Töreboda, then travelled by boat on the beautiful Göta Canal and across Lake Vänern, then past Trollhättan to Gothenburg. On 25 August the party arrived back at „lovely Carlsberg, which for all its size and magnificence looked wonderfully home-like after our three weeks of journeying".

„For all its size and magnificence ... wonderfully home-like." Nanna's words catch the essence of the Jacobsen dwelling. In his old age (in 1911) Carl Jacobsen wrote a brief memoir of his childhood home in which he recalled that when the house was completed, the father had said to his 12 year-old son: „I have built this house, Carl, not so as to have a magnificent building for my residence, but in order to make something beautiful." Such was the intention. It was a house with a programme built into it. Even while Jacobsen was planning his brewery at Valby the house was in his thoughts, as can be seen from one of the earliest drawings from his own hand in which the private dwelling-house is sketched in. However, he continued to live at Brolæggerstræde during the early years, partly because he had to earn money and partly because he wanted to prepare his ambitious scheme thoroughly. As a first stage, therefore, he contented himself with erecting a summerhouse designed by an architect named Nebelong.

Just as Jacobsen in a sense spent his whole life building his brewery, so also his private dwelling as it exists today – the Carlsberg Residence of Honour, as it is known – was created in stages over a period of about 30 years. The planning and the laying-out of the grounds began in 1848/49; Tyge Roth, by appointment gardener to H.M. the King, assisted him, and from his many travels Jacobsen brought back plants and trees to fit into the design, which was modelled on the English pattern and assumed more and more the character of an arboretum. He used the spoil from the storage-cellar excavations to introduce undulations into the terrain. The villa itself, the main building, was erected in 1851-54, and to this was added the conservatory (also on English lines) in 1858, and then finally in 1876 a greenhouse which was placed parallel to the railway and an Italian pergola built earlier from which there was an ample view over Kalveboderne and the Bay of Køge. The greenhouse is built in the form of a peristyle and was soon commonly spoken of as „J.C. Jacobsen's Pompeii".

Jacobsen did have technical experts to assist in the elaboration of his preliminary drawings: the architects N.S. Nebelong for the main building and P.C. Bønecke specialising on the architecture of the glazing for the conservatory and greenhouse. But otherwise Jacobsen's own knowledge of materials and structures was very important. The heating and ventilation system of the main building was his own design. He exhibited his system subsequently at the international medical congress on hygiene in Brussels in 1876. By then it had been functioning for 22 years. He displayed similar expertise when the greenhouses of the Copenhagen Botanical Gardens were being erected. His correspondence with the architect Ferdinand Meldahl concerning the reconstruction of Frederiksborg Castle shows something of the same sort. Greenhouses were Jacobsen's speciality. When the Danish architect Theophilus Hansen, who was internationally renowned and whom Jacobsen visited in Vienna on several occasions, inspected „Pompeii", he praised the classical Doric peristyle, but he did not like the Fakse stone from which the columns were hewn. Hence this dialogue:

„But it is full of holes."
„Yes, but we fill them with putty."
„Well, it seems to me it would be better to make the columns entirely of putty."

The master builder chivvied his architects. He could not stop interfering. He did the same with the artists commissioned to execute decorations for the building. An amusing example of this can be read in the memoirs of the sculptor Th. Stein. Stein – to whom Jacobsen also entrusted the important task of creating the gallery of portrait busts for the foyer of the Royal Theatre – was also commissioned to execute two reliefs depicting themes from the Iliad and Odyssey for the Brewer's residence. In the relief portraying „The Battle of Patrocles" Stein had given the onrushing Hector a small lock of hair on his forehead, which J.C. did not like – but the sculptor pleaded for his lock. When the relief had been mounted in its appointed place and Stein inspected the result, he found to his astonishment that the subject of the dispute was gone. Stein was totally taken aback. Jacobsen flourished his pocket knife and explained: „Now he looks more Greek." And that was that.

The main building of the brewer's residence was located on the central axis of the brewery establishment, and it was reached by driving through the brewery, not via the style elegantly laid-out grounds. And indeed this was typical of J.C. Jacobsen. He wanted to live where his business was, and did not by any means regard his brewery as a mere factory devoid of aesthetic appeal but as a place to be eagerly shown off to his guests: even such an ethereal lady as Johanne Luise Heiberg, who stood high in his esteem, was invited to inspect the storage cellars, brew-house and other installations.

Neither was the close proximity of the railway regarded as a nuisance. The railway age had just opened, and J.C. was a staunch admirer of this new mode of transport. The train was a feature of everyday life at Carlsberg. „I hear the train rushing past – but I must send my thoughts and greetings to my dearest love far away over the great waters," sighs Nanna wistfully in an evening letter to Brask. The train brings guests: „Aunt Faye came by train on Tuesday evening, and she is staying out here for now. She is nice once you understand her, even if she can be a little caustic. She does much to enhance our lives."

Carlsberg's location right alongside the railway line brought in time the great benefit that it enabled the brewery to get its own goods station connected up, but during the early years the new railway, with its terminus at Roskilde, was a „picnic" line. To travel by train was a popular amusement. The line between Copenhagen and Valby was double-tracked, and on Sundays in summer there was an hourly service. On ordinary days, however, there were only three trains a day in each direction. The historian Troels Troels-Lund, who spent his childhood at Gl. Bakkehus, recalls the prickling sensation at the back of the neck on arriving at Valby Station, the starting point for the summer holidays. At the bottom of the steep steps lay the station like a fashionable cocotte, „haughty in its new wooden dress, blinking in the sunlight. It knew what it had to offer: a peep at the wonders of the world, from Valby Hill and its honeycomb of diggings to the sparkling shoreline of Kalvebodstrand. And with every train came the ringing of bells, the whistling, the white clouds of steam puff-puff-puffing from the wondrous locomotive, swifter than any horses, that could pull the whole long line of carriages far, far out into the wide world."

The station had absolutely everything – including a fine cake shop and café where lurked temptations additional to those of the outing to Søndermarken and Frederiksberg Gardens.

Whereas the facade of Jacobsen's main building facing the yard matched the brewery, the facade towards the park was designed on more elegant lines. The style here was Italian. This was the countryside. Other denizens of Copenhagen built summer residences at Valby, but Jacobsen's house and park, with nursery and kitchen garden attached, formed a grandiose whole more reminiscent of the country houses of the well-to-do 18th century English gentry. The style of the house was late classical and the layout of the rooms symmetrical, with simple geometrical basic patterns.

The heart of the home was ordinarily „the Captain's room", i.e. the study. It was from his command post here – his writing desk – that he directed his numerous projects. Jacobsen did not employ a secretary for his correspondence but wrote all his more important communications in his own hand. Brief, clear, well-composed messages – „with the best will in the world I cannot write long letters" – in a neat, quick and legible hand. Jacobsen had a clear view of the brewery from where he sat. A large French window to the left led out to the conservatory, where pride of place was taken by a large Araucaria excelsa, which impressed all Jacobsen's guests. In October 1864 Nanna asked Brask to tell Lindahl the gentleman farmer that the Araucaria had now been moved to the centre of the conservatory. „Uncle is so delighted with the change out there that he cannot express his satisfaction in less than biblical language – and God saw everything that he had made etc." Another utilitarian item of furniture in the Captain's room was the drawing-board, which stood by the window. The decorations were dominated by Marstrand's great portrait of H.C. Ørsted, which hung above the sofa.

Laura Jacobsen's room lay opposite, with a view over the park. From the latter there was access through the French windows to the „garden room", a large salon forming the central room of the house and the one where guests arrived via the hall. Three doors led from the garden room out to the monumental garden steps. The garden room's wall spaces were in Pompeian red, and wall spaces and doors were adorned with floral decorations, birds, allegorical figures and candelabra. Leading off from the garden room was the largest room in the house, the assembly and dining salon, a two-storey interior, very carefully planned and strictly executed in its symmetry, with galleries behind Romanesque arches at either end supported by pairs of Ionic columns. From here music could be provided on festive occasions. The whole room breathed of antiquity. Like many others of his day, the Brewer loved and honoured Bertel Thorvaldsen. A copy of the Alexander frieze, the original of which had been made by Thorvaldsen for Christiansborg Castle, went around the room high overhead. Six reliefs by Thorvaldsen adorned the walls. The goddess Hebe, holding out the marble bowl of eternal youth, stood in a niche between the two doors of the dining salon, carved by H.V. Bissen from a design by Thorvaldsen. There were large mirrors, concealed in the walls during the day, with which the windows were closed on festive occasions and which reflected the candles and gaslight of the room. A costly parquet floor and an antique panelled ceiling completed the room. The dining table was decorated with Thorvaldsen's figures. „The gods are at table," as Professor Rasmus Nielsen, who was the family's favourite after-dinner speaker, expressed it.

It had long been the Jacobsen family's custom to hold open house for friends and acquaintances on Fridays, and this tradition was transferred to Carlsberg. Here the nucleus of their circle of friends would present themselves: the Steenstrups, the Djørups, Professor Rasmus Nielsen and his family, Theodor Lind the bookseller and family, the Vogelius family, the Roths, H.J. Lindahl, the Stillings and a few others. Erhard Kogsbølle, who later on became the Brewer's partner, was of course also intimately involved in the life of Jacobsen and his family.

In the summer of 1863 Jacobsen held Kogsbølle's wedding to Magnella, daughter of a dean of the church. It was a big celebration which little Nanna entered into with enthusiasm. The ceremony itself took place in Frederiksberg Church. Nanna was accompanied by one of Rasmus Nielsen's daughters, and the two young girls were in complete agreement that the church was not specially exciting, because they were bundled straight into the choir stalls up by the altar and so missed the procession through the church, „the only amusement the retinue have at a wedding". It was more enjoyable later on at Carlsberg, where the reception was held. Tea was served first, and then at 9 o'clock came a six-course meal with six kinds of wine in the dining salon. The Lachrimae Christi was tasted for the first time on this occasion. The guests took their leave at 11.30, and the newlyweds drove to their home at the brewery. Next day the bridal couple were at home to receive congratulations and presents from a host of well-wishers. Nanna gave them a pair of flowerpots with bas-reliefs by Thorvaldsen and already filled with rare and beautiful plants. From Laura and J.C. there was a mantel clock. It was a perfect day, quite idyllic. On the third day the Carlsberg family went over to dine with the newlyweds along with the Djørups, and finally on the fourth day the dean was able to set off homewards by train to Klampenborg and thence by ship to Rungsted and his home at Karlebo. Later on Jacobsen took Kogsbølle into partnership and built a house for him in 1875/76 opposite the brewery on Old Carlsberg Road, once more demonstrating his feeling for technical innovation and new materials. He decided on Fakse stone for building the house, which took its name from this material, being known afterwards as „The Fakse House".

In the day-to-day conduct of his life the Brewer followed his nature. The form of life was work, and its goal was the happiness which came from work, especially that work which lay beyond the narrow circle of the ego and had to do with the duty of the individual to society and the nation. It may sound hypocritical to speak of frugality in relation to Jacobsen, considering his surroundings. He certainly did live in high style, and he was proud of his house and its splendid setting. Yet it remains true that in the everyday conduct of his life he was frugal in terms of his personal needs.

It was a different story when he entertained guests in his home. Jacobsen's social life and interaction with others went through phases reflecting the shifts of his role and interests in life, which in turn illustrate the development of his personality. He knew that he was a one-man band, but he had a need to mix with others, especially those who could stimulate him and thereby develop those aspects of his being which he felt hampered him in his relations with others. He laboured to cultivate himself, and he took a great deal of trouble to create the ideal settings for his social gatherings and parties. He worked out his arrangements thoroughly beforehand, and his residence gradually changed character. After the war of 1864 the drawing room and garden room became more elegant with higher mirrors and new decorations: floating figures on the doors, a frieze with centaurs, mermen and bacchantes on the door cornices, and his pride and joy – „moonlight" illumination from the cloakroom of the conservatory. A pair of French candlesticks on brackets in the sitting room were the pièce de résistance.

The first showing of the redecorated interior was a great success. „My house and my arrangements made an agreeable impression on everyone, but most of all on the visitors, of course," he records of one of the great gatherings of parliamentary figures held at Carlsberg in the postwar period. This one took place on 11 November 1866 and was an official military and political gathering; its purpose was to bring together the most important members of the Military Commission, of which Jacobsen had been chairman and which had just devised a new organisation for the army and navy, and the leading politicians of the Rigsdag. The military establishment was represented by the directors of the Military Academy and the Naval Dockyard along with half a dozen other highly-placed figures from the army and navy. There were 14 influential politicians drawn from the two Houses of the Rigsdag. Finally, from among his own circle of friends Jacobsen had invited Michael and Frants Djørup, the two Steenstrups, V. Rothe and Martin Hammerich. The latter was not actually a personal friend but Jacobsen had long wanted to invite the headmaster of Carl's school, the Christianshavn grammar school.

A surprise awaited the guests. As they went in to dinner the Marseillaise struck up from the east gallery of the dining salon, where the host had stationed eight musicians and their „musical director". All through the meal they played a variety of overtures and operatic pieces, „very pleasantly", Jacobsen considered. It was table music. „I deliberately avoided melodies which had a definite significance." However, the inclusion of the French national anthem in the programme did echo Jacobsen's extensive tour of France the year before and at the same time was expressive of Denmark's hopes in the international arena with regard to the Schleswig-Holstein question.

They took their places at table. Prime minister Hall escorted Laura, J.C. two generals. A cascade of speeches and toasts followed. Had Nanna been sitting in the west balcony, she would undoubtedly have stifled a yawn or two and been thoroughly bored, as she usually was, by the floods of loquacity gushing forth over everything and everyone. But she was not there. She had left Carlsberg in the spring and was now established as a married woman in far-off Holstebro. The host was content. His first toast was to the new plan for the army and navy, „of which I jestingly declared myself to be the godfather. This occasioned much amusement and created a jovial atmosphere." Next Jacobsen proposed a toast to the armed forces, who were to translate the plan „into reality". He hailed Lehmann, the National Liberal politician who had taken the lead in awakening the Danish people to a sense of freedom and nationality, as „the chivalrous champion of truth, right and honour", as the words went. Then it was the turn of two opinion-makers of the time, Ploug and Hammerich, to whom „so much gratitude was due for the growth of the Nordic spirit on both sides of the Sound and Cattegat". He went on to pay tribute to the university „and its indirect influence on the non-studying classes of society". This toast he addressed to Professors Madvig and Steenstrup; by the prestige which their researches enjoyed in the outside world they had strengthened Denmark's name and importance. Lastly, he proposed a toast to Hall, to whom he ascribed an important share of the credit for the declaratory clause in the Prague peace settlement (following the Austro-Prussian War of 1866) providing for the return of Danish Schleswig.

Now it was the turn of the guests. Lehmann toasted the host's health, then later on in the meal proposed another toast to the young son of the house. This was sure to be a welcome gesture. Hall toasted the nation, then delivered the further obligatory toast to the host and hostess. Ploug, Hammerich, Madvig, Jonquières, Schaffenberg, Max Müller and Nyholm then all spoke – some of them several times in fact. „It all happened so quickly, the one after the other, that at this moment" – it was the following day – „I only vaguely remember what each of them said individually." „The atmosphere was agreeable in the highest degree. I formed the conviction that every one of those present would be glad to receive another invitation to Carlsberg," he wrote to his son, and added, with typical matter-of-factness, „which of course will be done in moderation."

It was a time when Danes could be tempted into heady eloquence once they got to work with knife and fork, and National Liberal bombast knew no bounds. Jacobsen had manifestly attained a point of his existence where he had begun to enjoy his wealth. „I regard it as one of the finest fruits of my diligence and my good fortune to have been able to gather such a circle around me." He goes on to say, very significantly: „I cannot help feeling pleased when I compare my standing of today, and my mental and moral outlook, with what I had when I wore clogs and washed out barrels in the yard at home and drove around to the beer-bottlers with the dray, and even for a long time, a very long time afterwards, when I used to feel so awkward and bashful with anybody whom I did not know well and when my horizons were so narrow that I was incapable of involving myself in anything other than brewery, a little chemistry and physics, and a little aesthetics. How could I have dreamt then that I should one day preside at my own table over a gathering of such men as I saw there yesterday?"

The young people of the household could be affronted now and then by the displays of luxury at these parties. „If it will amuse you," wrote Nanna to Jutland, „I shall recount for you the number of wines, which will give you an idea of the dimensions which such parties have gradually assumed, where the one does not want to be outshone by the other." „Chateau Latour, port wine and Golden Sherry St. Piray (drunk from shallow glasses, white and sparkling), Scharlachberger Rhenish wine, Chambertin Burgundy, Champagne, Malvasier, Cap Constantia and Cyprus wine. Is it not beastly? And 9 courses of food with it." Carl passed the remark that during the worst excesses in the age of the Roman Empire, no more than four kinds of wine had ever been served.

„This morning we have been busy washing up and putting away porcelain and glassware, and tomorrow we shall polish the silver." Such was the day after, downstairs.

But what was the use of all this? Jacobsen attached crucial importance to usefulness. It had shocked Nanna for one: „It strikes me as deplorable to hear someone whose external conditions of life are those of good fortune, pleasure and amusement saying that usefulness is what must be wrested from everything. Amusement does not produce anything in this life." The usefulness of entertaining consisted in the bringing together of people who in their day-to-day lives had no opportunity of getting to know each other personally. That was the answer. And social events at Carlsberg were well mixed.

The stream of guests increased, especially during the war when everyone drew closer together. „We have many visitors here, we are almost never alone any evening." Jacobsen's entertaining was into high gear. New acquaintances inspired him greatly. They did not need to be well-known figures, and they could well be young people as long as they had liveliness and depth. He was particularly interested in introducing artists and intellectuals into his home. There were his „Roman" friends: Carl Bloch, Christian Freund, Henrik Scharling and Olav Glosimodt. There were authors and poets, among whom it is hardly surprising to find Hans Christian Andersen, who loved being invited to grand residences and country houses.

Andersen had trouble finding the way to Carlsberg. He had taken the tram to Pile Allé and tramped through mud and slush – it was February – at the bottom of Søndermarken. First of all he landed at the home of Carl Weis, a high-ranking civil servant, where he learned that he must go through the factory in order to reach the brewer's residence. Once he reached the warmth indoors, however, it turned into a thoroughly pleasant Sunday. Andersen, who escorted Jacobsen's wife to table, noticed the statues and Thorvaldsen's bas-relief in the dining salon, and also observed the „machinery for lifting the food, gas in the jets and wax candles in the chandeliers". „Down in the conservatory there was a lamp shining like moonlight on the big green trees," he notes in his diary, „and there was Orla Lehmann's daughter Margrethe taking a stroll." Her dress was of blue gauze. „You look like the Woodland Fairy," Andersen said to her. Later on he blanketed himself in the smoke from an after-dinner cigar, to the vast amusement of Ørsted's daughter Mathilde, who was one of his faithful admirers. On taking his leave Andersen expressed much appreciation of the party and declared that he would be happy to come again, which he did.

The first visit was in 1868. The following year Andersen made another Sunday visit to the Jacobsen family. It was spring this time, the month of May, in fact, so he was shown round the garden, and he records in his diary that Jacobsen had made a miniature mountain range out of all the rubble from the fire and planted it with spruce, birch and beech. „I was up at the peak, it was cold, and I came into the room quite hoarse." The poet was always rather worried about his health, but we may allow ourselves to guess that in other respects Andersen found the industrial surroundings congenial. He felt at home in the machine age, with its engineering arts, bridges, chimneys, iron horses and iron ships, and he derided the dreams of the past cherished by the older romantics. For him reality was the most wondrous fairy tale of all.

It was gratifying, of course, that Carlsberg suited the much-fêted poet's taste, but what pleased Jacobsen even better was that at the same party in 1868 he had been able to introduce to the circle a gifted individual of much talent, to wit, Andersen's „Woodland Fairy", Margrethe Rode, the daughter of Orla Lehmann, along with her husband Gotfred Rode. They were both first-time guests, and of her J.C. wrote in a letter to Carl, who was abroad: „She does not have her father's liveliness and wit, but she does possess a rare degree of culture which is not apparent on the surface and which she does not take the least pains to show off. She expresses her ideas straightforwardly and naturally in her own words, and her observations are telling and fresh, not learnt phrases." „I was much gratified to discover that both she and her husband would like to visit us more often, as they are a valuable acquisition for our circle."

As we have seen already, Jacobsen was very receptive to feminine vibrations, and he was no mean talent spotter. Margrethe Rode undeniably had personality. She was an only child who had grown up in a political milieu, showing herself at an early age to be very alert and eager to learn. She had attended a girls' school headed by Natalie Zahle, a pioneering educationist, and after completing her schooling had attended a continuation course in literature arranged by Gotfred Rode. Profoundly influenced by the ideas of Grundtvig and Rasmus Nielsen, she and her husband started a folk high school in the country house of Skovgaard, in Ordrup, which she had inherited from her mother. In 1876, however, she left her husband, by whom she had had two sons, Ove and Helge. She married a Norwegian and became a well-known critic in Norway, her reviews being highly regarded by many. She reviewed Ibsen's „A Doll's House" very favourably in 1879; she was alert to the new ideas and artistic currents of the age.

Margrethe Rode fits in well with the bouquet of femininity which warmed J.C. Jacobsen's personality and in whose company he throve: Michael Lunn's lovely Norwegian lassie, his sister, whom Jacobsen called his „pearl", the independent, sharp-witted, very young Nanna Rygaard, Sophie Steenstrup. Later on Natalie Zahle, Agnes Berthelsen and of course the queen of them all – the great diva, Johanne Luise Heiberg.

One flower was lacking in the bouquet, his wife Laura.

J.C. and Laura

What was the relationship between Laura and J.C. really like? The accounts given by friends skirt round the subject for the most part. Jacobsen himself weeded his papers before his death and destroyed his son's letters among other things. No diaries have come down from him. Generally speaking he was not a person with any urge to confide or confess in the grand style. But the son did preserve his father's letters. They afford us the welcome possibility of probing a little deeper psychologically, with a view in particular to forming a better understanding of the very crucial, and for his son utterly staggering, dispositions which Jacobsen made during the last ten years of his busy life. Nanna's letters provide scattered glimpses from the private sphere but are somewhat limited in scope, and with their frequent mentions of Laura's migraines they probably exaggerate the wife's frailties and infirmities. From Laura herself we only have sporadic letters, sufficient to illustrate the intellectual gap between the spouses.

„When I see the daily life together of Uncle and Aunt, it often seems to me that such a relationship would make me unhappy in my Aunt's shoes," wrote Nanna shortly after her arrival at Carlsberg. „Uncle may be exemplary in a thousand other things, but he is not so in this. There is no tenderness at all there, more coldness, and so I often think with a shiver: does one really cool like that when the years have passed! I believe Uncle is too intellectual to be a sensualist, and that makes me sad for Aunt, who looks up to him like a god, that he does not respond to her feelings more. But I also believe he has thrown himself so much into public life that he cannot be expected to be anything to his wife. To be sure it is hard to say this, but in my opinion things are not as they should be, though of course a man has duties to fulfil towards the state and nation which are perhaps just as important as his duties to his wife."

Later on Nanna qualified her verdict by saying that Aunt Laura for her part did not sufficiently understand how to keep or capture her husband's attention. In particular she was jealous of some of the women in the circle of acquaintances, and „her displeasure and jealousy then express themselves in bitterness and sarcasm towards the females concerned in the presence of others, and that is imprudent and ill-advised". The result was that „Uncle ignores her in everything except money matters – it is vexing and distressing to see it – no, felicity she does not have."

When Jacobsen believed he had found something harsh and inconsiderate in his son's nature, „a high degree of selfishness and not a little arrogance", he ascribed this partly to „a lamentable inheritance" and partly to environment, i.e. „the atmosphere in which you have lived", and „the so-called 'fortunate' circumstances which have never taught you to want for anything or anyone". Of himself he used to explain to his son that life had taught him patience and resignation. He recommended others to acquire the same qualities. There was a solitary occasion when he spoke of „the evil in me which the frowns of fate have called forth", but otherwise he had little propensity for disclosing himself and his feelings. „You know that for choice it is my habit to let my feelings express themselves in deeds." His patent medicine for problems was intensive activity. „Nothing is so calculated to bring peace of mind as strenuous exertion in one's calling."

There is resignation behind all this advice to his son, an admission that reality had not measured up to the ideal. With regard to the feminine ideal Jacobsen was a romantic. He could say with Goethe: „Das ewig weibliche zieht uns hinan" (The eternal feminine draws us towards itself). He spoke to his son of the dream of „one day finding a strong and true love for a noble woman who stands so high that one must approach her with humility and a sense of reverence, a woman to whom you would not for all the world show thoughtlessness and selfishness, whom you must fear to lose".

The prerequisite of true love between two people, Jacobsen continued in his conversations with his son, is a certain degree of congruence; but there must also be a measure of dissimilarity, otherwise harmony will become boring, and boredom is the grave of love. In this connection he cites, surprisingly, the 18th century French writer, adventurer and libertine Beaumarchais, who had launched a provocative, witty criticism of the morals and manners of his age in „The Barber of Seville" and „Figaro's Wedding". The citation he chooses is

Count Almaviva's rejoinder to the Countess: „Je t'aime beaucoup mais trois ans d'hymen rendent l'hymen si 'respectable'" (I love you, but three years of marriage make marriage so 'respectable'). The Count is longing for a little piquancy of manners, even a rebuff once in a way; our womenfolk believe themselves safe once they have won us, but one fine day we are satiated when we ought to be happy. We have to conquer them, but they have to reconquer us. „This you scarcely understand, for you do not understand 'human nature', but one day you will experience the truth of it," he declares to Carl.

Both Jacobsen and his wife possessed an old-fashioned form of discipline in their marriage. Henrik Ibsen's „A Doll's House", which had its première at the Royal Theatre in 1879, put a torch to one of the bourgeoisie's sacred institutions, in Denmark as elsewhere. The Jacobsen family, who were ardent theatregoers, were among those who saw the play. We have an assessment of it in Laura's hand, set down in a letter to the painter Elisabeth Jerichau Baumann, one of the few emancipated women of the 19th century. The letter sheds light on Laura's own marriage and tells us a good deal about her character at the same time.

„You ask me if I am convinced by The Doll's House. No, by no means, I have positively grieved that nearly all my friends, but especially the women, can hold Nora to be within her rights when she leaves a man whom she has robbed of his honour because he speaks harsh words to her, and then when he repents of these harsh words and almost begs forgiveness for having said them, the writer lets her work herself up to a meaningless idealism which is quite grotesque. One can hardly help laughing at her where the author intends that we shall be moved and where most of the public are weeping buckets. True enough he has spoilt her, and yet he reprimands her properly because she did not tell the truth. It might well be thought that that could also have a good effect."

On the subject of modern times she continues:

„But it is like this nowadays, that young wives want to be spoilt, they want their husbands to pander to them in all the small things, and when they are confronted with the big ones, they have had no practice in suffering and enduring. The sense of freedom harms morality. There are no morals in The Doll's House, but it will have done some good if it brings many to regret letting some little white lie pass their lips."

And she closes by declaring that „Jacobsen is at one with me of course in this opinion of The Doll's House. He cannot be said to have spoilt his wife or given her too much independence." These last words were undoubtedly true.

Patience and resignation were qualities for which Laura had had much need ever since she first made her home in Brolæggerstræde at an early age.

She suffered much grief a year after the marriage when she gave birth to a son who died when only 10 days old. Laura was then 21 and J.C. was 29. Her next confinement was a year and a half later, on 2 March 1842, when Carl came into the world. The couple had no further children. Thus Carl was an only child, with the problems that that brought: exaggerated solicitude and an excess of zeal in watching over the child's talents and signs of development. The classical symptoms rapidly showed themselves. The lad developed a stammer and bit his nails.

In 1854 the parents and their 12 year-old son moved from Brolæggerstræde out to the big house at Carlsberg, a home which in its every aspect was the father's work and the father's pride. The wife was scarcely consulted as to its design. Even Laura's own room bore the impress of Jacobsen's aesthetic taste: for instance, it was provided with a series of prints by Italian Renaissance masters, who for him represented the absolute zenith of the history of European painting.

Here Laura filled the traditional womanly role of mistress of the house with the keys at her girdle. In day-to-day life all went well, but when they were entertaining it was hard for her to retain command. Only exceptionally did Jacobsen abstain from interfering, though it could happen. „Uncle has left the entire affair to Aunt, and she says: 'That will be pleasant.'" As we have already noted, her sister often lived in the home, and Laura also had a lady's companion to read aloud for her and lend her a hand in other ways: this was usually a young girl, such as the dean's daughters Magnella and Emilie, Nanna Rygaard, then after her one Marie, and finally Agnes Berthelsen, who had been recommended to J.C. by Natalie Zahle and who as the years went by became institutionalised as „Aunt Bertha". They travelled with Laura on holiday every year, to the family in Jutland, to Marienlyst for the bathing or to some German spa to take the waters. In this sphere too, the paterfamilias had a decisive voice in the family councils. „Uncle has remarked to Aunt that Marie is boring. She has no personality or vivacity such as is needed here," Nanna reported of her successor towards the end of her sojourn. „Aunt thought, as was reasonable, that the principal aim should be to get one to her taste – but no notice will be taken of that, I imagine."

Even though Laura was far from personifying J.C.'s ideal of woman, her status as the brewer's wife, Carl's mother and the lady of the house was solidly founded. Her greatest asset was indubitably her own family, the nucleus of the circle of friends who stimulated and formed Jacobsen personally and whom he could not do without. In a multitude of matters J.C. was thoughtful and considerate towards his wife. He instructed his son to send little presents from abroad. „Buy something for your mother. She could do with a shawl, white for preference and like the one I gave to Magnella but got burnt. If you write anything to me which you do not wish your mother to read, then write it on a separate sheet, because your mother becomes displeased if I do not want to show her your letter to me, and she gets Miss Berthelsen to read to her what is written in French." Both parents corresponded with the son during his lengthy sojourn abroad, sent their letters together and exchanged news from Carl with each other.

Another little domestic scene unfolds in Nanna's account of her last Christmas in the bosom of the family at Carlsberg, when Laura lavished items of equipment on her for her future home in Holstebro. Uncle presented her with two pairs of ornamental cups and saucers, „one pair for the husband and one for the wife", and among other things Laura gave Nanna an automatic samovar in brass, „so beautifully designed that I have never before seen the like. Aunt Laura declared the machine was also from Uncle, which he would not hear of, but marched up with a very curious coffee pot constructed in tiers, with glass tubes, steam and taps." Christmas presents were showered on Nanna that year, and yet she felt that „in this wealthy home we are holding a very poor Christmas". „Uncle's unreasonableness and remorselessness drive Aunt into a subdued and abject mood – sometimes her jealousy breaks out too, and now and then not without reason either." Laura wondered about Nanna's outspokenness towards Jacobsen. She herself explains it in terms of tone. „I present a gentle face to him and tell him the truth in jesting fashion and indirectly. It is always pleasanter to hear it thus than in a sharp tone and with a fiery light in the eye."

Another of the pinpricks was the English mistletoe tradition which J.C. introduced after his son had described it from England and sent a mistletoe as a Christmas greeting. With almost childish glee he dragged the attractive ladies, especially the young ones in the group of acquaintances, under the green bough with its white berries and gave them a smacking kiss. It was probably also a disappointment that J.C. gave up dancing, whereas Laura enjoyed having a whirl. And that he invited young Emmy Moltke to ride in the countryside around Carlsberg as his guest and practised assiduously beforehand on the Arab mare „Leila" in order to cut a good figure.

Patience and resignation were indeed qualities for which Laura had good use during her marriage to this overpowering and gifted dynamo of a man. Once upon a time he had been able to conclude a letter to her with „A kiss to you and one to Carl and so farewell." That was on the trip with Little Møller in 1844, but it was so long, long ago. As the years went by, and especially as the relationship between father and son became so tense that in the end they each went their own way, there loomed before her the prospect of losing both son, daughter-in-law and grandchildren. Carl's wife, Ottilia, chose to stand by her hotheaded husband. She did so with the remark that „there is not going to be another unhappy marriage at Carlsberg". The psychosomatic pyre within Laura then flared up.

In a moving letter to Carl, penned in Laura's somewhat awkward schoolgirl handwriting, she dissects her despair frankly and confides in her son. Her instinct tells her that her son's character is changing: some harsh and ruthless element has taken command of him; his smile has become „cold and over-hasty". She herself is sometimes very rancorous and bitter in her mind:

„But as I cannot bear to harbour this bitterness, but in the strangest way become physically ill from it, I am forced to look at that which embitters and grieves me from another side. So this severe test, which is what poor health really is, can still do great good. I do not always know how I am to bring this other side forth, but then I seek solitude in my room or amongst nature. I am formed neither for giving thanks nor for praying but nevertheless I do it, and my will to do so is so strong that like the singer who sings herself into the mood, I bring myself to thank God fervently for all the joys and blessings which for a while I had forgotten I possessed. Then I feel like every kind of miserable wretch, but along with this I am vouchsafed the hope that God will help me if I only ask him humbly to do so; that he will give me such a clear view of my own faults as to make my will strong enough to put them aside; and the miracle does happen, and for a while I am able to look at life from a religious standpoint again. The blessing never fails to be granted. I find myself loving people with their virtues and failings because I have been afforded a view of my own faults. And that which I previously felt as a crushing weight bearing me down now washes easily over me. Faith, hope and charity have then conquered … Dear Carl, hold fast to these three jewels and you are in possession of the highest happiness and the most blessed sentiments. Your loving Mother."

„Here at Carlsberg, God's word and God Himself are seldom topics of conversation," Nanna had observed during her sojourn there. „I do not believe that they lack faith – Aunt least of all, she is humble and possesses just that proper childlike faith – Uncle likes to have visitors here on Sundays, and so Sunday mornings are taken up by many other things. He never goes to church himself – he is too much of a rational person to be capable of feeling edified by the words of a priest. He believes in God as the Guide and Creator – but I think he probably draws the line at Christ. That is certainly fairly common in our day! This is not the case with Carl, however, but he rarely goes to church."

The theologian whom Jacobsen understood best was J.H. Paulli, who was one of the most admired preachers of the age. „He was one of the few, I believe the only one of our parsons, who understood the business of preaching Christianity to thinking and enlightened Protestants," J.C. wrote to his son from France on receiving the news of Paulli's death on 11 July 1865. „He knew how, as smoothly as the Church's rules and parsons' vows permitted, to slip past the inessentials of dogma and hold fast to that which is the essence of Christianity, the rules for the conduct of life, and he also presented these in the true Christian spirit: with gentleness and seriousness and not as a thundering Zealot."

A fortnight later Jacobsen amplified his religious ideas in a further long letter written from Rheims in a mood inspired by the view of the cathedral opposite. It was written specifically for his son, who had asked his father to acquaint him with his attitude to God and the Church.

Jacobsen begins by declaring that he does not wish to be his son's religious teacher but „merely to inform you of my religious outlook as it has evolved step by step". Jacobsen is a Protestant, and a Protestant does not believe blindly as a Catholic does; his faith is the result of his own testing and scrutiny. He reflects upon the preachings of the priest and forms his own philosophy of life. His „church" is not some fixed entity or organisation with a pope empowered to determine the content of faith. For the Protestant self-activity is a right and a duty. The faith of the individual therefore assumes a more or less individual character.

Dogma is unimportant and in part contrary to common sense, with many alien elements: oriental conceptions, myths and metaphorical tales interpolated into the so-called sacred writings by the earliest church fathers. The doctrine of the Trinity Jacobsen does not understand. Christianity does not need „this nimbus" in order to substantiate its divine origin. The doctrine of the Atonement is contrary to common sense. „I believe as little in that as in the Trinity." That the heathen should be condemned to hell, for example, he feels is an unchristian idea. There must be a life after this one, and here the conditions for a higher perfection must exist even for those who have never heard Christian doctrine proclaimed.

After this, what is there actually left?

„I believe in one God, Who created the world, Who bears at all times the impress and tokens of a wisdom before which Man must bow down in humility and awe. By the world I understand not merely this earth and all the spheres which move in space but also the spiritual life which moves in time: the life of humanity. Here too eternal wisdom reveals itself as standing infinitely high above man's shortsighted knowledge, so that humanity, despite some errors, despite setbacks, apparent or real but transient, yet moves forward to a higher existence, so that gradually, despite mistakes and wickedness, the true and the rational will conquer. To me this is God's dispensation."

What Jacobsen called „the special dispensation which the individual invokes in the individual instance" he would not accept. It was contrary to common sense. God could not respond to the individual's prayer by acting against world order in H.C. Ørsted's sense or performing miracles. He would not disparage prayer, „understood as the warm, humble, sincere appeal to the Supreme Being", when its goal was broader in scope, viz. to seek „wisdom, patience and humility". But if its aim was to solve a specific problem in an individual instance, he declared against it.

The doctrine of immortality cannot be proved philosophically, nor can it be understood any more than the infinity of time and space can be understood. Nevertheless Jacobsen assented to it unconditionally. Without immortality the whole of human life appears to him senseless. Without immortality there can be no eternal justice. The wicked will die without receiving their punishment: the virtuous will die without receiving their reward. Human life positively presupposes some continuation after death. „Man cannot possibly have been vouchsafed a divine spark in his inner self merely to eat, drink, sleep and die." „The goal of man is spiritual and moral perfection." This is the key. To attain this is salvation, but to neglect it produces remorse, pain, eternal torment. In figurative terms it is called God's judgment, God's wrath. The powerful urge for perfection cannot be satisfied here on earth. Many die when still young, children are snatched away: common sense says that for them there must be some continuation beyond the grave. Jacobsen concludes that there must be such continuation, and adds „with an awareness of the life lived here below". But he declines to speculate over the form of a continued existence. Thought cannot penetrate eternity, but it is possible to daydream – and this is tempting, provided only that it is kept clearly in mind that it is imagination and not thought that produces these pictures.

Laura's relationship to God was intimate and uncomplicated. She held to her childhood faith and used prayer as a lifebelt in time of crisis. J.C.'s Christianity was coloured by his sharp intellect and scientific ponderings. The teaching of H.C. Ørsted, who believed in the ultimate identity of all the forces of nature, influenced him more than testaments and dogmas. Add to this his inheritance from his childhood home, which followed the rationalist principles of pastor Bastholm, with the doctrine of duty near the centre. But the life of church and congregation was peripheral to Jacobsen.

All through his life Jacobsen felt himself to be inhibited in his social relations. This may seem odd considering his wide area of contact with society. In his professional field he was on home ground both in Denmark and abroad, and he blossomed as a politician as well: his circle of acquaintances was deliberately wide. He wished to make his home a gathering point for „a broad selected circle" – he did not use the word salon – but his aptitudes and other factors stood in the way. He felt wanting in humour, in refined forms of light and harmless wit, in the facility to order and manoeuvre his ideas. „All this is lacking in your home," he wrote to his son, and expressed the hope that Carl would acquire these accomplishments on his educational grand tour. „I hope that your lengthy sojourn among Frenchmen will have made you acquire something of the polished manner which to them is inseparable from the idea of education and indeed also constitutes one of its noble aspects."

The need to consort with people possessed of the capacity to untie the knots inside him was great. As the years went by there grew in him also a great need for friendship in the not merely convivial sense of the word. He once confided to the young Johannes Steenstrup that Thomasine Gyllembourg's short story „Montanus the Younger", published in 1837 and one of the authoress's celebrated and much-read „Everyday Stories", had taught him much. It tells of the young, self-confident Conrad, who comes home to Denmark after a stay in England and takes over his uncle's old textile mill, which he immediately sets about modernising energetically and singlemindedly on up-to-date principles of increased productivity, product development, efficient marketing, financial planning and so forth. Conrad attacks Denmark's fossilised institutional and business structures, points to the economic liberalism and the new spirit of enterprise in England and the United States, where initiative is not fettered by rusted chains. All so true, so true. Nevertheless things go wrong for Conrad. He is toppled by his headstrong, overweening arrogance and not least by his pent-up emotional life vis-à-vis his family, and especially his sweetheart – who loves him with quiet intensity and whom he in fact also loves – until he realises at last that „that man is not a man who has never yearned to pour out his own soul to another kindred soul".

That was, and remained, J.C. Jacobsen's problem all his life.

J. C. Jacobsen at 35. Daguerreotype from 1846.

J. C. Jacobsen at 57. Photograph from 1868.

◀ *Laura Jacobsen. Photograph from the 1850s.*

J. C. Jacobsen and his employees, 1885.

The citizen

As is well known, present-day industrial leaders and founders of business concerns are conspicuous by their absence from the organs of public decision. They cannot afford to participate, nor do they have the time, excusing themselves on the ground, for example, that their interest groups and organisations serve to offset this under-representation. Matters were quite differently ordered in the early days of representative government during the last century. Interest groups had not yet become rigidly organised; businessmen and industrialists took part personally in the legislative process at national and local level. The citizenry joined wholeheartedly in the National Liberal movement which brought forth the Constitution, and which demanded reforms and self-government in local affairs. J.C. Jacobsen was part of this powerful and variegated movement.

At the time Carlsberg was founded, Jacobsen was in his fifth year as a member of the Copenhagen city council. He had been elected in January 1843. Seven councillors were up for election on that occasion. „Fædrelandet" (The Fatherland), the National Liberal movement's leading newspaper, urged its readers to re-elect five of the retiring counsellors, and in place of two who were not available for re-election to vote for Georg Bloch, a merchant in silks and cloth, and J.C. Jacobsen, brewer and at that time a lieutenant in the civic guard.

The Industrial Association and the Trade Guild put forward other lists in which Jacobsen did not figure, but it was „Fædrelandet"'s list which triumphed. The journal expressed its satisfaction with the election results, although not everyone on its list had got in. Jacobsen was referred to on this occasion as „an able, broad-minded and independent man". Jacobsen's co-representatives were J.C. Lund (agent), N. Meinert (merchant), H. Kyhl (watchmaker), who were old hands, along with Troels Lund (scene painter), P.G. Vörmer (master painter) and P.C. Olsen (distiller and graduate in surgery and pharmacology), all newly elected.

The assembly in which they took their places reflected the liberal interests of the day. Among the members were Orla Lehmann (graduate in laws), D.C. Monrad (master of arts), P.F. Lunde (ironmaster) and Joseph Owen (merchant). Lehmann and Monrad later became ministers. When Jacobsen entered the Rigsdag as a deputy the following year, he became close to them both. The strong and sure chairman of the city council was councillor of state L.N. Hvidt. He became one of Jacobsen's great idols. In 1865 J.C. had a bust of Hvidt made by the sculptor H.W. Bissen to put in his residence at Carlsberg.

L.N. Hvidt was the pivotal figure and political spokesman of Copenhagen's liberal bourgeoisie. In 1834 he became vice-president of the Roskilde Assembly of the provincial Estates and retained this post as long as the assemblies of Estates remained in existence, i.e. until 1848. He was one of the older generation of liberal leaders along with such men as Professor J.F. Schouw, Professor H.N. Clausen and the influential manufacturer J.C. Drewsen. These men found themselves opposed to the absolutist government; they wanted a constitution which would give decisive power, including that over finance, to popularly elected representatives, but they regarded this as a goal for the far-distant future and were ready to work towards it by collaborating with the government and its representative in the Roskilde Estates, Anders Sandøe Ørsted.

In December 1846 there was an election of deputies to the Roskilde Estates. „Fædrelandet" published a list that included J.C. Jacobsen and Lunde the ironmaster as candidates. They were the only industrialists on the list, and again Jacobsen figured as the newspaper's declared candidate. He stood high among businessmen in his education and competence, „and for his constitutional convictions and independent character we would vouch as for our own", as the journal put it.

In the test ballot in the Industrial Association and Trade Guild, Jacobsen secured the nomination and was then elected. His gratification was short-lived, however. The Roskilde Estates were summoned in April 1848, but the assembly, which was the last assembly of the Estates, was already over by May. Eight meetings were all that they managed to hold before political events, both in Denmark and abroad, overtook the assemblies of the Estates of the Realm.

King Christian VIII passed away on 20 January 1848, whereupon events accelerated.

Orla Lehmann, whose eloquence was especially appealing to the academic classes, now became the leading light of the National Liberal agitation of 1848, when addresses and resolutions poured in from mass meetings all over the capital. Lehmann believed that the hour of the bourgeoisie had now struck: they must seize political power and lead Denmark into the future. „The heart of the Danish nation resides in an enlightened and worthy middle class, which has absorbed into itself all the higher estates and thereby inherited their intellectual, moral and political merits." An academically educated élite was destined to become the leadership of a broad representative government.

It was not as easy as that, for there were other forces in Danish society which wanted a free constitution. Lehmann assembled a committee of National Liberals under the chairmanship of L.N. Hvidt, and one of its first acts was to arrange a meeting at the Casino on 11 March, the tickets for which were snatched up. 2300 people came to hear the main speakers, Orla Lehmann and H.N. Clausen.

The day after the Casino meeting, a group of young artisans arranged a meeting at the Hippodrome. Many of them had been in Paris and discovered socialism; they wanted universal suffrage as an absolute condition of any future constitution, and they reproached the National Liberals for betraying this demand. Lehmann, who had been invited, sprang up and declared that universal suffrage would be a common programme for all. The card was played.

The Copenhagen city council became involved. It assembled on the evening of 26 March for a meeting at the Town Hall, at which Lehmann secured assent to an address of no confidence to the government. The address opened with words to the effect that the advisers whom King Frederik VII had inherited from his predecessor did not enjoy the people's confidence in the current situation, which was also a fatal one from the foreign policy standpoint. It went on: „The hour of decision approaches by leaps and bounds, and the state will disintegrate if Your Majesty does not forthwith surround the throne with men equal to the magnitude of the task and capable of bringing an energetic will to bear on government." Denmark's honour and the nation's liberty were at stake. There then followed an undisguised threat of revolution: „We appeal to Your Majesty not to drive the nation to desperate measures."

The next morning the city council – all to the man – marched to Christiansborg Castle; even the conservative chief magistrate, Michael Lange, had decided, after some temporising, to march with them. The procession set off peacefully and in good order. It turned into a mass demonstration as a vast throng of people joined in on the way. At Vimmelskaftet they encountered a solitary gentleman walking on the pavement in the opposite direction. It was minister Anders Sandøe Ørsted, in full uniform. He was on his way home to his residence on Gammel Torv after the meeting of the King in Council at which the government had submitted its resignation. In point of fact he could easily have avoided the marchers by turning up one of the side streets but, like the serenely self-confident person he was, he passed by unmolested by anyone. On the corner of Knabrostræde, Grundtvig stood at his second-floor window watching.

The demonstration reached the square in front of Christiansborg Castle. Little by little something like 12-15,000 onlookers had gathered. Hvidt handed in the address: there was tension in the square while the reply was awaited. Hvidt came out and announced the King's reply: „The ministry is dissolved." His thin voice could be heard only by those nearest to him, but when it was realised what had happened shouts of joy broke out, and a cry of „Three cheers for the King!" It was a disappointment, to be sure, that the King did not come out on to the castle balcony himself to acknowledge the people's ovation.

The castle square emptied quickly as people went their various ways. Many of the demonstrators followed L.N. Hvidt back to the Town Hall, where he announced the King's reply yet again. Next he went to the stock exchange, as was his habit between 2 and 3 p.m., and then to his office at the National Bank. The Copenhagen chief magistrate, who along with Hvidt had led the demonstration against the former government, went to have dinner with Anders Sandøe Ørsted.

Thus peacefully was the revolution of 1848 accomplished in Copenhagen.

The birth pangs of the new government were severe. For a while the National Liberal leaders, who held a conference in Professor Schouw's office at the Botanical Gardens the day after the mass demonstration, expected that having regard to the situation abroad they would be joining a caretaker government alongside some of the former ministers. J.C. Jacobsen and P.F. Lunde, who were both reckoned to be „Hippodromedaries", turned up in the room during the meeting and spoke in forceful terms of the ferment among the populace of Copenhagen. They advised strongly against adopting the idea of a caretaker government. While they were speaking, P.G. Bang, one of the former ministers, entered the room, and at sight of him Lunde exclaimed: „Up to now you have done the talking: now you will see that we others have something to say as well." But Bang parried with the retort: „Mr Lunde, I am only asking you to tell your friends that the men here present are summoned by the King to assist in forming a ministry."

The result was a Conservative-Liberal government, the Moltke-Hvidt ministry, whose stand on foreign policy was based on the Eider programme, which held that all territory as far as the Eider river, i.e. the southern boundary of Schleswig, belonged rightfully to the Danish monarchy. The King declared that from now on he regarded himself as a constitutional monarch, and thus the days of absolutism came to an end.

Jacobsen did not himself play any prominent role in the political turmoil that preceded the establishment of the Constitution of the Kingdom of Denmark on 5 June 1849, but it engaged his active attention both as a city councillor and as a deputy to the assembly of the Estates. Jacobsen was critical of the upcoming Farmers' Party, although he did favour universal suffrage. At one of the meetings at the Hippodrome which he attended along with his friend Frants Djørup, the leader of the Farmers' Party, Balthazar Christensen, and Lunde the ironmaster, who was much more radical than Jacobsen, earned the wild applause of those present by advocating the introduction of a constitution with only one legislative chamber. Jacobsen sat silent, did not vote, and later on when discussing the issue far into the night at his friend's home, insisted in opposition to Djørup that there ought to be two chambers. Only in this way, in his view, could the essential conservative forces in a society be given the importance which was both necessary and their due.

Turning to local politics proper one of the first issues to be tackled by the Estates of the Realm was the drafting of a new system of local government for Copenhagen and the provincial towns. The outcome, known as the Local Government Act of 1840, became a milestone in Copenhagen's history. The old self-elective council of 32 members was replaced by an assembly elected by citizens, a municipal council totalling 36 members and given the name of Borgerrepræsentation. One sixth of the members were to retire annually. Voting was direct, but with the limitation that voters must either own real property of a certain minimum value or be substantial business taxpayers. In reality this meant that only a bare 2000 of the city's 121,000 inhabitants had votes or were qualified for election. Moreover, half the members of the municipal council had to be freeholders. Smaller property owners did not slip through the eye of the needle, the argument being that these could not be expected to be of sufficient intelligence for their participation in local government affairs to be beneficial.

The Borgerrepræsentation was advisory. It helped to draw up the budget and granted the taxes and other imposts which determined the budget's revenue side, but the budget had to be approved by the Chancellery. Above the municipal council stood the magistracy, or corporation, consisting of one chief magistrate, three burgomasters nominated by the government and six aldermen elected by the citizenry. The latter were thus unable to decide for themselves who should be burgomasters of their own city. Furthermore, certain matters were placed under special commissions, which meant in practice that a number of important local authority affairs, such as the roads, the inspection of buildings, the water supply, and public assistance were excluded from the municipal council's immediate influence.

Thus it was no revolutionary change in the city's administration that was introduced in 1840, and the King also underlined this when a deputation from the municipal government assembled to express thanks the day after the promulgation of the new system. He said: „I have let the correct situation remain in force, that the corporation is responsible for the administration of the city, but that no expenditure can be incurred and no tax imposed without the consent of the municipal council."

Nevertheless the local government reform of 1840 opened the door to a new era. At the very first election a National Liberal minority gained admittance to the municipal council. They were dubbed the „new citizen" class, signifying not people engaged in the trades associated with formal citizenship but those who had taken out trade licences in order to participate in the election. There were only about 50 such persons in 1840, but of these no fewer than 6 were elected, including L.N. Hvidt, Orla Lehmann, Balthazar Christensen, Tage Ahlgreen-Ussing and C.N. David. The „new citizen class" consolidated its position in the local elections of the following year: D.G. Monrad was elected, and – more important – L.N. Hvidt became chairman and Orla Lehmann deputy chairman.

Thus the municipal council became in reality clearly National Liberal, which heightened the tension between the municipal council on the one hand and the mainly Conservative corporation on the other. Step by step the National Liberals strengthened their position in the years that followed. „Fædrelandet" was assigned the right to publish the official reports of debates in place of „Berlingske Tidende", and a number of new faces made their appearance. H.H. Kayser, a master carpenter by trade and destined to be the municipal council's strongest man of the second half of the 19th century, was elected in 1848, the same year in which the lawyer A.F. Krieger also became a member. In 1848 the National Liberals had their way over one of their key issues when the meetings of the municipal council were opened to the public.

J.C. Jacobsen, who as already noted was elected in 1843, took up his duties eagerly as a municipal councillor, and good use was made of him. The year after his election he became a member of the standing committee of the municipal council, to which he was re-elected every year. In 1853, when L.N. Hvidt retired and was succeeded as chairman by H.P. Hansen, director of the National Bank, Jacobsen and Krieger were candidates for the vice-chairmanship. Krieger was elected, but left the municipal council two years later, whereupon Jacobsen took over the vice-chairmanship and retained it until he himself left the council in 1857.

He sat on numerous special committees and for brief periods was a member of executive or administrative bodies: for example, he was an interim member of the Port Authority in 1844 and on the Public

Assistance Board from 1845 to 1847. Immediately on election he became a member of an interim committee considering the establishment of butchers' stalls at Nikolaj Tower. Then followed in quick succession committees on the weighing of corn, coal and salt in 1845, reorganisation of the corporation in 1848, port authority resources in 1850, municipal cleansing in 1851, the system of dues and taxation in 1853, the farming out of toll-bar duties in the same year, the establishment of bathing and washing establishments in 1854, the erection of gas- and waterworks in Copenhagen in 1854, the organisation of local government administration in the city in 1855, and the commission on land tax assessment in 1856.

One special field for which Jacobsen was a natural choice was that of building. In 1850 alone he was involved in reorganising Copenhagen's chimney sweeping, in establishing government loans for people living on land within the city glacis, and in the fire commission. He also helped to reorganise the city surveyor's office in 1854. In addition, Jacobsen and Kayser were appointed by the municipal council to two commissions set up by the ministry, viz. the commission to consider a new building law for Copenhagen in 1852 and the commission to consider building development on sites outside the city ramparts in 1855. Finally, there were a couple of matters on which J.C. Jacobsen submitted proposals himself, one in 1851 being for the provision of better wharfage for steamships plying to and from Copenhagen and another in 1856 for an improvement of roads and watercourses outside the city.

As a local government politician and later on in the Rigsdag, where Jacobsen sat from 1854 onwards and was involved in handling much legislation bearing upon local government and arising out of the work of the aforementioned committees and commissions, he manifested clearly his fundamental dissatisfaction with the 1840 system of local government for Copenhagen. Neither did he find it possible to support the local government reorganisation of 1857. It was true that it gave the municipal council the right to choose both burgomasters and aldermen. From then on the capital had four burgomasters: one for schools, one for finance, one for public assistance and one for roads and the technical departments, plus a similar number of aldermen. In fact Copenhagen was being allowed a special privilege in this, for the provincial towns still had their burgomasters appointed by the government, a system which continued until 1919. But the magistracy was retained, thus perpetuating a division of power which in Jacobsen's view was unnecessary. It was one of the fundamental weaknesses of the reform.

Jacobsen's ideal was the English system of urban administration with its far-reaching independence of the state and with unpaid officials selected from among people with high ability and above all personally independent of interests and of money. In local administration there was no ground for practising a division of power between a legislative arm and – as he put it – „one of God's Elect sitting on the other side" (by which he meant the chief magistrate).

As far as the franchise was concerned, Jacobsen could not countenance the idea of multiple electorates. When the constitution of the local government of provincial towns was changed in 1860, two classes of voter were introduced: the Lower House voters and an electorate consisting of high taxpayers, and these elected the major and the minor proportion respectively of the municipal council.

On the contrary, what he proposed was a general extension of the franchise in local elections to include all taxpaying citizens. The point was to link „a much larger body of the inhabitants of the local authority district to the nation and evoke among them that public spirit which is the firmest foundation for the whole of our constitution", as he said in 1856 in one of his many contributions on the subject, which was one of his hobby-horses. The constitution's surest defence „is the public spirit which is developing among the lower orders of society – where it is developing to a better and higher degree than among the other orders". The local authority district should be a unity, and the nation should be built up of such unities. Free local government districts would be the bulwark of freedom in Denmark.

It has been said that Jacobsen was a class politician, meaning a middle-class politician. In his eyes the middle class was identical with the people, and the middle class ought not to be split by setting „rich and poor against one another". „If a local council be divided into two corporations, and if they be reminded that they are two different parts which may have two different opinions, then they will have two different opinions," as he expressed it during a Rigsdag debate in

1867/68. Universal suffrage to him was the suffrage of the middle class.

The independence of public officials was also a key issue for him. The new local government act prescribed elected burgomasters for Copenhagen, who were to be salaried, with tenure for life and a pension. This was not Jacobsen's cup of tea. If indeed there were to be salaried burgomasters, then they ought to be appointed by the king, however odd that might sound, „for it is a truth that representative assemblies, especially where the numbers composing them are large, are least of all suited for assigning offices". This was not a popular thing to say, but it was his firm conviction that anything else opened the way for horsetrading and incompetence in the filling of offices. On the same grounds he was opposed to the city treasurer's being a member of the municipal council. The treasurer who had to account for the use made of local government funds could not himself sit in the assembly which had the duty of supervising his discharge of his office.

He raised a similar criticism during the Rigsdag's deliberations of 1862-63 on the building law. Although it was stated clearly in the instructions to housing surveyors that they were not to act in an official capacity if they were themselves involved in a building venture, the reality was different. Many builders were very eager to order drawings for their projects from the surveyors in return for payment, and the latter then made a pro forma survey after building had been completed. Similarly it was the accepted practice not to sign building drawings, so concealing who had made them. Altogether, because of the inefficiency of the municipal clerk of works to whom the surveyors were responsible, „this most honest dotard is not in a position to perform the duties laid on him by his office, on account of his age and decrepitude". This was the broadside which Jacobsen fired at the 75 year-old Copenhagen clerk of works. After 50 years in office, the latter would not feel inclined to familiarise himself with the rules imposed by the new law, declared Jaocbsen in the Lower House.

Lack of professionalism always got the Brewer's blood up. In 1851 he became a member of a royal commission charged with formulating proposals for a new and up-to-date organisation of the Copenhagen fire service. The commission's report was pigeonholed. By 1863 the Rigsdag still had not dealt with it, and Jacobsen decided to raise the issue by means of a question to the minister of justice. He began by remarking sarcastically that he was reluctant to be accused of an ill-timed ardour for reform, but the fact was that Copenhagen's firefighting arrangements were thoroughly obsolete. They dated from 1805. During the intervening period the population of the city had grown by 50,000 and it had acquired many new industries presenting high fire hazards of which the old system simply knew nothing. The fire appliances were hopeless, and the city's reserve corps of 5000 men was undisciplined and in any case was never exercised. What Jacobsen advocated instead was a small, highly trained fire brigade with a technical expert as its permanent chief. He demanded new equipment, and he also wanted the firefighting forces of the suburbs to be brought under Copenhagen. The costs of the fire service should be divided between the local authority and the fire insurance companies. It was the fixed and personal property of citizens, their lives, limbs and well-being, that were at stake. Therefore it was impossible, in his view, to shift all the costs on to the fire insurance companies, who would in that case demand control of the fire service, and that would not do.

There were good grounds for Jacobsen's impatience. Fires were an everyday occurrence, and they not infrequently developed into catastrophes. In 1834 Hillerød was heavily damaged by a big fire, and on the night of 16/17 December 1859 Frederiksborg Castle was burned to the ground. In 1865, at the height of the summer heat wave, a fierce fire ravaged Valby. In the course of a few hours the fire turned the entire town centre into a sea of flame, reducing 4 farms and 35 houses to ashes. Two of the homeless families, along with their numerous children, were given food and shelter at Carlsberg. In April 1867 Jacobsen himself was touched by catastrophe when his own brewery burned down. This happened while he was a member of the Upper House, where even yet nothing more had come of the deliberations over Copenhagen's firefighting arrangements.

He lived to experience yet another catastrophe, this being the Christiansborg Castle fire of 8/9 October 1884. The 73 year-old Jacobsen inspected the site the day after the fire. He wanted to see if Thorvaldsen's Alexander frieze had survived. „By pushing my way up to floor level" he was able to ascertain that the frieze had escaped.

The marble had taken on a brownish tinge but was otherwise undamaged, he reported to J.J.A. Worsaae the archaeologist. „It is almost a miracle really." Jacobsen had donated a steam-operated fire engine to the Copenhagen Fire Brigade the year before. After the fire at the royal residence he paid for an engineer to travel to Germany to seek inspiration for further development of the capital's fire precautions.

The Copenhagen municipal council had adopted a large-scale programme in the spring of 1853 for providing the city with water, gas and sewerage systems, all to be installed at the same time. Local expertise had been supplemented by consulting a prominent authority, James Simpson, a civil engineer from Britain. The chief magistrate proposed that the sewerage plan should be laid aside and only the gas and waterworks schemes implemented. The municipal council rejected this. A cholera epidemic struck that same summer and carried off 4737 of the city's inhabitants. Under the impact of this catastrophe attention was concentrated on the water scheme, which was given top priority, but after further deliberation the municipal council brought the gasworks into the programme again, whereupon Anders Sandøe Ørsted, who at this time not only combined the offices of prime minister, minister of home affairs and minister of ecclesiastical affairs and public instruction but was also a close friend of the chief magistrate, said no, thus effectively blocking the sewerage scheme.

On 19 April 1854 the municipal council set up a committee to pursue the work on the gas and water schemes. It consisted of burgomaster A.L. Casse, J.C. Jacobsen and V. Rothe, a railway director. A loan of 3 million rix-dollars was raised, 2.4 million of which were assigned to the installation of the two works. On his visit to Britain in the summer of 1855 Jacobsen contacted James Simpson, who was again appointed to supervise the entire scheme, and through him the undertaking was entrusted to the English contracting firm of Cochrane & Co. The contract was signed on behalf of the local authority by the banker C. Hambro in London on 20 February 1856. The contractor's operations in Copenhagen were headed by a young Scot, John Aird, who subsequently carried out similar projects in other large towns and also directed the construction of the Aswan dam in Egypt.

The task was tackled at once with vigour. By that same summer 900 men were already at work. Operations sometimes continued at night, a phenomenon never previously witnessed in Royal Copenhagen. On 16 May the following year it was possible to lay the foundation stone of the engine room at the glacis outside the moat of Vestervold, the western rampart. It had been decided to recognise Jacobsen's involvement in this great affair by getting him to lay the stone. After that he and Aird made the obligatory speeches to mark the occasion. Thus was inaugurated a new chapter in the city's history. A technical reform of the most far-reaching importance to the life of the common man had taken place. Now it was possible to open a tap in the kitchen and let fresh, pure water stream out. It was a miracle: there was none who regretted the passing of the old order. At such a moment, a citizen could feel pride.

In the same year the Lower House considered a proposal concerning gasfitters and plumbers. Jacobsen demanded that these should either be licensed by the local authority or have proved their qualifications. Although he was a supporter – and a wholehearted one – of economic liberalisation and the Freedom of Trade Act which was adopted on one of the last days of the year, freedom still had its limits. Where the exercise of economic freedom could threaten the interests of the community at large, it must yield. He wanted a similar restriction in the insurance sphere; he was a determined opponent of insurance business being conducted by the private sector because the social aspect was too important.

In matters concerning Copenhagen's building laws Jacobsen advocated uniform building regulations. He felt the situation with regard to building on the outskirts of the city to be particularly dubious; the sanitary arrangements were not satisfactorily implemented, and planlessness in conjunction with legislative dilatoriness, especially in the Rigsdag, meant that new quarters were being added to the city, for example the Blaagaard quarter at Nørrebro, where housing speculation had free rein.

The year of destiny

„We live in the most important period through which Denmark has passed since the Reformation. The times have not been so turbulent for three centuries," wrote the young Frederik Hammerich, parson of the parish of Starup, near Kolding, to his younger brother Martin at Christmas 1840. He went on: „People against king, Schleswig-Holsteiners, Holstein-Lauenburgers, Pan-Scandinavians, friends of national unity, pro-French, pro-Norwegian, liberals, royalists, ecclesiastical conservatives and champions of liberty – all oppose one another. Scarcely any other country the size of Denmark displays such sharp conflicts."

There was a ferment in society all over Europe. In 1848 the tensions triggered a wave of insurrection that washed over the nations. It began in February in France, the motherland of revolution, in the form of a bloody revolt by an urban proletariat resolved to fight for better living standards. From there unrest communicated itself to the German states, to the similarly fragmented Italy, and to Austria-Hungary.

The national liberal middle class was the leading element in the storm. It was likewise the middle class that reaped the first fruits of the insurrections in the form of new liberal constitutions giving it a share in political power. The underlying ideas were those of popular sovereignty and the demand for recognition of the nationality principle. The body politic ought to be founded on and sustained by common language and national culture, assembled in unitary states or in firm federations of states. The movement for unity was especially strong in Italy and Germany, where it profited from one of the other tendencies of the time, viz. the desire for a liberalisation of economic life and, with the help of tariff policy, the breaking down of ancient local barriers in favour of larger and more dynamic national markets. The rapid progress going on in transport and industry gave strong encouragement to this tendency.

The Constitution of the Kingdom of Denmark of 5 June 1849 can be set into this new European context. The assembly of Estates of the Realm was replaced by a parliament, the Rigsdag, consisting of a lower and an upper house known respectively as the Folketing and Landsting. The franchise was the same in both cases. All males of good character „with their own cloth and table", i.e. householders, had the vote. The difference between the two chambers lay in the mode of voting. The 100 seats in the Lower House were filled by direct election in single-member constituencies, while the 51 members of the Upper House were elected by indirect voting in county constituencies. There were also differences in the qualifications for election. It was possible to be a member of the Lower House at age 25, but the age qualification for the Upper House was 40 and an annual income of at least 1200 rix-dollars was required. Women had no vote and were not eligible as candidates.

The constitution laid down that Denmark was a constitutional monarchy with a king free from responsibility and responsible ministers nominated by the king. The sovereign powers were separated, civic and religious freedom constitutionally guaranteed, and abolition of censorship likewise. A series of declaratory clauses set out a programme for the coming years. The administration of justice was to be reformed, economic freedom established and independence of local government introduced. Entailed estates were to be converted to freehold ownership, and the status of the national church would be regulated by future legislation.

The constitution contained one clause which was not subjected to any major discussion in the national constituent assembly but which gave rise to fierce tensions later on in the century. This was the right of the king, in special instances when the Rigsdag was not in session, to promulgate temporary „provisional" laws.

The constitution of 1849 was carried into effect without a revolution. Blood was shed in Denmark nonetheless, for the nation was at war, and there was no time to celebrate the new constitution. Because of the First Schleswig War, the provision that the constitution was to be valid for both Denmark and Schleswig had to be scrapped – and what was worse, the war did not settle this vital issue. After the conclusion of peace, Denmark was left with the most democratic constitution in Europe but had not arrived at any clarification of the monarchy's final structure. Where was the constitution to apply? Its fathers had acted as politicians but neglected their role as statesmen.

The next decade showed that in Germany too, the national sentiment which liberalism had nourished was growing vigorously. The demand for a unitary state was not to be denied. The King Wilhelm I, and still more so his chancellor, Otto von Bismarck, exploited this situation in order to create a strong Germany under the leadership of Prussia, with all Germans embraced in a single nation. The ideological basis of the Schleswig-Holstein movement was affected by this. Similarly, Danish national feeling, partly as a result of an exaggerated conception of what had happened and what had been achieved during the First Schleswig War, had become so dominant that any division of Schleswig in accordance with linguistic criteria was politically impossible.

Another contributory factor was the growth of Pan-Scandinavianism, a variant on Nordic soil of the unification movements of the day. Its aim was similar to that of the German and Italian movements. Denmark was to be the guardian of the Nordic frontier against the advance of Germanism, and the frontier was along the Eider river – the river boundary between Schleswig and Holstein. The universities were the hothouse of Pan-Scandinavianism. Whereas it had been a non-political, mainly literary and humanistic movement prior to 1840, with landmarks consisting of such events as the laurels awarded to the poet Oehlenschläger at Lund in 1829, the publication of Frederik Barfod's quarterly journal „Brage og Idun" (from 1836 onwards) and tentative small-scale meetings between students from Lund and Copenhagen, after 1840 the movement became more and more political. One of its new instruments, The Scandinavian Society, of which in fact J.C. Jacobsen was one of the founders, was established in 1843.

After the end of the First Schleswig War the Danish government endeavoured to bind Schleswig more closely to the kingdom, firstly by changes in the Schleswig administration and secondly by a new language system in those districts of Schleswig where Danish was hard pressed. Danish was made compulsory in schools and confirmation classes. However, the closer integration of Schleswig into the kingdom depended to a large degree on the great powers – especially Russia, which had intervened in the war to Denmark's advantage. The Tsar's rule was absolutist, and the great Russian Empire was brimming with nationality problems, Poland and Finland being vast foreign provinces for example. The Scandinavian student meetings in Uppsala were observed with uneasy attention in St Petersburg. There was no sympathy at all in Russia for a Denmark extending to the Eider, and still less for the June constitution. The Russian government let it be known in Denmark that the price of continued friendship was „to shake free of the remnants of the national revolution". For the good old days were coming back in Europe. After the revolution followed the reaction. In France, Louis Napoleon established personal rule by a coup d'état. Austria was moving towards the reintroduction of absolutism.

Under this pressure, successive Danish governments had to set about re-establishing the United Monarchy under constitutional forms, and a conservative constitution was what foreign powers demanded. In January 1852 the June constitution was restricted so as to apply only north of the Konge river: it was thought that this would meet the requirements of „the European imperative". This step did not command agreement. Grundtvig called its proclamation a breach of the constitution and disputed its necessity. In his poem „Kærlighed til Fædrelandet" (Love of the Fatherland) he propounded „the Danish imperative" as a counterthrust: „Fear not the world's imperative of steel, so called." However, the A.S. Ørsted ministry, led by the old statesman and father of the assembly of the Estates, went a step further. Ørsted was one of the few who had voted against the constitution in 1849. He had little understanding of the National Liberals and got rid of three of their leading figures, Hall, Andræ and Monrad. In July 1854 he promulgated a constitution which included the Two Duchies and thus restored the conditions of absolutism in joint matters concerning the monarchy. These joint matters were to be handled by a State Council of only 50 members, 18 chosen by the Rigsdag of the June constitution, 12 by the assemblies of the Estates of Schleswig-Holstein, and 20 nominated by the King. The executive authority of the State Council was restricted to joint taxes and the raising of state loans. The remainder of its functions were only advisory and its meetings were private.

In the Lower House there was talk of a coup d'état and a breach of the constitution. The protests against the ministry were vociferous. They precipitated an election on 2 August 1854.

J.C. Jacobsen was active in the protest movement. He was a co-signatory of an invitation published earlier that summer in „Fædrelandet", the main organ of the National Liberals, to all citizens to join a newly-established Association for the Defence of the Constitution. Other signatories were N.F. Bonnesen (tobacco manufacturer), C.A. Broberg (merchant), G. Brock (supreme court advocate), Martin Hammerich (school principal), H.P. Hansen (merchant and bank director) and Moritz Melchior (merchant). But next he stood as a candidate for the Lower House. In his election address, which was reported in „Fædrelandet", he declared himself a faithful friend of Denmark's liberty under the law. He had never feared the existing electoral law nor did he wish it changed. It had never been any more abused than any other law would have been. The Rigsdag, in Jacobsen's view, had done sensible work, not least by putting forward useful reforms and by controlling the national finances and introducing economy into them. It was contrary to the constitution for the government to have tried to push through a joint constitution outside the Rigsdag.

Jacobsen won the election and thus embarked on a political career at national level. He never attained a place in the direction of national policy: in English terms he was a „backbencher". Nevertheless there are good grounds for dwelling on Rigsdag politics, for they led him forward to the catastrophe of 1864, Denmark's year of destiny, which set a deep and quite crucial brand on him. The year 1864 created in J.C. Jacobsen the sense of a new „national imperative" which is essential to the understanding of the patronage of his later years.

J.C. Jacobsen is easy to place in the political line-up. He was a National Liberal. It is true that when he sought election to the Rigsdag for the second time in 1861, he declared that he stood in isolation as a politician and that he had never been able to commit himself wholeheartedly to any party, but that he nourished a warm attachment to the constitution and freedom of elections, which alone were capable of nurturing national sentiment. „Fædrelandet" did not report this election address, for which one must turn to „Berlingske

Tidende"; nevertheless everything in Jacobsen's actions and circle of acquaintances points towards the National Liberals, and he continued to feel linked with „Fædrelandet". Thus, in 1864, he was co-arranger of the grand banquet held to celebrate the newspaper's 25th anniversary.

The National Liberals were not a party in the modern sense. There were many who, like Jacobsen, protested at the idea of enrolling – Madvig and Monrad, for example – and even if the National Liberals were not without organisation, regarded as a group they were not habituated to discipline. In that respect the largest Rigsdag grouping, the Farmers' Party, were better placed. It has been said of the young Rigsdag that it was inexperienced, which is a truism, and that it still lacked the fields of force that can be generated inside strong party frameworks, which contains a measure of truth. The gallery of personalities is large, the shifts of scenery many, and there was no lack of jealousy between the actors with all the fortuitous happenings which that can produce. Viewed thus, it can be difficult to chart and understand the manifold subtleties of the play.

However, the main themes delineate themselves clearly enough. The new government which succeeded Ørsted's ministry devised a kind of mixed constitution keeping the Duchies within the monarchy and limiting the June constitution so as to make it apply only to the Kingdom and the affairs specific to it. It was also proposed that the State Council should be enlarged. The Rigsdag adopted the proposal, but not by an overwhelming majority since 54 voted for and 44 against. Jacobsen gave his support with the observation that it was important and significant for Denmark to retain the link with the economically more highly developed Holstein.

The German customs union, the Zollverein, which was extended to the frontiers of Holstein in 1837, was attractive in many respects in terms of the economy of the Duchies, but of course the Duchies also occupied an important position within the Danish Monarchy. Their area accounted for about half that of Denmark proper, population density was greater and urbanisation more advanced, a number of the Monarchy's biggest towns being situated in Schleswig-Holstein: Altona, Flensburg, Kiel, Schleswig and Rendsborg were all bigger than Odense, the second largest town in the Kingdom. The Duchies differed in terms of occupations too. Agriculture was more advanced there than north of the Konge river. The Flensburg trade with the West Indies was the biggest in the monarchy. The town supplied not only Copenhagen but also large parts of Schleswig, Funen and the east coast of Jutland with foreign- and home-produced goods, in increasingly intense competition with Hamburg.

The events of the next few years showed that the problems of the United Monarchy were insoluble. At the beginning of the 1860s Schleswig came back on to the great power agenda after the Prussian chamber of deputies had raised the question. A fierce Schleswig-Holstein propaganda campaign provoked a counter-movement on similar lines in Denmark. Pan-Scandinavian aspirations received new impetus. Carl XV, Regent of Sweden-Norway since 1859 and personal friend of Frederik VII, lent his ear to the movement; the Swedish envoy in Copenhagen, Count Henning Hamilton, was an ardent adherent of the idea. Council president Hall came under increasing pressure from the Eider movement led by Orla Lehmann. The „Dannevirke Society" was founded, named after the old fortification line south of Schleswig. A parliamentary address demanding a constitutional union between the Kingdom and Schleswig in an indivisible and independent state was supported by all political parties and attracted 71,000 signatures from all over the country, far more than any previous Danish address had achieved. In September 1861, Lehmann, leading figure of the movement, joined the government.

Jacobsen, who in his disappointment over the outcome of the Rigsdag's deliberations on the Local Government Act of 1857 had not wanted re-election, decided to stand after all. In June he offered himself as a candidate in Copenhagen's seventh electoral district (having represented the first district in his first period). Whereas on the previous occasion he had felt called upon to defend the constitution, the issue this time was Schleswig. He declared that he would work to see that what was Denmark's, Denmark should have, and that Holstein should have what was Holstein's. He would rather have war than a feeble climbdown which would make the people slaves. These sentiments echoed Lehmann's. Again he was elected. He sat in the Lower House for two years, then was nominated by the King to the State Council's Upper House in 1863. This brought him closer to the fateful events which led to war.

On 28 September 1863 the government submitted proposals for a constitution covering the joint affairs of the Kingdom of Denmark and the Duchy of Schleswig. This was called the Eider constitution and was the Danish counterblast to the obstructionism of the Schleswig-Holstein majority in the Schleswig Estates. On the Scandinavian plane the government had suffered a disappointment. The proposal for a treaty with Sweden-Norway for a relief force of 20,000 men in the event of Holstein's being besieged by the Germans had foundered because of resistance within the Swedish government.

Nevertheless there was jingoism in the air, and this included Carlsberg. With his accustomed hospitality, J.C. Jacobsen had invited his new colleagues on the State Council to dine at his home. „On Sunday we shall be having grand company from the State Council," reported Nanna on 29 October. „Aunt Faye and I are pleased that we shall be spectators up in the gallery. We are giving up our places for a couple of state councillors and are letting Aunt Laura preside. If the others are drinking champagne down there, no doubt we shall have to content ourselves with the corks." Brask asked for a more detailed description of the party. This followed with the next letter:

„Yes, I had a bird's eye view of it all – many different toasts were drunk. Good and bad speeches were made as is customary at other dinners. Krieger gave an excellent one for Count Hamilton as the man he considered best suited to get some results from the Scandinavian idea. Burgomaster Larsen maundered on about the Council of State and then dried up. L. Skou from Haderslev spoke with warmth and inspiration of our fatherland. Uncle must have proposed a dozen different toasts – for the King, for the Schleswigers, for the ministry and others – but I am really beginning to yawn, so it is about time I went to bed. I will just tell you that I was able to pick out Liebe straight away from the whole mass of people because of the resemblance to his brother. Unfortunately he gave no proof of his much discussed and brilliant eloquence; in spite of Uncle's repeated hints he found no cause to say anything."

The constitutional proposal was adopted on 13 November. Henceforth the State Council was to be the legislative assembly both of the Kingdom and of Schleswig, with two chambers. The 130 members of the lower chamber would be elected according to the same rules as the Lower House of the Rigsdag, while the upper chamber would consist of 18 representatives nominated by the King and 65 elected in accordance with the census rules of the 1855 constitution. The adoption of the proposal was announced by the president amidst a storm of cheers from the spectator benches.

No one could be in any doubt that the November constitution would lead to war. Naturally Jacobsen voted in favour. „Today," wrote Nanna on 13 November, „the big battle has been fought in the Rigsdag – all the politicians were agog over what the outcome of the debate would be, especially since Hall had said that the ministry would resign if the draft fell through. Tomorrow Uncle is to have dinner with Count Frijs Frijsenborg, who lives here in town when the State Council is in session."

The drama rolled on. Two days later Frederik VII died at Glücksborg Castle. The King had not yet appended his signature to the November constitution. His successor Christian IX, the first Glücksborger on the Danish throne, had no ready-made popularity to draw on. He believed in the old constitution and was a conservative, aloof, marked in his being and culture by his German origins. Quite unjustly, his Danish sentiments were suspect in the eyes of many. The new monarch availed himself of his constitutional right to request time for consideration and consultation, but no one dared to advise him to refuse to sign the constitution. He put his name to it on 18 November.

„There is such suspense here among all classes – and the report of his signature today brought the smile back to the faces of the whole surging mass of people filling the streets. Tomorrow the State Council will be admitted to the King's presence to express thanks." And there was mourning apparel to be sewn. „We are as black as ravens," declared Nanna. „The students are wearing crape with hanging ends round their caps, and the students' union flag mourned at half mast when all the others were raised to pay homage. And it is still mourning," she concluded her private report to her sweetheart in Jutland. A couple of days later she wrote: „Everyone in this house is so politically minded just now, of course. No one thinks of anything else or speaks of anything else, and even when we read the newspapers we only trouble ourselves with whatever concerns our Danish-German dispute or the new and the late king."

Then during Christmas: „I cannot really accustom myself to the idea of war, of course I hear everyone saying we are going to have one, but my innermost self keeps saying: it will not come to anything" ... „Aunt is melancholy with apprehension that Carl's turn will come, which it certainly will, whether Uncle decides to buy a substitute for him or not. Of course it is not a matter of money but of a sense of duty to the fatherland" [Carl was called up later in the year, in July] – „Sophus M. has volunteered as a doctor in a camp hospital." „Ludvig, the foreman at the brewery, will be going tomorrow, and one of the others." They were given a home-knitted kerchief for the journey. Winter was making itself felt early, and it was bitingly cold.

Saxon and Hanoverian forces crossed the frontier on Christmas Day. The Danish army retired without a fight behind the Eider to the Dannevirke position. On 31 January 1864 Prussia and Austria informed the other great powers that they were now proceeding to the occupation of Schleswig. This was done without any declaration of war. On 5 February the Danish army evacuated Dannevirke. These events caused a shock wave. The evacuation of Dannevirke was a staggering blow to the population. No one had expected the ramparts to be abandoned without a real struggle. There were rumours of cowardice and treachery on the part of government and generals. Riots broke out in Copenhagen. The police had to clear the streets around Det gule Palæ, the „Yellow Palace", where the Regent and his wife were still living.

„On us out here the news ... made an overwhelmingly disheartening impression, and the idea of treachery instinctively thrust itself on us as on most others." Jacobsen was afraid that the Jutlanders would make some composition in order to escape the burdens of quartering soldiers. He wrote about this to his friend Lindahl. Brask reassured Nanna: „Tell your Uncle that he is wrong in his opinion of us Jutlanders. Although I mix with many persons of different classes, I have never heard a single utterance to suggest that we should give up anything in order to have peace. On the contrary, I believe that we are agreed to stand and fall to the last man rather than sacrifice voluntarily any of our just rights. Have we ever done otherwise?" Jutland had exerted itself in the First Schleswig War and its turn had now come round again. „The fine gentlemen of Copenhagen know too little of the common folk." Carl went around being vexed with the English. „He gives vent to his disgust with the most incredible variations on the word 'scoundrel', blackguard etc."

Jacobsen himself was prepared for the war to last three years. „He goes violently on the warpath against the newspapers and correspondents who taint our cause by their blusterings. If the soldiers get hold of these papers, they will destroy discipline," wrote Nanna as the siege of Dybbøl was getting under way. The first of the wounded came from Horsens to Valby and were taken on to nearby Frederiksberg Castle, where a camp hospital had been established.

The mood vis-à-vis the King continued to be negative, although Christian IX's „terse, lucid and patriotic words which he had signed the other day at the adjournment of the Rigsdag made an excellent impression. There was a private party at Schwalbé's (as he now calls himself) on Østergade in the evening, where a dozen Rigsdag deputies were assembled along with Hall, and the cheers for the King were so hearty that Uncle was hoarse the next day."

A couple of days later, on Easter Monday, a party was traditionally held at Carlsberg. The company was assembled in the garden room when Japetus Steenstrup's young son Johannes, a student, arrived with news of the sortie from the redoubt and the warship „Rolf Krake"'s intervention in the battle of Dybbøl. The shells from the ship had exploded in the midst of the enemy's columns. Hopes rose a little.

At a later party we find the gentlemen in the Captain's room, now in subdued conversation; the mood is depressed. Then one of the guests, a highly-placed official with a confidential post in the Ministry of War, rises to his feet and reveals that „Aarøe's corps" is to make a landing in total secrecy on the North Schleswig coast and take the enemy in flank – an excellent plan, well thought out and prepared. It ought to succeed and may have great significance. Carl Jacobsen, who related the episode, adds:
„How typical: a trusted official from the Ministry of War tells a large

company at dinner the secret plan which is to surprise the enemy!
Aarøe's plan foundered because the enemy, curiously enough, had
received news of it! It is certainly not so remarkable that we did not
hold our own in this war."

At the students' union the actor Wilhelm Wiehe declaimed No. 15
Stolt, by Runeberg, and Asgaardsrejsen, by Welhaven; Hans Christian Andersen read six stories; the students sang exquisite songs in
chorus. At the university edifying lectures were delivered by
Goldschmidt, Frederik Hammerich, Hauch, Worsaae, Rasmus Nielsen and Japetus Steenstrup. „I think everyone is agreed in giving
preference to Nielsen's words on 'Shame and honour'. It was an
extraordinary occasion," Nanna felt.

Vaccination against smallpox … bazaars … collections… auxiliary
work.

„Uncle has given 5000 rix-dollars under the pseudonym „A Citizen"
and 1000 publicly for the dependants of the fallen … All sorts of
people come with private petitions which he cannot cope with. His
name has become known through his gifts to the army."

Jutland came under occupation. „Oh, these Prussians! How I hate
them." Brask was taken hostage and removed to Aarhus, but was
quickly released once the armistice was agreed and peace negotiations
opened at the conference in London. But the conference ended on 25
June without any result. The Prussians crossed Alssund and conquered the island of Als.

It was a loss which had crippling effects, especially in the capital.
The restaurants of Tivoli and Klampenborg had had record numbers
of guests. Now panic gripped the Copenhageners. If Funen fell too,
and if an Austrian fleet should appear, then the enemy could be
expected at any time. Stock Exchange prices plummeted. There was a
run on the savings banks.

The State Council was summoned to an extraordinary meeting, at
which Jacobsen ranged himself with Estrup, Chr. Jensen Jr, Mourier-
Petersen and Rosenørn-Lehn in proposing an address to the King.
They wished to support the King's offer to cede the territory situated
south of Slien-Dannevirke in return for recognition of the country's

sovereign independence. This minimum, the partitioning of Schleswig, must be the prerequisite of „the Danish people's being able to lead not only a material but also a spiritual and moral life, a prerequisite of their being able to fulfil their mission as an independent member of the comity of European nations and as such to work in unity with them for the furtherance of civilisation and culture".

The proposal for an address did not win unmixed approval, but on being considered a second time was passed by 41 votes to 14. However, at a confidential meeting the ministry asked for the address to be stopped, since peace negotiations had been resumed.

The peace treaty came before the Rigsdag for consideration on 8 November. It involved the cession of all three Duchies: Schleswig, Holstein and Lauenborg. As expected, many harsh and dismissive words were spoken about the treaty. Monrad, whom the King had forced out of the government at the beginning of July in favour of more sober-minded spirits, would not vote in favour: „It is said that it would now be madness to offer resistance, but has not madness, then, achieved the most in history?" He was a sick and broken man; his bombast bore the marks. Hall and Lehmann, on the other hand, now looked reality in the eye. They both warned against a resumption of the war and hoped that in time the nationality principle would prevail. The Lower House of the State Council adopted the peace treaty by 75 votes to 21, the Upper House by 55 votes to 4. There were 4 members of the Upper House who abstained. One of them was Jacobsen.

On 12 November 1864, then, Christian IX signed the peace treaty in the State Council. He declared that it was the unhappiest day of his life and spoke of abdicating the throne, but the ministers replied that it was his by absolute right.

The National Liberals felt that they were the men of the defeat. Even so they determined to celebrate „Fædrelandet"'s anniversary in November with a grand dinner at the Skydebanen restaurant. Martin Hammerich made the main speech and J.C. Jacobsen proposed the health of the King. „It is comical," commented little Nanna. „Uncle was not the King's friend before this – however, judging by his words this evening he seems to want to steer a seemly middle course while still throwing some sops to those who are so sharply opposed to him [the King] – so that when he ends with some graceful good wishes for the King and the people, it will be possible to get a decent enough cheer." There is something of Uncle's voice behind this letter, an echo of some monologue in the bosom of the family. The same letter mentions the writings of the Danish-French journalist and unofficial diplomatic agent Jules Hansen, the purpose of which was to influence the French press and thus the French government in favour of Denmark, „a strict secret. Uncle has forbidden me and the rest of the household to talk about it."

The year 1864 also marks a dividing line in Danish domestic politics. New groupings and new parties appear on the scene during the struggle of later years over the constitution and the legislative process. At the war's end Denmark was in the ludicrous position of having two constitutions, one dealing with home affairs, justice, and ecclesiastical and education matters and a second covering foreign, military and financial affairs. Both the Rigsdag of the June constitution and the State Council of the November constitution met at Christiansborg, and each consisted of two chambers, lower and upper. It was said that the country was driven four-in-hand. About a hundred of the elected representatives were „doubles". They sat both in the Rigsdag and in the State Council.

Some simplification was necessary. While there was no problem as far as the two lower houses were concerned, since they were both elected in exactly the same way, there was disagreement about the upper houses. Was the upper house of the June constitution or the November constitution to be chosen? The electorate for the latter was considerably smaller than that for the former. The Conservatives and the National Liberals preferred the narrower franchise. Only in this way would it be possible to guard against „the evil instincts of the plebeian spirit", as Lehmann had expressed it in a speech in 1860. It was a matter of securing a decisive influence in the upper house for what he called „Denmark's best men" – the gifted, the educated and the wealthy.

Jacobsen, who stayed on in national politics until he resigned his seat in 1871, was an unconditional adherent of the Lehmann line. He supported the revised constitution of 1866 and advocated a strong and independent upper house.

In matters pertaining to financial appropriations he asserted the equality of the two chambers. He wanted the upper house deputies appointed by the King to serve for life. Independence was one of his key concepts, and it was from that standpoint that he proposed the abolition of all parliamentary salaries. To one of his colleagues, the director of the Carlsberg Laboratory's physiology department, he wrote in 1879: „It is my conviction, which has grown ever stronger with my increasing experience of life, that no society and no institution can be carried on, indeed it can scarcely stand, if the fundamental basis on which it is built be tampered with too often and too easily. I admit that in my view insufficient conservatism has been shown in this direction." What leaps to the eye in the statutes of the Carlsberg Foundation of 1876 is the provision that the director of the laboratory may not accept election to the Rigsdag. Once again it is a matter of ensuring integrity and independence.

Two factors are crucial to any understanding of Jacobsen's later political outlook: North Schleswig and the defence question. In 1879, when Copenhagen University was planning the celebrations of its 400th anniversary, the North Schleswig issue suddenly reared its head with the news that Prussia and Austria had repudiated clause 5 of the Peace of Prague giving the North Schleswigers the right to vote themselves back into Denmark. The University had had in mind a gathering to include guests from all European and North American universities and learned societies: now the University's governing body changed course and wanted to confine the invitations to Nordic guests so as not to have to receive German and Austrian representatives. However, Fischer, the Minister of Ecclesiastical Affairs and Public Instruction, faced the University with the choice between the international celebration as planned, for which a grant would be made, or a „normal" university celebration without foreign guests. The University decided to defy the minister. In a letter to Professor Edvard Holm, Jacobsen undertook to meet the deficit on a „Nordic" celebration, and did so.

The situation on the national plane was marked by the struggle for the introduction of parliamentarism. This intensified during the first half of the 1880s. During J.B.S. Estrup's premiership, to the annoyance of many Conservatives, the government had found itself on a starvation diet because of the opposition's policy of obstruction. Now it went over to the offensive, for example by appointing Colonel Jesper Bahnson, a vigorous spokesman for the fortification of Copenhagen, as Minister of War, and by introducing in March 1885 a proposal for a provisional finance act giving the ministry greater freedom of action than the provisional finance acts brought in earlier. The crunch came in April 1885. A provisional finance act was promulgated giving the government authority not only to defray expenditures on which the two chambers had been agreed but also „expenditures necessary for the proper conduct of state administration" within the amounts set out in the government's proposed finance act.

This financial diktat aroused the violent wrath of the opposition. Mass meetings were held, rifle clubs were formed and in some places there were attempts at organised tax refusal. In right-wing quarters the prevailing mood was one of satisfaction that the government had at last pulled itself together. Jacobsen for his part fully supported the Estrup line. He attacked the Lower House's policy of obstruction, which, applied to defence, seemed to him a surrender of the nation's independence and honour. He refused to admit the claims of parliamentarism. He considered the constitutional power of the crown an effective safeguard against the abuse of freedom.

He maintained his political involvement to the last. He was present at the great Conservative meeting at the Riding School on 19 April 1885 and gave a lecture to the League of Conservative Workers and Voters at Frederiksberg the following year. The meeting took place at the Valby Inn and caused Edvard Brandes, in an article in „Politiken", to express regret at Jacobsen's attack on „old pals'" networks – among which the Brewer counted freemasonry in the French parliament.

Jacobsen's conservative profile is depicted best in his letters of 1885-86 to Holger Drachmann, to whom he opened his mind on political issues. The defence question had brought the ill-assorted pair together. First Jacobsen settles the question of the meaningless designations „Right" and „Left". In a letter to Holger Drachmann on 8 June 1885 he writes:

„Since you make use of the current expressions „Right" and „Left" in discussing political differences, I cannot omit to remark that these names are highly misleading to many who believe that Leftists are democrats and Rightists are the opposite. Nothing could be more false, however, for the struggle on the part of the Left turns not at all on the implementation of democratic principles but only on the desire of a few power-hungry mercenaries to become ministers and their consequent dissemination of hazy notions of the delights which, when they come to power, they will secure for their supporters and helpers. And the so-called „Right" has only accepted the name as being the opposite of „Left". In fact it is not a party in the ordinary sense, for it does not seek anything for itself but merely enters the lists as citizens in order to safeguard the nation as a whole against an oppressive hegemony of the self-serving leaders of the Left. Neither have the great majority of „Rightists", as our legislation ever since 1849 shows, ever opposed democratic proposals but on the contrary have lent them much support, while on the other hand they have opposed – though far from sufficiently – self-serving proposals for the benefit of a particular party."

He continues:

„Fortunately our Constitution has introduced a genuine two-chamber system (the best in Europe), which gives to all classes of the population, i.e. the whole nation, equal rights and participation in law-making, but excludes Parliamentarism and thereby guards against the despotism of a single class. If in spite of this we have suffered somewhat during recent years under a particular party's peevish attempts to revenge itself because it has been unable to seize power, then this is purely and simply the result of excessive good nature and lack of energy on the part both of the government and of the Conservatives, who from sheer peaceableness have tolerated many encroachments, thus giving the agitators a fair wind and reinforcing in them the idea that they could storm their way to power. This bubble was burst on 1 April, and the spell is thereby broken. The agitators' impotence can now be concealed no longer, and accordingly their role will soon be played out. The next regular Upper House election will certainly expose this."

The letter concludes:

„I have not in fact regarded the situation in recent years with as much disquiet and impatience as many others have done, for how can one expect a people who in a political sense are quite immature – indeed childish, to put it bluntly – to understand straight away how to use a comprehensive political authority properly? None of the European peoples who have received free constitutions since the French Revolution has learnt it yet. I therefore believe in a happy future for Denmark, even if I do not live to see it."

Jacobsen advises the poet not to let himself be hitched to the Conservative party wagon. Drachmann should be wary of his new friends. He should be himself, be the poet „who describes the wickednesses of the age good-humouredly from a superior standpoint. I am thinking here of Heiberg's 'A Soul after Death', for example." „Our age furnishes material enough for satirical comment." And once more Jacobsen expresses his confidence that a political turning point has been reached. People's eyes are about to be opened at last to the danger of modern despotism in „the name of the Sovereignty of the People". The best safeguard against „Mob Absolutism" is to divide the „People's" power into two parts.

So far does the old gentleman go in his new-found optimism that he assigns a civilising role to Denmark. Perhaps it will fall to the nation's lot to teach the world how all classes of society can be brought to share in freedom without society's being destroyed thereby.

„But I must not neglect to add that another condition is required, a strong hereditary royal power. It is France's misfortune, under which she still groans, that in 1793 she severed her historical thread by cutting off the head of the king. The last hundred years have exposed clearly what the principle of Sovereignty of the People has been able to create, and now France lacks the historical foundation for a strong royal power and can only put its hopes in Caesarism; but the prospect of that is distant and will scarcely open itself until ethical and moral corruption has reached its uttermost limit and provoked the reaction with manifest power."

„The air of all Europe, and therefore of Denmark, will therefore probably remain filled for a long time with noxious infections, and exertions are accordingly needed to cleanse the mental and moral atmosphere of all the poisonous organisms or to render these harmless, just as Pasteur has taught us to do in the physical world. This must now be the noblest task of the popular speaker, the author and the poet – and therefore of yourself."

Thus, at the end of his days, the Brewer came to the extraordinary conclusion that Pasteurisation was not merely useful in brewing but might equally be a sovereign remedy against the pollution of democracy.

La Belle France

On 1 May 1865 J.C. Jacobsen travelled to Korsør by the evening train and took passage on the steamer for Lübeck. From there he went directly to Holland, where Amsterdam and Rotterdam were his first stops on a lengthy foreign tour, the longest he had ever undertaken. He permitted himself an absence from his business of more than four months.

He travelled alone, hurried through Germany, and with the bitterness of defeat still rankling was irritated when people in Holland and Belgium mistook him for a German and answered him in that language. It was his custom to go travelling every year, but the war had shut him in. Now he had to get out. A distinct feeling that time had not been standing still in the outside world drove him to go. As always he combined tourism with business. Wherever he went he visited breweries, made his observations, cemented his contacts. The tour of 1865 turned out to be one of the turning points of his life. It stimulated him as a technician and an industrialist.

The real goal of the tour was France, La Belle France, the hope of Denmark with respect to the future of the lost duchy of Schleswig. This hope was fuelled the following year, when at the instance of France the Peace of Prague of 1866, by which the Austro-Prussian War was brought to an end, was made to include the declaratory clause 5 providing for the northern districts of Schleswig to be ceded to Denmark whenever the inhabitants showed by a free ballot their desire for such union – which the North Schleswigers at last received the opportunity of doing in 1920. „I think as little as possible about politics," wrote J.C. to Laura from Paris, „but have not been able to avoid the subject altogether because 'The Ferret' has met me a number of times and told me a good deal, which indeed was quite interesting. He has really good connections and access to reliable intelligence." „The Ferret" was Jules Hansen, the journalist and diplomatic agent already mentioned, who lobbied for Danish interests in the French capital. In Paris too Jacobsen received the results of the election just held in Denmark. He did so with the remark: „So we shall be threshing the long straw again in the autumn! Phew! That is trying, but I do not want to think about it now."

Whereas Jacobsen's first visit to France had been a short one, this time he wanted to achieve a deeper understanding of that country. „Not to drop in casually for a few days to skim the cream off the top ... [but] on the contrary, to make a steady effort to get to know people in town and countryside, *tel qu'il est*".

France's economy expanded vigorously during the Second Empire. Two features especially leap to the eye: urban renewal and the expansion of the railway network. Paris was the leader in town planning. Under the direction of Georges Hausmann a system of great boulevards was laid out around which new residential complexes were planned. This triggered off a veritable building boom with its associated effects on employment. The provincial towns rapidly followed suit.

The expansion of the transport sector was even more far-reaching. A national market was being swiftly built up. The capital market was dominated by the great railway projects, both at home and abroad. Europe's aggregate network of railway lines more than trebled during the course of the 1850s and 1860s. In this golden age of „railway mania" France asserted itself as the leading Continental nation. While Europe's old railway builder, England, concentrated its efforts overseas during these years, in Egypt, India and North America, French engineers and financiers were responsible for most of the new construction in Spain, Italy, Switzerland, the Danubian countries and Russia. Closely bound up with this was the development of a technology which had a knock-on effect on other branches as well. French researchers and engineers secured for their country an internationally recognised position, especially in steam technology and a range of metallurgical industries. The engineering industry's exports of tools and apparatus soared, supported by brilliant marketing notably in the form of great fairs and world exhibitions of which those held in Paris particularly attracted many foreigners. And naturally it was by no means a drawback that the city's cultural life, including its theatres, hotels and restaurants, was flourishing. Paris was in fashion, and Paris created fashion. *Tout le monde* met there and amused itself. It was the Paris of Offenbach.

Jacobsen swiftly perceived that the wind of change was sweeping over France. The old city centre was yielding before the new age. „Embellishment is in full swing here too, and soon Morlaix will be a modern town – its greatest pride is the railway viaduct, which goes right over the town at a height of 180 feet from the ground and a length of 900 feet," wrote Jacobsen from Angers. As far as his own métier was concerned, there was particular food for thought in the fact that bottom-fermented Bavarian beer from the breweries of Alsace was now finding a market not only in the capital but also in the provinces. Right down in the southwest corner of France, in Biarritz and in the Pyrenees, he came across the Alsatian beer. Thus, from the wine city of Bordeaux he recorded: „Everywhere I have been, even here in Bordeaux, lager beer is the most common refreshment in the cafés, both morning and afternoon. The beer is as a rule excellent and admirably clear. It comes from Strasbourg and other places in Alsace, which I absolutely must visit on my journey north. Shall therefore abandon Chamonix and Auvergne. Yesterday visited a brewery in Poitiers which also makes lager beer. It was not bad!"

On arrival in Paris Jacobsen sought out the editor of the *Journal des Brasseurs*, a Monsieur Bourgeois, with whom he got on to good terms and who introduced him to the country's leading brewers. „I have received much interesting information, which has given me a good deal to think about, so that sometimes I fall into a reverie and forget that I am in Paris." For the same reason he put off his departure for some days. On his way home two months later he continued his discussions of what he had seen with Bourgeois, and with the chemist Esquiron, to whom he had been introduced. They dined together, both *en famille* and at Jacobsen's hotel on the Rue Lafitte. One evening the three of them sat talking until midnight at the Café du Grand Balconilol. The next day Jacobsen drove from end to end of the town studying air compressors, rotary pumps, galvanised mash tubs and other brewery equipment.

One of the breweries which Bourgeois had recommended Jacobsen to visit was Brasserie de Méditerranée in Marseilles, owned and managed by Eugèn Velten. It was a visit he was never to forget.

Velten was a professional after Jacobsen's own heart, on the go personally everywhere, in his office, in the brewery, in the town. He showed his guest round graciously and knowledgeably, ending up by inviting him to dinner along with the Danish consul in Marseilles, who was a friend of his. However, Jacobsen declined on a pretext „because I am ashamed of not being able to speak French properly and would have cut a poor figure in company".

The brewery was a steam brewery. It distinguished itself by its direct use of steam in the mashing process, i.e. by conducting the steam into the mash. Velten said that he had used the method for fifteen years without any problems. Step by step he had extended the application of steam in the processes. Jacobsen, who had played with the idea but never ventured to put it into effect, was impressed. „His whole mashing operation is original too," he reported home, and posed the question: „Whether it is the best method? That must be tested. From a rational standpoint there is little or no objection."

Velten boiled his wort by indirect steam, which gave an even distribution of heat and therefore a better boil. The condensed water was conducted back to the steam copper with the aid of a supply pump, „an idea to which I have devoted much time," Jacobsen observed. The power loss, according to Velten, was insignificant, and the system better than that employed by the brewer Boucherot at Puteaux, near Nanterre outside Paris. Again Jacobsen discovered that „the boiling of the wort is done in the very way which I had thought of using". Another innovation was the use of compressed air for transferring beer from storage barrel to storage barrel and for transporting beer from the storage cellars for barrelling upstairs prior to being despatched from the brewery on the sales drays, „another of my ideas carried out in practice". Velten's method of accelerating clarification of the beer was also superior to Jacobsen's. Velten's fermenting tub was different, being made of brick and lined inside with sheet glass. The most remarkable feature, however, was that Velten produced cold water for cooling the wort and kept the temperature low in the fermenting tubs with the aid of a large etherising apparatus in which the ether was vaporised in a vacuum. Jacobsen put a question mark against this system, adding: „it is dearer than Danish ice, but cheaper than Norwegian." When the winters in Denmark produced insufficient ice to charge the ice cellars of the lager beer breweries, the import of ice from Norway had to be resorted to.

The visit to Marseilles acted as a spur. Jacobsen galloped north on his iron horse to Strasbourg and Lutterbach, where there was another steam brewery, then on to Boucherot's aforementioned brewery at Puteaux. In Strasbourg he considered for a moment whether „to swing right from the Rhine" down to „my friends in Stuttgart, Munich and Vienna, with whom I have so much to discuss, but there is no time for it this year since I have far too much to do here and in Paris". Gone was the distaste for the German tongue; vanished was the tourist. True enough he took a route via Rheims in order to see the famous cathedral and tried to put himself into the romantic-historical mood again, but to no avail. The drama of Joan of Arc failed to strike any real chord in his imagination. All at once the enchantment of ancient historical monuments had evaporated. „I am now far away from the Romantic, I am living in the Real, which after all is my true element. If that is where I can swim around well, like a true fish, then I shall not worry if I cannot fly in the air like a bird. To each his own." The holiday was over.

„To travel is to live," wrote Hans Christian Andersen, Denmark's most cosmopolitan poet. He travelled abroad thirty times, mostly during the years 1840-57, but even in the 1860s he travelled far and wide. In 1861, for example, he made his fourth visit to Rome, in 1862-63 he visited Spain, a journey described in his last great travel book, in 1866 he was in Portugal, and two years later he went to the world exhibition in Paris. Another Dane whose writings stimulated the urge to travel by bringing the great world into the living room was Meïr Goldschmidt. Henrik Scharling, best known as the author of „Ved Nytaarstid i Nøddebo Præstegaard" (New Year at Nøddebo Parsonage) (1862) published „Breve fra Holland" (Letters from Holland) in 1864, to which Jacobsen refers in his first letter from the Netherlands. He does so with the remark that he cannot find anything worth reporting, for the family at home know Holland better from Scharling's book.

The tourist's bible in the mid-19th century was the „Red Book", compiled by John Murray, which first saw the light of day in 1836 and afterwards came out in one edition after another, revised and enlarged. It remained the Victorian vademecum for a long time. Jacobsen had Murray in his pocket and followed his advice – „I skipped over Nantes, since Murray says it is dull." He had cause to regret it, in fact, when he saw from the train that a big popular festival was going on in the town. But Murray does not cover everything: what Jacobsen misses especially is historical information. He reproaches himself for not being better acquainted with French history and wishes his friend Rasmus Nielsen were making the tour with him. To remedy the deficiency he gets himself a French travelling companion, Monsieur Duruy, who lives „in my suitcase, where I can accommodate him quite easily, since he is in three volumes". Victor Duruy was a historian and was also France's minister of education in 1863-69. His history of France was a popular book in its day.

Jacobsen's own travel letters fall into two categories. The brewery-related ones are written to Carl; the general ones are addressed to Laura. The letters are devoid of literary pretensions but are nevertheless unmistakably intended to be read aloud to a circle of friends, as, for example, with this conclusion to a long epistle dated Auranches/Morlaix, 9 June:

„This excursion really belongs to the description of Normandy, but firstly there is insufficient room for it on this sheet and secondly, also, I should like to be piquant for once and break off at a really exciting point like the serial writers; thus, the wondrous, fantastic, famous etc. Mont S. Michel will not be reached until our next issue. Please be so good as to have patience until then! Farewell to all friends! J.C. Jacobsen."

The English Victorian gentleman and his family dominated tourism in this, the first era of middle-class travel. Jacobsen came across them everywhere, in museums, churches and hotels; there they sat and „grimaced without uttering a word to any stranger even among their own countrymen". The phlegmatic Anglo-Saxon was hopeless, whether you led him or drove him. In point of fact Jacobsen upheld the same principle himself – „I have no wish to seek out my fellow-countrymen when travelling" – though the principle was frequently broken, depending on whom he met. With foreigners a different principle applied. Here he shared the tourist's eternal desire to get to know the guaranteed genuine local population as they really were.

The only trouble was that, however much he willed the end, he had difficulty with the means. He had a communication problem. Two factors were responsible, the one psychological, the other linguistic. Jacobsen confessed that he found „small talk" hard, even in Danish. By „small talk" he meant the capacity to chat, to gossip about this and that, to converse. Whenever specialist topics came up, on the other hand, he was fluent in his mother tongue – indeed there was no stopping him, and he could get along in French. But „small talk" – „in that direction I have much to learn," and he adds, „it can only be learned from ladies, and how am I to approach French ladies? On the railways it does not happen, for there are coupés for *Dames seules* everywhere (cigars are responsible for that). So there is nothing else for it but for me to go hunting for them (the ladies) at one of the Pyrenean bathing resorts, or at Vichy or somewhere like that, but unfortunately the saison does not begin at these places until next month." At one place he did hire a guide to accompany him when sightseeing, but not much took place in the way of conversational exchanges. Jacobsen returned home from his sojourn in France firmly resolved to study the language further and to write exercises regularly, and this he did. As the years passed he did gain a command of this language that so captivated him, as witness, for example, his correspondence with the Frenchman who later came to play perhaps the greatest role in his life, Louis Pasteur.

Jacobsen the tourist was as persevering as Jacobsen the brewer. He travelled neither to eat nor to relax. He often skipped his meals in his eagerness to experience or discover. Arriving in a new town, he would at once set off on foot early in the morning, not returning to the hotel until sometime in the evening. Museums, concerts, opera and the theatre were all included in the repertoire. Tours around the countryside would last all day as well. When he finally decided, after a fortnight of intensive travelling from place to place in Normandy and Brittany, to rest for some days at Tours in order to digest his many impressions and only undertake minor trips from the town, in the event these turned into day excursions of 10, 12 and even 16 hours' duration under the burning sun. He lost weight. „I now weigh 138 pounds, which is 18 pounds less than when I set off. There is probably not very much fat left on me. I think I now consist of bone, sinew and muscle, which cannot melt away. I wish I could always keep myself like this," the 54 year-old writes with gusto in one of his letters from the Pyrenees.

Jacobsen's physique was good, in fact, for most of his life. He was tough and had staying power: a strong man. Many years later Johannes Steenstrup had experience of this during a walking tour when the other participants were palavering about a rest and a snack, while Jacobsen refuelled with the aid of a small piece of liquorice from a box in his pocket and doggedly trudged on.

Holland was the first stop after Copenhagen, as we have noted. From the touristic standpoint the country did not manage to avoid boring Jacobsen a little. „If one is not an enthusiastic lover of Flemish herring or Dutch cheese or Schiedam gin, I do not know what there is to be excited by in Holland, where everything is flat and smooth and solid, more or less as it is with us too." He found the life and manners of the people ponderous and dull; musical life in the form of public promenade concerts did not exist; and neither Amsterdam nor Rotterdam could boast a decent changing of the guard. He remembered the Dutch barrel organs with horror. Only the chimes were an experience. Dutch cleanliness did impress him, or rather made him wet. Saturday morning was the day of the week for washing the housefronts in Rotterdam. „Never walk on the pavement on a Saturday but down the middle of the street, unless you want to be subjected to an involuntary washing," was the good advice he gave his friends in his letter home.

In Belgium there was a shift of scenery. Things became livelier and jollier. Jacobsen waxed enthusiastic over a concert in Antwerp's Société Royale d'Harmonie in a large new concert hall in its own grounds just outside the city. The orchestra played well, the William Tell overture being particularly good. Enjoyment was enhanced by the presence of female members of the public in their elegant toilettes, „a luxuriant garland of beautiful flowers", to invoke the Jacobsen terminology.

In Brussels he admired the Grand Place and the imposing town hall.

Here the right romantic-historical mood prevailed. In his imagination he saw the Spanish Duke of Alba from a window of the town hall watching the execution of the two champions of Netherlands liberty, Egmont and Hoorn. On the opposite side of the square was the ancient building where they spent their last night before being put to death. „Who can stand in this place without rehearsing Goethe's Egmont in his mind and lingering over his Clärchen, surely the loveliest female form ever drawn by the hand of a poet?"

Around the middle of May the Brewer arrived in Lille. From there he went on to Paris, where he stayed for two weeks. He visited the museums, saw the great fountain of Versailles, listened to military music by the Zouave guards, went to the Théâtre Français, where he caught two pieces by Molière and one by Racine in a single evening, to the Opéra Comique, where they were playing „The Daughter of the Regiment" and „Fra Diavolo" – „these were not much better than when they were shown in Denmark; only a little livelier" – and finally he found time to attend mass in the Tuileries chapel, where he saw the Empress and the Prince Imperial, „for that was why I went, of course, and I did not take notice of anything else during the half hour. I had an excellent place and stood no more than a couple of feet from her as she went to and from the mass, and both times I received a gentle and gracious greeting from her."

On 5 June he left the capital by train for Caen, „a very pleasant route … only a shame that it goes so fast!" From there he went to Rouen, whence he set off on a two-week tour through Normandy and Brittany. The inhabitants of Normandy struck him as very pleasant. In Auranches one evening, where Jacobsen was enjoying the view over the sea to the rocky island fortress of Mont St Michel, he was fascinated by the crowds on the promenade. Seldom had he seen such exquisite young girls, „absolutely lovely creatures with Roman noses and high foreheads, dark eyes and eyebrows etc., the eldest, of about 15-17 years, strolling along primly, but the younger ones romping about playing tag etc. on the undulating greensward, under the supervision of their parents and *bonnes*. I found it difficult to tear myself away from this sight, and it was not until a considerable time after the glowing sun had gone down, when 'the aureate skies that swim above though far horizons hide the orb of day' also began to lose their golden glory, that I continued my ramble to other points of vantage so as to see the valley from the other side in the clear moonbeams that succeeded the daylight."

Another picture of popular life and manners comes from Angers, where Jacobsen arrived on 18 June from Brittany. „An endless stream of people, driving, riding and walking, was returning from the racing at the municipal common and passed along the boulevard outside my windows." It was Sunday evening. In an open space encircled by beautiful trees military music sounded from a brilliantly lit pavilion. In the middle was a fine fountain in a large ornamental pool „with clumps of rushes, in which masses of gas lights shine out of arium lilies and suchlike – it is both splendid and tasteful. A number of sweet little girls, 'some red, some blue', danced the polka and galloped around the music pavilion, and down at the end of the boulevards was a large market with stalls and Harlequin and Punch and Judy. I can tell that I am in France again, in Brittany it was more like being on Danish ground than French."

Along the river Loire our traveller, still with Mr Murray to hand, tours the great chateaux, which refresh the spirit after the stern monotony of Norman architecture. The goal of one of the excursions is at Leches, the ancient royal castle of Charles VII, where the principal sight is the sepulchral monument to Agnès Sorel, the king's mistress. „France's historians ascribe to her the credit for having raised the king, who from youth was weak and insignificant, to a higher mental and moral level, indeed for having completely remade him, so that he ended as a strong king, but the tradition dwells especially on her gentleness and kindness and on her noble beauty – *la plus belle des belles* – Frenchmen do not mention her name without employing all the tenderness and grace of intonation which their language possesses – and in truth one cannot imagine anything gentler, more feminine and more beautiful than the picture of her in marble that lies on her gravestone."

We catch Jacobsen pressing a kiss to her white forehead before he leaves the place.

The beauty of the Loire landscape, on the other hand, does not satisfy Jacobsen. It is flat as in Denmark. He finds no fine flowing lines of horizon and woodland. The aesthetic criterion, as with the

Norman women, is Italian. To be good it has to be picturesque. To head south is a help. By the end of the month he has reached Biarritz. Now the mountains come into view on the horizon with their plentiful changes of line and shape and their shifting light. He is out by the ocean again, the great, mysterious ocean that casts its spell over him. Here too he finds that the population contains many „elements of beauty and not a few real beauties of both sexes; there is much to remind one of Rome: the girls collecting water from the public fountains in big pitchers carried on the head, and the fisher-girls and women carrying great flat baskets of fresh sardines on their heads with one or both hands at their sides and with a walk so fast and sturdy that Napoleon's Old Guard could scarcely have done better and in any event not with such plasticity. The shriek with which they call out 'Sardines fraîches' is fearsome." He had expected bathing to be in full swing, but saw only the bustling preparations for the season, „like the day before a market".

At the beginning of June he travelled by rail from Bayonne to Pau and the charming route up through the fertile Adour valley, now with the Pyrenees in the foreground. He stayed a couple of days in Pau and devoured „a mouthful of historical memories", including the castle in which Henry IV was born. His cradle, a hammock in the form of a huge tortoiseshell which had been saved during the Revolution, was one of the objects of interest. Another was the bed of Abd-el-Kadir. This Arab emir, who had stood against France in the war of 1832-47, had been interned in the castle at Pau, transferred later to that of Amboise, and finally released in 1852. He ended by becoming the friend of France. He was one of Jacobsen's heroes, „the noblest character our century has produced". A visit to Versailles always included a moment of homage before the battle painter Horace Vernet's painting of the Arab regent. Abd-el-Kadir was also one of „The Corsair's" heroes. That journal frequently published stories of the cunning emir's game of cat-and-mouse with the French military.

From Pau Jacobsen went up into the mountains, where he installed himself at Bagnères-de-Luchon for a fortnight, partly to take lessons in French and partly to walk in the mountains. He made a good number of trips, some of them above the tree-line with a 75 year-old mountain guide leading the way. The old man's performance stimulated Jacobsen. From one hike up to the glacier edge he paints a picture of the mighty Pyrenees glittering in the clear light as far as the eye could see. The sky was cloudless, „deep dark blue and so transparent that I thought I could see the stars through it. The scene was accompanied by the combined purling and frothing of the mountain streams sent down by the glaciers on either side of me." To the rhetorical question whether this was really worth all the exertion he replied very characteristically: „Well, you know, there is another benefit as well; to test and exercise one's powers is an indescribable delight; to struggle against difficulties and obstacles and overcome them is a sensual pleasure accompanied by the instinctive feeling that it is not only the body that is strengthened, not only muscles and sinews and nerves that take on an increased resilience, but also the capacities of the soul that are developed, as well as the heart, which is enlarged by coming nearer to heaven and receiving the impression of the vastness of all that surrounds us. Pettiness cannot flourish in such a place."

On his last excursion he climbed Pic-de-Entecade, from which he had a front-row view of Maladette, the Mont Blanc of the Pyrenees, and the extensive system of valleys with no fewer than 32 villages.

„This brings my excursions in the Pyrenees to an end; on Monday morning I am leaving. Farewell! Jacobsen."

The journey took him westwards to Marseilles, where the Brewer took over from the Tourist. At Arles he saw the Roman remains, including the amphitheatre, and kept an eye open for the women so highly praised by Mr Murray for their beauty, but was disappointed „either because my thoughts were somewhat beery or because too much hearsay on the subject had raised my expectations too high," he explained to Laura.

On the outward journey Jacobsen had sent his son a letter in which he touched on the dispositions which ought to be made at home in the event of his sudden decease. Under the impact of a violent thunderstorm which he had admired from his hotel window, it had struck him that he had never put his affairs in order. Carl was disturbed by the letter and thought his father was feeling ill. Jacobsen reassured him from Paris that he was in top form but nevertheless gave him some practical instructions.

Should the event materialise, Carl and his mother should rely on Kogsbølle until Carl had completed his studies and qualified himself in the brewery trade, undertaking as part of his training a visit to South Germany of at least nine months covering breweries in Vienna, Munich and Stuttgart, and one of the Rhine breweries. In that case Kogsbølle's contract must be improved in the form of higher remuneration (Jacobsen suggested 24 skilling per barrel of beer sold) and a suitable residence, and he should be given an inspector to assist him. If Kogsbølle wanted it, he should be taken in as an associate or partner. The main thing was to hold on to Kogsbølle. His practical skill and exceptional meticulousness along with his unusual capacity for handling people were indispensable. Jacobsen mentioned that he had in fact had it in mind to help Kogsbølle to become independent one day. If Kogsbølle nevertheless would not venture to undertake the management function for such a lengthy period, then Jacobsen suggested Th. Schiøtz of Odense. „He is now involved as a sort of partner with the people who have founded the brewery [Albani] in Odense, but it would not be difficult to offer him much better terms than he has now, and if to this were added the prospect of helping him to establish an independent position after some years, I dare say he could be got." As adviser and trustee, finally, Jacobsen assigned August Vogelius, who was a relative of Laura's. He was inspector at Carlsberg from 1852 to 1856 and had then managed the brewery in Brolæggerstræde as tenant, after which – with Jacobsen's assistance – he built a brewery in Rahbeks Allé which had been inaugurated in 1861 at the same time as brewing in the old brewery premises was closed down.

To these pieces of advice on head-hunting Jacobsen added something that was more important: a settlement of status and a rule of conduct – a strategy for the future, one might say. Let us call it Jacobsen's mid-course will and testament. It drew much of its inspiration from the visit to France. It represents the conclusion formed from the observations and numerous visits he made during the tour of 1865, which in fact included the breweries of Holland and Belgium as well. In Holland he had made „a couple of very pleasant acquaintances", one of them being with Feltmann of the Heineken brewery, a connection he maintained all the rest of his life. Belgium on the other hand was a disappointment, the breweries poor, the beer poor and „the brewers surly and old-fashioned in outlook".

This is how his „testament" to his son reads:

„I appropriated the experience of others (the Bavarians) and applied it in Denmark at just the right moment, and luckily I had acquired sufficient knowledge and sufficient insight to understand tolerably well what it all meant, at any rate better than most brewers in Germany and better than all of them in Denmark. But the world does not stand still, knowledge broadens and insight increases everywhere. Many of the fundamental conclusions handed down by the Bavarians are disputed; it is certain that their correctness is not unqualified; the metamorphoses during malting, mashing and fermenting are demonstrably not as simple as was previously supposed; there now appear to be different substances and different changes of substance which we had not dreamt of before but which we must now know about if we are to explain the phenomena we see and if we wish to direct the progress of our operations with a clear awareness, not stumbling forward in the dark like the crude empiricists until we happen to hit on the right path."

„This, the task for brewers at the present time and in the most immediate future, lies beyond my capacities because I was not fortunate enough to fulfil my wish to go through a complete course at the Technical University and become a real chemist and physicist. For this reason I am well on the way to being overtaken as a rational brewer and indeed perhaps already have been – not in Denmark, certainly, but in Europe. He who possesses the most thorough knowledge of chemistry and its auxiliary sciences along with the necessary practical proficiency and insight will be Europe's leading brewer of the coming generation. This ought to be your aim, otherwise you will soon decline into the rightly despised class of empiricists of which I shall be one before long, unless you can take me under the arms and keep me above water."

On 28 August J.C. Jacobsen returned to Valby full of plans and ideas which he at once set about realising with his customary energy. Carl did not recognise him when he met him at the station. His father had become thinner, sharper in his features, his hair almost white – and he had grown a full beard. The latter seemed quite strange to the family, but Nanna thought it really suited him quite well.

An engagement

Jacobsen's return from France was awaited with misgivings at home. Carl had secretly become engaged during the summer to his cousin Emilie, who was the daughter of Christian Djørup, dean of Karlebo, and the sister of Kogsbølle's wife Magnella. Everyone knew that when J.C. got wind of it the fat would be in the fire. They were not mistaken. „As you can imagine, tempers are all blazing here in the family," wrote Nanna the same day. „Everything has come out into the open, and Carl is furious with Aunt Faye, who has been running about casting aspersions on Emilie and telling all sorts of lies about her." The barometer stood at storm.

Carl, who became a student in 1861, had been smitten with his cousin for a long time, if we are to believe Nanna, who was the confidante of both and was blessed with the alert eye of an expert when Cupid's darts were flying. The house invited infatuations – not only the park but also the conservatory. Carl Jacobsen spoke many years afterwards of the conservatory as a „dangerous" place, where young couples, sheltered beneath exotic trees in the gloaming, waxed amorous by moonlight, natural or artificial. On the wall was a relief by Thorvaldsen: Cupid and the Three Graces. From time to time Cupid exchanged his lyre for bow and arrow and went hunting in the grounds. „The writer of these lines has vivid memories in this respect," recalled the old gentleman. In fact the arrow scarred him for life.

Nanna reports from one of these parties – at Christmas 1863 – that Carl escorted Emilie to table. „Uncle went pale and puckered his brows and became silent. Aunt was so disconcerted that she forgot where she was both in the conversation and in the tureen." And Nanna continues: „However, Carl was with her the rest of the evening with one ear and half his senses, although no one noticed it except me, the silent observer."

The following spring Emilie was staying in the town with Frants Djørup. „It is amusing to hear what a dance they, Carl and Emilie, are

Carl at 10 years of age with his playmate Sophus Møller (standing). Photograph 1852.

Carl as a student. Photograph from 1861.

Emilie Djørup. Photograph from 1867.

Carl in his early thirties.

leading the old ones." This is Nanna reporting again. „I am her confidante – they go to museums and walk into the town together when Emilie is out here with Magnella. There is not a single person who suspects that he cares for her. He is nonchalant and argumentative with her, and she is cold and hard, laughing and scoffing, whatever seems to suit best."

Emilie came to Copenhagen again in January 1865. Her sister Magnella did not dare to have her living with her. It was Frants Djørup who provided her with accommodation again. „Uncle will hardly look at her and spies on Carl's movements in the most ridiculous way when she is here, for which of course there may be reason," wrote Nanna on 13 January, and then added: „There is mischief in this situation if you ask me! Embarrassing at the time and not nice to watch in the long run. I am afraid that at bottom Carl's attachment is not so much love as loyalty, which he takes pride in possessing. Perhaps it has not even occurred to him that it is not love. God help her! In the long run he will never feel content at her side – or at all! God help whoever does get him one day. In the first place because of his own character and individuality – and because of the in-laws! Phew! I would not have Aunt as a mother-in-law for anything in the world!!" Nanna considered the relationship between mother and son to be an unhappy one, and likewise that between father and mother – „and that casts a gloom over their entire life together."

One summer evening she sat with Carl discussing the life of the family. They went on until the other side of midnight, and she was surprised to find that „he sees more clearly than I had thought". It ended with Nanna believing that Carl's love for Emilie was genuine and profound.

Genuine or false, J.C. was against the engagement. In his eyes Emilie lacked the natural freshness and openness by which he set great store in other young girls. That did not matter, however – after all it was not his own engagement that was in question – but what was crucial was that in J.C.'s judgment his son was an immature person, weak of character and quite unformed, without training and therefore totally unfitted to think of engagement and marriage. True love, in Jacobsen's opinion, could not exist at all between quite young and immature people. To believe in it was a delusion. Here he was referring to his own experience, but he never removed the seventh veil for his son, remaining silent about his own love-life prior to marriage with Laura. Not until one's own personality had been shaped was it possible to take one's bearings in the garden of love and find the consort to complement oneself. For that was the crux: the consort ought to complement the man. This Emilie did not do. On the contrary, she was a replica of Carl himself: silent, withdrawn, devoid of humour. Carl's nature, formed as it had been in a sheltered environment, was weak and in his father's view needed to be tempered in the school of life. Only then should he look for a wife, who ought to be a woman capable of nurturing and strengthening his weaker sides.

The son's upbringing outside the nursery, and his subsequent education, were wholly the responsibility of the father. It was self-evident that Carl was to be a brewer: family tradition dictated it. J.C. himself was the son of a brewer and an only child, and Carl was the heir to an enterprise which was considerably bigger than the original family business in Brolæggerstræde. Carlsberg had a powerful inbuilt growth potential. Therefore it was absolutely imperative for the son to receive a solid theoretical and practical training which would also include a thorough knowledge of the international brewery industry.

In its social aspects too, Jacobsen viewed his son's upbringing and education in the perspective of the generations. The grandfather had belonged to the age of the guilds, and notwithstanding the fact that he had been a pioneer in his field whom his son admired, the dominion of the guild inside the Copenhagen ramparts represented for J.C. a comfortable but uncultivated and vapid world. He had liberated himself from it and climbed upwards through the ranks of society. He ascribed his success to an inherited urge which had driven him „like the bee to seek honey instinctively from every flower I encountered on my way". By self-activity and tireless labour he had developed his talents and capacities, especially those in which he was naturally weak.

This was the mirror he held up to his son in season and out. He did it in the name of an all-consuming paternal love. The son was to be shaped to fit the ideal of a human being and technical expert as visualised by his father. Jacobsen Senior thought he knew which were Junior's weak sides, where intervention was needed and by what means. His son's ideas on the subject were largely swept aside on the ground of his youth and his utterly immature outlook. The old man's hope was to see in the crucible one fine day the clear picture of a man of the world, a gentleman, a scientist and a brewer, all in one and the same person, the dynasty's third generation. He dreamed of making his son his scientific colleague at Carlsberg, where they would work together year after year until at last, when the father withdrew from the world of affairs, the son would take over. A pretty dream – which never came true.

At the age of five Carl was enrolled in „Borgerdydskolen" (The School of Civic Virtue) a grammar school in Christianshavn, whose headmaster, as already noted, was Martin Hammerich. After the family moved out to Carlsberg the way to school was long, but the father took great care to ensure that suitable arrangements were made. He was in constant contact with Hammerich and Carl's teachers concerning the boy's performance.

Jacobsen, incidentally, considered the upbringing which the lad received to be liberal by the standards of the time. „You have not been accustomed from childhood to a strict, respectful relationship in your parents' house." The father attempted at an early stage to inculcate in Carl a feeling for history, the visual arts and architecture. The parents took the boy along with them on their journey to North Italy in 1851. Eleven years later father and son went to Rome together, and the father also took him travelling during the summer holidays, for example on an 8-day trip to Schleswig. The Copenhagen museums, art exhibitions and theatres also figured in Carl's programme.

All this was part of a deliberate attempt on the part of the father to prevent his son, bred in wealthy surroundings, from developing a narrowly materialistic bias. Later on, when Carl had grown up and displayed a marked interest in the art of the day, his father's anxiety shifted direction. Now he was afraid he might have given the boy an overdose of aesthetics, with indulgence in art having become an end in itself at the expense of work. „Vigorous activity is the best form of pleasure both mental and physical." „In the sweat of thy brow shalt thou eat bread" – that is God's message for mankind's own good. Only after that shall you enjoy the blessings and joys of life as a fruit of your toil: so ran the father's admonitory words.

An example of the Jacobsen pedagogics is provided by a letter to Carl on the latter's 13th birthday, when the father writes that his son was to have had a watch as a birthday present but must now be content to have it on loan. He must promise not to take it out of his room until he has regained his previous place in class. In 1859 Jacobsen also attempted to cure Carl's stammer by sending him on a trip to Switzerland and Paris with K.H. Schow, an able and well-liked teacher at the school who had just been appointed head of the Slagelse secondary school; Schow's task was to improve Carl's fluency of speech.

To Carl himself J.C. wrote: „It depends on the successful outcome of this cure and on your subsequent efforts to maintain the results which I hope will have been achieved whether you can usefully continue on the path on which you have started, for without a reasonable prospect of passing your examination with honour, you know that you will never become a student with my consent." Carl was provided with a small diary and told to keep it up to date. At the back his father had noted the route of travel, times, hotels – the instructions covered everything down to the packing of the special rucsac for the walking tour in the Swiss Alps. All this chaperonage is touching but depressing and at the same time typical; it was not the mother but the father who fussed over the tiniest details of socks, shirts and underwear. All too late did Jacobsen admit that he had overburdened his son with advice and comments, but this self-knowledge was more academic than real. Jacobsen persisted in his endeavours to instruct and direct to the point where one might say he placed the boy under tutelage out of sheer eagerness to make him independent.

At the instance of his father, Carl embarked after matriculation on theoretical studies in chemistry and physics at the Royal Veterinary and Agricultural College and the Technical University of Denmark. But his studies were not altogether successful, partly because of difficulties with mathematics. His father was dissatisfied, and with the disclosure of Carl's secret engagement the situation became untenable.

The storm broke, and Laura, whose composure always shattered instantly in such situations, became unreasonable beyond all endurance in Nanna's eyes. It was difficult to do anything to her liking, and Nanna got one dressing-down after another. „As long as I was in her house, I was to leave the affairs of the household out of my correspondence." Laura became so wild with rage „that she was like a Fury".

It came to a trial of strength. The brewer and the dean discussed the matter together, back and forth. Then J.C. wrote a long letter to Emilie explaining that the relationship must come to an end, and at the same time Carl was told to break off the engagement. Emilie was brokenhearted and Carl furious, but he toed the line and severed contact.

It was cold at Carlsberg. „Scarcely anyone could feel more unhappy than Aunt," wrote Nanna in her Christmas letter to Jutland, „although none of her material wants are unsatisfied, but she does not have her husband's love, and it becomes worse every day. The relationship between father and son does its part as well – it is sad to see a family's life so torn to pieces and really an ordeal to live through, but I am learning a great deal from it," she added matter-of-factly. It was Christmas 1865.

Then came the dances after Christmas and New Year, and the preparations for the big carnival at the Students' Union. For a while the gloom was relieved a little, but in fact positional warfare still went on. In the early spring Laura attempted an action. She pressed her husband to accept that Carl had a relationship with Emilie. She also wanted him to talk to his son. She was afraid of losing Carl, who had threatened to seek an appointment at a chemicals factory in the United States so as to make himself completely independent of his father, who, he believed, did not love him.

One morning Carl took himself off to Karlebo and talked to his sweetheart. In the evening he went with his father to a concert at the Philharmonic Society and while there told him of the visit. He would not let Emilie go. Jacobsen exploded. „He looked absolutely thunderstruck." More talks, more complications. Carl visited Emilie again, and Jacobsen had to recognise that he could get nowhere this way. He then decided that Carl should break off his studies in Copenhagen and embark at once on the foreign part of the programme of education planned for him. Carl Jacobsen called it being sent into exile, and so it must have seemed to him.

„I do not know what else to say," wrote Nanna. „It seems as though everyone is agreed that they are not suited to each other, that she is too old and he is a complete child in that direction. Even the two doctors Djørup and their wives say the same, and they think that the match was really made by Magnella and perhaps by Emilie as well, and that in any case Carl was being led up the garden path." It was Nanna's last report from Carlsberg in March 1866.

Carl departed in April. Four years were to pass before he was allowed to return.

„Jacobsen's best hope"

„Jacobsen's best hope" was what Frants Djørup had called the 12 year-old Carl in May 1854, when the circle of friends had been invited for the first time to a party in the Brewer's new home at Carlsberg. J.C. frequently harked back to this toast to his son by Djørup. Now, 12 years later, a crisis had arisen in the relationship between father and son. Measured by the standards of the last century the breaking off of a secret engagement at the father's behest was trivial enough, but the conflict went deeper in this instance.

Carl's educational tour had been brought forward. What this really signified was that J.C. had had to give up the idea of Carl's undergoing the theoretical training which J.C. had once wanted for himself but had not been free to bring to fruition. When one remembers the vital importance which Jacobsen attached to „insight into the laws of nature", and not least his belief, confirmed in the course of his travels in 1865, that the future of the European brewery industry would belong to the industrial leader who thoroughly understood the processes underlying production; and when account is also taken of his ingrained reluctance to re-cast plans once made, it was in fact quite a drastic step he took when he sent his son into exile. But „Jacobsen's best hope" was being threatened, and the first priority was to get the two young people separated from one another.

The operation involved guidance by remote control from the command post at home in Valby. The Captain's desk was the headquarters, and the guidance mechanism consisted of the stream of weekly letters that flowed steadily from father to son over the next few years. They make a formidable file, running the gamut from affectionate fatherly injunctions via anxious enquiries, solicitous advice and practical guidance to sorrowful reproaches, wrathful outbursts and peremptory ultimata. They also contain technical discussion, and this element of brewery expertise increases and in time comes to dominate the correspondence. Finally, in March 1870, on Carl's 28th birthday, the sorcerer eyes the picture of his apprentice in the crucible: „You are now as fully equipped for the fulfilment of your task as almost any young, or even older, brewer in Europe can be, and with an interest in your calling which warrants the highest hopes. And what higher hope can there be for me than to see the goal which has seemed to be before me since my earliest youth, realised through you?"

Lofty words, and certainly well meant, but there is an undercurrent running the opposite way. If the son has at last become in his father's opinion a mature and fully-educated man, a new idea is forcing itself more and more strongly on J.C., namely the suspicion that he and his son are not well matched. Their mentalities and temperaments cannot be made to harmonise. It is part and parcel of a growth in Jacobsen's self-understanding during these years. He is beginning to recognise his hyperactive nature and little by little is moving away from the idea (if he had ever really entertained it seriously) of retiring for Carl to take over. „I am no good at pottering about," he says in plain words in one of his last letters to his son. „To cease working would be the same as deliberately to put an end to my days." He has discussed the matter with his friend Frants Djørup. „Only by vigorous exertion can my strength of spirit be sustained, and on that the body depends."

But on top of this there is a distrust which has been lurking in his subconscious and now swells forth. When it reaches the surface he dates it back to an episode in the Spithoever art gallery in Rome in 1862, when the son had had what the father considered to be an attack of hysteria. Over what is not known. Had J.C. refused to purchase some work of art to which Carl had taken a fancy? Ever since that scene, the father declares in a letter dated November 1867, he has feared for his son's lack of character. He adds too that a son will find it difficult to collaborate with an active father „especially when he as a son has not been accustomed from childhood to a strict and respectful relationship in his parents' house".

When it came to the pinch, J.C. was unwilling to relinquish command of his life's work.

Jacobsen accompanied his son to Korsør and there took leave of him as he departed on the steamship to Lübeck. He stayed pacing the quay until the vessel vanished into the night. He had assured himself by enquiry of the chief officer that the voyage would be a calm one and that the ship would be in Lübeck at 9 o'clock next morning according to plan. He put up for the night at the station hotel. Next morning he met a couple of travellers from Lübeck, who told him that they had had a quiet voyage. They had slept well, which relieved him.

Back in Copenhagen he immersed himself in work, made preparations for building extensions at Carlsberg and was busy in the Rigsdag, where the chairmanship of the Defence Commission was making heavy demands on his energies. In his first letter to Carl after the latter's departure his feelings are allowed free rein for once. He confides to his son that in the evening, when he is sitting at the drawing board or the desk, he is overcome by a crushing sense of emptiness, „which often brings tears to my eyes". It is worst when he goes up – as he frequently does – and sits in his son's room, where they have so often talked together. Before sending the letter off, however, Jacobsen reads through it one more time and adds: „I am completely well otherwise. I shall write to you every Sunday as a rule." So everything was under control again as before.

Carl's travels took him first of all to Paris, but the hastiness with which everything had been done is evident. J.C. had been unable, as otherwise was his wont, to organise his son's tour in detail. He had to make do with recommending Carl to seek help from his friends Bourgeois, editor of the *Journal des Brasseurs*, and Esquiron the chemist, who would help him to make a start on theory. With respect to language studies, counsellor of embassy Haxthausen, a Danish acquaintance in Paris whom J.C. had met at the Athenæum, had recommended a lady who could be found at the Café de la Régence. Most Danes took lessons from her.

Progress was very slow to begin with, however. A stay at the breweries in Puteaux, outside Paris, proved impossible to arrange. There was no brewing during the summer. In fact the first half-year passed with nothing achieved from the vocational standpoint. During the autumn Bourgeois managed to gain access for Carl to a couple of the Strasbourg breweries, where he got to know the Ehrhard and Hatt families and struck up friendships with the sons, who like himself were under training.

Carl's long odyssey next took him to Velten's brewery in Marseilles, then to Munich and Vienna. In the latter city he stayed for part of the time at Anton Dreher's brewery in Schwekat. After having made visits to breweries in Pest and in some of the Austrian towns, he returned to Munich, where he met his friends from Strasbourg. Together the young people made a lengthy tour of breweries in Bohemia, Silesia and Prussia. After a short sojourn in Paris the next stop was England. J.C. wanted Carl not only to master the manufacture of bottom-fermented beer but also to familiarise himself with the top-fermented English and Scottish types. England was the classical beer-making country, from which even the Bavarians had learnt much, and Jacobsen had a dream of getting his own beer introduced into Britain. That would be the definitive stamp of quality. Moreover, he nourished an expectation, widely shared in those days, that English export beer – which went all over the world – would find favour on the Continent, including Denmark. It was therefore necessary to be prepared for such an eventuality.

It was more difficult to tear asunder the bonds between Carl and Emilie than Jacobsen had expected. After the passage of something like nine months J.C. found that he was no further ahead than when he had started, and that his son's refractoriness was blocking his vocational progress. „I had expected that your letters from Strasbourg would breathe nothing but brewery. You have not even made any reply to the matters I asked you to look into. By Christmas your letters were already showing the marks of idleness and haste," J.C. fulminated at the end of February 1867. „If you think to be my successor at Carlsberg, you must make yourself worthy of that position. Otherwise affluence will be a curse upon you. Only a proficient and energetic brewer, with the ability and the will to continue what I have begun, and who wants to be ever at the forefront of progress in brewery in Denmark and Scandinavia, shall come into possession of this place after me, which is dedicated to this undertaking. God forbid that it should be anyone but my son."

The young people had been exchanging letters, of course. Carl thought that the relationship had now withstood the test of time and distance. The fact that they still loved each other must at last convince his father of the genuineness of their feelings. What had started as a „childish romance" had ended as a true relationship. J.C. rejected this point blank. In a birthday letter to Carl, who was now 25 and accordingly of age, Jacobsen declared that his responsibility for his son from now on was only moral. Money would still be sent to Carl for his education, but his father required accounts. He demonstrably omitted to send Carl a birthday present. The thermometer stood below zero.

Next the Captain introduced censorship into the family. He forbade Carl not only to write to his sweetheart but also to exchange letters with her family. Kogsbølle was ordered to put an end to his correspondence with Carl forthwith. The Djørups were given the same message. All communication was to be channelled through Jacobsen from now on. He declared that he would talk to Emilie when opportunity offered and would do so „as if I were her father".

Jacobsen tells of this strange meeting, which took place at Michael Djørup's home, in a bizarre letter to his son dated 16 March 1867. Emilie had faced him as the strict, harsh uncle who was angry with her because she had acted against his will. But she capitulated at once „when I put my hands affectionately to her face and patted her". They embraced one another, „a pleasing parallel to my last meeting with you on the journey to Korsør". He assured his son that „she now has trust in me and real affection. I want to see her and talk to her very often. This must take place gradually, however. Yesterday she came out here and visited your Mother while I was in town. Tomorrow a small circle of the Nielsens and Djørups will be with us here at home. She will come then." However, so that Carl should not think that his father had now reconciled himself to the idea of an engagement, he added that „as the two of you are now, you would never be able to find happiness together". In a postscript he sends his son a special greeting after the friends' visit to Carlsberg: „If you had seen E. this evening sitting on my knee for a couple of hours with her head on my breast in affectionate conversation, you would certainly have been red with embarrassment over your errors." Whether this rhapsody from the animal trainer's workshop made the expected impression on the son seems doubtful.

Several times over the period that followed Carl raised the question of his coming to Denmark for a visit. This too was rejected. „You must be 28 years old and have made good use of your years of learning and rehearsing. I therefore cannot under any circumstances give my consent to your making a visit home before then. The trial period must be completed first," he wrote in December 1867. Provided that all went well the father would help his son to become his own master. He promised to set him up in a business of his own.

The disharmonies between father and son continued. In a bitter birthday letter to Carl dated 28 February 1868, J.C. writes: „The year's red-letter days are days of anything but happiness for me, for there is little of happiness, but much sorrow, or rather worry, that they remind me of" ... „However far you may be from understanding me because you do not understand yourself, however much 'disharmony' you may see where there is only a lack of self-criticism and resignation, however unloving and ungrateful you may show yourself towards me," Jacobsen yet believes that one day his son will thank him, because „I put four years between the youth's dream and the man's decision". He asks Carl to understand that the disharmony will vanish when he no longer has to ask his father for anything, when there is „no longer the need to beg me to give in to your ideas". There is hope in the fact that one day Carl will be independent and will enjoy a position of his own in the community. On this occasion a gift accompanies the letter, however: a drawing made the same morning by Carl Bloch – of J.C. Jacobsen.

During the spring and summer of 1868 the tune changes. Ideas have clarified themselves, and the father now intends to carry on with his own brewery while setting up his son independently. Characteristically enough, J.C. tackles the business at once and sets out his plans. The correspondence between the two becomes more and more filled with the project. For a while Carl entertains the idea of introducing a beer similar to the „Strasbourg young beer", so called, in which he is very interested and for which a future is predicted in Strasbourg, but Jacobsen dismisses this. It would be impossible to found a brewery in Denmark on this beer alone, neither in Elsinore nor in any other of the provincial towns, and not in Copenhagen either, where there is no room for more breweries at all. His son ought to go in for making beer for export. This is the task which Danish brewers must solve instead of sending excellent Danish barley to England, where it is brewed into ale and porter, and then exported to British colonies all over the world. „Go to England, the sooner the better. That is where you will find your future by learning the brewing of high-grade top-fermented beer for export and ship-victualling as well as for drinking at home." Jacobsen mobilises his English connections both in Denmark and elsewhere: Melchior, Adler, Suhr, Burmeister, Pontoppidan, Westenholz and old Aird in London.

The diffusion of technology and know-how between the large European breweries was already quite effective even in this initial phase of the rise of the modern brewery industry. The channels were many – exhibitions, congresses, journals, schools of brewery, to name a few of them – but personal contact in the form of apprenticeship, traineeship and study visits was always the most important. Introductions were required, however. The breweries did not open their portals to all and sundry, and the families which owned and managed the businesses helped each other.

As we have already seen, J.C. Jacobsen was the „pupil" of Gabriel Sedlmayr the Younger in Munich. Just as Carl was being sent off on his study travels Sedlmayr published a couple of articles in *Journal des Brasseurs* and *Der Baierische Bierbrauer* in which he mentioned Jacobsen of Copenhagen and Anton Dreher of Vienna as two of the most important names to have studied at his „Zum Späten" brewery in the Bavarian capital. Bearing this in mind, J.C. suggested to his son that he should write to Sedlmayr and ask for an introduction to Dreher in Vienna, which he was given. The old boys' network functioned.

Arriving at a brewery without warning or introduction was more tricky. Some breweries would not countenance such visits. J.C. Jacobsen himself was rebuffed during a visit to Holland in 1860, „even though I presented myself with my ribbon in my buttonhole, which otherwise was a good talisman! And at Liesing in 1865 I was unsuccessful as well." Carl had the same experience, for example when he wanted to visit the breweries in Liechtenstein, and arising from this his father gave him a correspondence course in the etiquette of brewery visits.

Carl was accustomed to openness at home. „Secrecy is something I have never needed," J.C. wrote to him in his instructions, „because I knew that I was superior to my competitors in insight and skill, and because to some degree I wanted competition, for having a virtual monopoly was simply not to my taste." Jacobsen added, however, that he required reciprocity. „Thus I will in no circumstances give access to my brewery to any emissary from Owen of Aldersro, because he does not deserve such courtesy."

In towns with several equally matched breweries, market shares often depended upon minor details of the treatment of the beer, J.C. explained to his son. So the brewer thinks twice and asks himself whether the visitor might just possibly be after something on behalf of a local competitor. Be a psychologist when you are a guest is Papa's advice. „With those who let their lights shine gladly, hide your own light under a bushel and ask questions quite innocently as though you were an ignoramus; with those who like to listen, you should talk a good deal but not praise other brewers' methods too much and never tell what you have seen in the same town without exercising considerable caution. In this way you can gradually gather together, piece by piece, everything you want to know. Take no notes on the spot, unless you are certain that this will not be taken amiss, but avail yourself of the first opportunity of doing so elsewhere. Do not ask too many questions at once, but ask them as though at random, without definite purpose etc." Attire, manners, language and the giving of presents are also included in the course.

The fact is that these visits could develop into what we would today call industrial espionage. There is a droll example of this from Gabriel Sedlmayr the Younger's own journey to England thirty years earlier in company with his friend of the same age, Anton Dreher of Vienna. British brewers were rather reserved towards their guests and as a rule refused to disclose their methods to strangers, but the two young brewers, with the help of a letter of introduction from David Booth, a British technical writer on brewery, gained admittance to a large number of breweries in England and Scotland. Here they acquired much knowledge of the installations, which were technically advanced and far superior to those on the Continent. In letters home to their fathers they related all the subterfuges they had employed in order to prise the Englishmen's secrets from them. These ranged from thermometers for surreptitiously measuring temperatures to hollowed-out walking sticks with vent holes, with which they provided themselves with samples of wort and beer for subsequent detailed analysis. Of one of their visits – to a brewery where, into the bargain, they had been very well received – they wrote home triumphantly: „Die Brauerei stahlen wir aber doch so gut als möglich aus." („But we still stole as much as we could from the brewery.") The notes were passed down through the generations too. When Carl came to Burton-on-Trent accompanied by his friends from Strasbourg, the young Hatt lent him one of Sedlmayr the Elder's „monographs" (from 1836) dealing with the special English malting technique, which Carl copied.

Jacobsen tried to use Carl as his eyes and ears. His letters fire volleys of questions. Why is the hop room kept secret in some breweries? Is a clarifying agent being used? Have you talked to Louis Hatt about it? Do they boil the hops in Vienna as they do in Strasbourg, in partial admixtures? Do all the hops come from Bohemia? Or from Saaz, Anschar, Leitmeritz? What is the percentage of wort to lager beer at Lilienthal? How long do they still keep old lager beer from last winter? How do they fill the beer into the storage barrels? Very slowly and distributed between many barrels? Or rapidly? How do they do it at Erhard's?

Little by little Carl's tongue loosened. „It was a surprising piece of news that the brewery in Pest was not a steam brewery," J.C. wrote back to him on 4 February 1868. „I should have been very pleased to have more details about its layout and operation so as to be able to compare it with mine, which of course became a complete steam brewery only this winter." „I confidently believe that the theoretical grounds which suggest steam boiling to be workable for lager beer as well will hold good in practice. Although some of the results elsewhere have not been very successful, this will not deter me, for the malting and drying may have played a part in those instances. Furthermore, no one except myself has steam-proof closed coppers in which the wort is boiled at 1 to 2 pounds pressure, i.e. at a temperature above boiling point." If Carl should get an opportunity of talking to Sedlmayr about this, he may tell him of Jacobsen's newly-gained experience at Carlsberg and report back with his comments. It also occurs to Jacobsen that it might interest Sedlmayr, „my teacher and master", to learn „that I have never changed my yeast, but that the yeast I am using today is in unbroken line of descent from the tin of yeast I brought home from his yeast cellar in 1845."

In Munich Carl met the next Sedlmayr generation, which at once triggered a fresh barrage of questions from home. Has the young Sedlmayr learnt chemistry properly? Is he a proficient analyst? Has he visited Kaiser or Liebig? Can he introduce you to either of them? Even if it is of no immediate benefit to you, it would serve as a recommendation in England, perhaps an important one, that you know Liebig. A word from him may secure you admittance into places where it would otherwise be impossible. Ask Sedlmayr about the best writings on English brewery.

The journey to England went via Strasbourg and Paris. „While I remember, let me say that any clothes purchased in France before you go to England must have been used before you pass the frontier sufficiently for it to be visible to the eye or for you to be able swear to it on oath. Otherwise you will be regarded as a smuggler." The solicitous father was running true to form.

Carl is also given the task of buying a work of art, viz. a bronze cast of an ancient statue, while in Paris. Here he is on his home ground, and for once J.C. deals with him as an equal from whom he is seeking advice. „You have made me waver very much between „Diana" and „The Swordsman", since I cherish a personal affection for the former because of its gracefulness and its *je ne sais quoi,* which gladdens the mind, while the latter undeniably has a much higher artistic value and would be a much greater adornment for Carlsberg inasmuch as it can also have a worthier place on the small lawn which you suggest. Rather than toss up to arrive at a result I shall leave the choice to you; and you shall have some small recompense for the inconvenience. I shall be equally satisfied whichever you choose." The choice fell on „The Swordsman", and Carl received great praise from on high for his manner of arranging the transaction himself. The statue was mounted in front of Jacobsen's villa.

In Britain Carl was installed as a trainee at Younger's brewery in Edinburgh. The Youngers were an old-established brewing family founded by William Younger in 1749. In the middle of the 19th century the firm was very prosperous and was reckoned to be one of the best and most modern ale and porter breweries of the age, with a growing export business both to the United States and the colonies.

For example, Younger's Ale was the favourite beer of the 91st High-landers and other famous Scottish regiments. It followed the soldiers wherever their service took them, whether to the Crimea, to India or to other stations overseas. „Bread, Beef and Beer are the charters of Britain's supremacy," ran a contemporary encomium of the brewery's products.

The Youngers had opened an office in London in 1866. The brewery disposed of two plants in Edinburgh, one in Holyrood close by the palace with Arthur's Seat in the background, the other in Canongate, not far away. Carl worked at the Abbey establishment in Canongate, whose speciality was porter. He spent about a year at the Abbey Brewery and described this as the most instructive of his numerous sojourns abroad. The manufacture of porter later became one of his specialities.

From Scotland Carl went to Burton-on-Trent in Staffordshire, where some of Britain's most famous breweries were and still are located, including Bass and the Alsopp brothers. Carl had a place at the somewhat smaller Evershed Brewery.

Altogether Carl's interest in his calling was now thoroughly awakened. From Edinburgh he sent an article on his experiences with the kiln-drying of malt to Bourgeois in Paris with a request for it to be published in the *Journal des Brasseurs.* His father was delighted. „Your observations of the degrees of heat during drying are classical and have scarcely ever been undertaken in such an exhaustive manner. They bear witness to a thoroughness and perseverance which pleased me greatly when I received your report. It is over now, of course, and you have not taken any harm, but it was a little venturesome to spend so much time in an atmosphere heavy with sulphurous acid. Did it not trouble your lungs?"

J.C. and Laura visited England in the summer of 1869. They arrived from France and were accompanied by two young ladies, Anna Steenstrup and Agnes Berthelsen. Carl met them off the Calais boat train at Charing Cross Station. „I found him in all respects as I had hoped and expected," Jacobsen wrote home to Kogsbølle. „In France he has learnt to be courtly in manner and in England the goal he has set himself is to be a complete gentleman, in which direction he has indeed made great progress. This development in formal aspects has not had the least influence on his straightforward attitude towards his nearest and dearest, and there is not the slightest difference to be detected between our mutual relationship 5 years ago and now." It was very satisfactory.

At last, now that Carl had attained 28 years of age, he could come home again. This happened at the end of May. Father and son had been conducting an intensive correspondence over the fitting up of the new brewery. The winter of 1869/70 had been very hard and had slowed up the building work, which had only reached ground level by the time of Carl's return home. Carl had chosen red brickwork, and he took the motif for the ashlar substructure from the riding school at Piacenza, but it was largely his father's tried and tested constructional principles and techniques which were employed, except that Jacobsen's system of brew coppers with sealed-in steam could not be used for English beer types. Ordinary coppers, heated by „open furnaces", were used instead. Carl had ordered some of the machinery in England. The old architect, Nebelong, made the detailed drawings. All was ready by the beginning of 1871, and the first brew was made on 17 February. The brewery was so equipped as to be capable of being rapidly converted to brewing Bavarian beer.

During his time in the beautiful city of Edinburgh Carl had enjoyed hospitality at the home of C. Stegmann, a merchant, where several members of the Danish colony were regular visitors. Carl mentioned in one of his letters home that Mrs Stegmann and her two young daughters were intending to go to Denmark, from where the Stegmann family originated, and Jacobsen asked him to keep him informed of their arrival, since he wished to thank them for their kindness to his son. He asked Carl to send a telegram when they set off, but felt it unfitting to specify the family's name in the telegram, so he instructed his son simply to send the laconic message: „Goods despatched today by steamship."

The steamship, and therefore the „goods", made a swifter passage than expected, the wife and her daughters turning up at Carlsberg as early as 18 May, to the Brewer's surprise. „I was somewhat disconcerted at having to plunge into English on the spur of the moment, and I made an extremely poor showing – at any rate I know I made some colossal howlers – but fortunately Miss Berthelsen speaks very good English, so that I was able to hand the young ladies over into her care, although they were so sweet and charming, especially Miss Ingeborg, whom everybody fell in love with, that I should have been more than willing to chat with them." He ran true to form in this situation too. „Uncle is a serious man, but he still likes jokes, life and youth," as Nanna had once observed.

Jacobsen found Mrs Stegmann to be a very beautiful woman of excellent deportment, perhaps a little distant. Soon visits were being arranged to the art gallery, art exhibitions and museums, and on Sunday the household's English-speaking social circle was assembled for a party and dance for the young people at Carlsberg.

In 1874 Carl married Ottilia, then 20 years of age and the youngest of the Stegmann daughters. He himself was now 34. The wedding took place in Copenhagen, whither the Stegmanns had moved in 1870. The wedding reception was held at the Stegmanns' residence in Dronningens Tværgade. The marriage proved fruitful, there being eight children in all, of whom four died during infancy. Carl, who loved symbolism and could occasionally take it to bizarre and eccentric extremes in his industrial building, erected a monument to the four survivors in the celebrated Elephant Tower of 1901 (designed by Vilhelm Dahlerup, who had become his favourite architect from 1880 onwards). The elephants took their initials from Theodora, Paula, Helge and Vagn, while in due course Ottilia and Carl themselves, in the form of a double bust by the sculptor Ludvig Brandstrup erected shortly after Ottilia's death, took up their position gazing out over the whole establishment from a point of vantage between two pillars of the loggia. The memories of the children who died were perpetuated in the names of the four bells of the Church of Jesus: Alf, Thorvald, Erland and Beatrice.

The story was rounded off when Emilie also married in 1874, her husband being a Dr Arendtz, a Norwegian.

Public Spirit

Patronage and philanthropy have deep roots in European civilisation extending far back into Antiquity. Mæcenas (whose name is still used as a synonym for a patron of the arts) was the counsellor and friend of the Emperor Augustus; he was the patron of Horace, Virgil and other poets. The word „philanthropy" is derived from the Greek *phil:* a friend, and *antropos:* a person – in other words it connotes a form of love of mankind.

The Italian popes and princes of the Renaissance sought to outdo one another as patrons. The emperors and kings of the Age of Absolutism continued the tradition, which was carried forward by the bourgeoisie in their turn during the 19th century, especially in the Anglo-Saxon world. In Britain such patronage flourished alongside the sure faith of the middle classes in the efficacy of private enterprise in virtually every department of the national life.

J.C. Jacobsen encountered this public spirit during his travels, and it inspired him. The Crystal Palace in London was not merely a technical miracle, it was also remarkable in being the creation of nine private individuals working on their own account without the use of taxpayers' money. For him it served as a model both in the building of his own private conservatory and in his biggest undertaking, the great conservatory of the Copenhagen Botanical Gardens. A similar impression was made on him by the great zoological gardens in Brussels situated on the heights overlooking the city. This was the work of a private company, and it was „a pity that with us public spirit is so little developed in such directions or indeed in any direction apart from charity", he wrote home from one of his visits there.

To his son he sent the news in 1868 that the Royal Danish Porcelain Factory had been bought by a consortium consisting of Suhr, Holmblad and a couple of other rich men with a view to maintaining the factory's artistic tradition. Had he not himself been hit by the catastrophe of the fire the previous year, he assured Carl, he would also have wanted to participate in the fulfilment of this task, „but now I am doubly pleased that this can be accomplished without me. Up to now I have stood virtually alone in that direction."

The hour of the bourgeoisie had struck. „Our nobility are neither numerous nor rich, you know," he explained to Carl on the occasion of his first and very costly donation, the Oratory Suite, which J.C. commissioned from the painter Carl Bloch, „and those we have are for the most part insufficiently educated and insufficiently high-minded to make such sacrifices for the public weal. But all the greater therefore is the duty of every citizen who has an ample income beyond his own modest necessities to act in this direction, and one ought not to hold back from it even if one finds oneself standing alone for a long time. For the force of example will gradually have an effect." *Noblesse oblige* was no longer valid, and the golden torch had now been passed to the well-to-do bourgeoisie, who ought to feel in duty bound to bear it forward.

The opinions of social thinkers and writers with regard to the phenomena of charity and philanthropy have not been unanimously kind. Some have asserted that the generous donors themselves, by their own previous conduct and activities, have helped to create the very hardships which they subsequently seek to alleviate by their charity. Others have called philanthropy a kind of moral greed on the part of acquisitive man, who first scrapes the money together and then, by the act of giving it away, begins to amass gratitude. Psychologists and sociologists have analysed the array of motives for charitable works and have come up with a long list ranging from guilt feelings and the desire to be loved via vanity and group consensus to the wish to secure a fine posthumous reputation in history, a niche with a marble bust.

What moved Jacobsen to perform his civic duty? It has been postulated that he nourished a lively fear of hubris, and that he had a dark foreboding that the wrath of the gods would fall on him who had too much; it was this Greek spirit in him that supposedly actuated his decision to give away large sums for socially beneficial purposes. Support for this belief in nemesis can be found in a letter which he sent to his son with the news of the fire at Carlsberg which ravaged his plant in 1867. On the very day of the fire he wrote to his son and among other things said: „Almost like Polycrates I have been afraid of my material success, and now nemesis has struck, suddenly and unexpectedly; but I am well prepared for it and feel almost pleased to have to start afresh in part." However, this is the sole example and scarcely suffices on its own.

It was not only the gods on the summit of Olympus who watched and pondered over the accumulation of affluence under liberalism. The philosopher F.C. Sibbern, for example, professor at Copenhagen University, published in the university programme on the occasion of the King's birthday in 1849 a paper containing some observations concerning state and church, in which he discussed the reverse side of the liberal constitution just introduced and so highly lauded by all. Whereas in Sibbern's view the previous paternalistic rule had set internal bounds to the exercise of the various occupations and thereby diffused incomes broadly through the reaches of society, the newly established liberalised economy and the competition associated with it would result in the amassing of exceedingly large fortunes in the hands of individuals. Sibbern here raised the question whether it was not then the duty of the state to step in with the demand that when fortunes over and above a certain level were acquired in this way they ought to belong to the state and be used by the latter most especially for the fostering of art and science.

The historian Troels-Lund says in his memoirs that Sibbern's words on the imposition of taxes on great fortunes for the sake of the nation's art and science „spread like seeds and fecundated responsive hearts. Some few years later the brewer Jacobsen the Elder gave the first remarkable example of voluntary self-taxation of this kind." This is an alluring fancy too, but it is undocumented in the mass of Jacobsen's own utterances.

It is perhaps more fruitful to follow a third trail. Jacobsen's far from church-centred religious sense was very much influenced by H.C. Ørsted, whose writings he cites. Rasmus Nielsen, C.T. Barfoed and Japetus Steenstrup were also among his „church fathers". A goodly portion of utilitarianism was mixed in as well, for example in the conception that in the last resort Divine Providence is propelling mankind towards a higher state of being. This optimistic faith, coupled with the principle of self-activity which we find everywhere in Jacobsen's world of ideas, viz. that men must work actively for their own mental and moral perfection, opens the way for the ideal of the useful citizen in the service of the community at large. It is true that no one will be able to attain the ideal during this earthly life, but there is the possibility of continuing afterwards in the beyond, and the individual will then confront the table on which his earlier strivings and the results thereof are recorded.

It is no overstatement to say that J.C. Jacobsen and his son Carl were the greatest patrons seen in Denmark up to the time of the First World War. J.C. himself did not care for the term patron, and he hated the word millionaire, which the newspaper „Socialdemokraten" accordingly liked to pin on him and tease him with. In the Brewer's eyes a millionaire was a „moneyed plebeian". But he regarded himself as a son of his city and country who did his civic duty and gave of his wealth with an objective before him and an idea behind. His gifts were not in themselves ostentatious, designed to impress, but were stirring and inspirational, serving some idea.

J.C. Jacobsen's patronage reached a peak during the 1870s with a series of donations to the nation of an order of magnitude never seen before. It is characteristic of him that the money now and then limped behind the plans. He financed his patronage out of what he called his „savings". Now and then they ran out, and he had to take a pause. The patronage was always in competition with the financing of new plant at the breweries, but only rarely did the two interests find themselves on a collision course.

These considerations are quite central. For this is not a case of a rich man deciding towards the end of his life to turn his wealth into something monumental that can live after his death. What we have here is an individual deeply involved in the affairs of his nation and striving the whole time to carry into effect a succession of idealistic undertakings while simultaneously practising his own calling. He is engaged on a series of tasks which he wants to accomplish and which he gets to grips with quite early in life. Rather than subconscious forces such as nemesis, self-taxation or a celestial balance sheet, his patronage springs from his own activities as brewer and citizen. In fact his contributions are immediately comprehensible and his monuments highly transparent. They are what he is and what he does. They grow out of his being, in close harmony with his life and experiences.

This may be difficult for a present-day collectively-orientated mentality to grasp, let alone accept, and it is therefore tempting to resort to mystical explanations in order to understand the phenomenon. But the source of Jacobsen's patronage is obvious. It is the political revolution of 1849. It is the conviction that the introduction of the free franchise alone can awaken the community sense of the people. It is also the bitter hour of military defeat in 1864, and it is the scientific discoveries and their practical application both in Jacobsen's own field and in society at large. And finally it is the belief in the force of example and in civic duty. All these are founded on his own experience and reflect phases of his life. In fact it is all very down-to-earth and tangible.

In 1871 Jacobsen was elected to the committee of the Copenhagen Botanical Gardens. Japetus Steenstrup was the figure behind his nomination. The other members were Johan Lange (professor of botany and director of the Botanical Gardens), Anders Sandøe Ørsted, university bursar L.V. Gade, the jurist, Professor J. Gram and Th. Friedrichsen, head gardener of the Botanical Gardens. At this time the committee had been deliberating for many years – since 1857 in fact – over an exceedingly complicated matter which was loaded to bursting point with the stuff of conflict. The University's botanical garden was at Gammelholm, a location in which it was impossible for it to remain because that quarter of the city was to be expanded. But where was it to be moved to?

In 1870 the committee suggested moving the garden to Glaciset, „The Glacis", i.e. the filled ground in front of the old moat along the extension of Gothersgade. Others wanted the new botanical garden to be placed out at the Royal Veterinary and Agricultural College, and there was fierce wrangling over this even after the Rigsdag, in the Finance Act of 1871/72, had made the first appropriation for the transfer of the garden to The Glacis. Shortly after his election Jacobsen took over the chairmanship of the committee as a purely temporary measure after Professor Gram was taken ill and then died. Then Professor Lange also took sick and had to take a long period of recuperation abroad. In December 1871 the Ministry of Ecclesiastical Affairs and Public Instruction appointed Professor J. Nellemann, a member of the University Senate, as chairman, but he and Jacobsen were soon in disagreement, over an exchange of real property among other matters, and when the Ministry handed down a decision supporting Jacobsen, Nellemann resigned. The committee managed without a chairman for a time until Lange returned from his convalescence and took over again. The real power in the committee resided in the executive subcommittee, and this was chaired by Jacobsen. He strengthened it by bringing in as „co-opted members" a couple of old acquaintances from the laying-out of the garden grounds at Carlsberg, two gardeners named H. Flindt and Tyge Rothe.

The task to be accomplished included not only the laying-out of the gardens but the erection of buildings and greenhouses as well. There was a set of drawings for a museum building by the architect Christian Hansen, whose designs had included the Municipal Hospital (1859-63) and the Zoological Museum on Krystalgade (1863-69), the latter in close collaboration with Japetus Steenstrup. Jacobsen was not satisfied with Hansen's drawings. Hansen had not ventured to deviate from the traditional rule that partition must rest on partition, „but I dare say his misgivings could be set at rest if he could once be convinced that it is possible to build with complete safety on iron girders". Thus did Jacobsen saddle and trot out his hobby-horse from the brewery, iron girders. In fact he romped about among design and technique questions generally. As was his wont he was for ever meddling, and Hansen prudently left the arena. The greenhouses were at the forefront of Jacobsen's interest. Over and over again he fussed over them, making sketches of heating apparatus – another of his specialities applied in his own house – calculated wind and snow pressures, corrected Professor Hummel's tables, and so on.

In the middle of all this the Copenhagen bricklayers went on strike. This was a strike that started in April 1872 and inside a month, on 6 May, led to a large-scale clash on Nørre Fælled, the North Common, known in Danish history as the „Battle of the Common", and to the imprisonment of the socialist leader Louis Pio. The journeymen bricklayers employed at the Botanical Gardens kept out of the strike but were abused and mobbed by their striking comrades. Jacobsen wrote a vehement letter to the Copenhagen chief of police, Vilhelm

Crone, demanding police protection for the working journeymen. „Should the police, contrary to my expectation, find themselves unable to provide these people with the requisite security, then it will be necessary as far as the Botanical Gardens are concerned to organise without delay a form of security guard capable of protecting the workers both at the building site and on the way to their homes," he wrote, and sent a courtesy copy of the letter to the Ministry of Justice. The threat of thus taking the law into his own hands provoked an acrimonious rejoinder from Crone, and the episode branded Jacobsen once and for all as a vile capitalist in the eyes of the labour movement and press, which did not care a fig about all his good deeds.

By 1 June 1874 the gardens were ready and were handed over by the committee to the University and so to the public. Copenhagen was now enriched by an institution which united the useful with the beautiful. It put a modern and necessary working tool into the hand of botanical research, and the city got a splendid garden which has since become one of its lungs. The jewel in the crown was the greenhouses, Copenhagen's Crystal Palace in miniature. When the University was celebrating its 400th anniversary in June 1879, Jacobsen sent as his personal greeting – and at the same time a quid pro quo for the honorary doctorate which he had had to be persuaded to accept – a sumptuously got-up monograph entitled „A Description of the Greenhouses of the University Botanical Gardens of Copenhagen, with details of the Layout and Establishment of the Gardens 1871-74". The co-author with Jacobsen was Tyge Rothe.

To complete the story it may be added that the funds granted under the Finance Act were insufficient and that Jacobsen put in almost 18,000 kroner to make up the deficit.

The busts in the foyer of the Royal Theatre were another of Jacobsen's donations that suffered prolonged and severe birth pangs. Here too he irritated many people by setting his conditions and meddling in matters which were felt not to be his concern. The first performance at the new Royal Theatre was held on 15 October 1874, but the theatre was not yet complete, one of the deficiencies being that the foyer in the loggia overlooking Kongens Nytorv was empty. Jacobsen had promised six months previously that he would embellish it with marble busts of the dramatists Holberg, Ewald, Wessel, Oehlenschläger, Heiberg, Hauch and Henrik Hertz, of the actors Ryge, Lindgren and Mrs Anna Nielsen, and of the composers Weyse and Kuhlau, twelve in all. The sculptors Vilhelm Bissen and Th. Stein were to execute the busts and pedestals. One of the conditions of the gift was that the rectangular foyer area should be decorated in a manner to harmonise with the busts. The offer was formally placed before the screening committee established under the Theatres Act of 1870, one of whose duties was to evaluate private contributions to the artistic embellishment of the theatre. Jacobsen was himself a member of the committee.

The acting theatre director, A. Linde, was less than enthusiastic about the condition for the gift. He wanted the space to be fitted out as a coffee shop, partly in order to generate an income for the theatre, and the Minister for Ecclesiastical Affairs and Public Instruction, Johan Fischer, supported him. The semi-circular foyer would be best for Jacobsen's busts: the rectangular foyer was originally planned by the architects as a „refreshment area" decorated with paintings.

Jacobsen went up in the air. The rectangular foyer, he argued, was intended as the theatre's „ceremonial hall". It was not to be given over to beer and aquavit but was to be the entre'acte point of assembly for an elegantly-attired public. Foaming beer tankards and fizzing soda-water siphons were incompatible with ladies „en grande toilette". Once more he resorted to his usual trick of imposing his will by topping the gift with a further gift. As well as the busts he would donate a further 20,000 kroner for the decorating of the foyer: that would take care of the finances. If his gifts were not accepted on his terms, he would withdraw them and keep the busts, which were already commissioned and being executed by the sculptors. In that way they might possibly end up via the Carlsberg Foundation at the Frederiksborg Museum or in some other public collection.

The equally temperamental Fischer would not yield. The foyer was leased out to Gianelli the confectioner. The minister took the view that a private individual was not going to impose an easement in perpetuity on the theatre. There matters rested until 1880, when Fischer was forced out of office because of his conflicts with both the National Liberal and the „Venstre" (Farmers') parties. He had also fallen foul of the University, for example by attempting to obtain an appointment for Georg Brandes, the critic and man of letters, and also endeavouring to give the University's 400th anniversary celebrations a more European slant; this was construed by the University's governing body as interference in its autonomy, even though Fischer, in his capacity as a Rigsdag deputy, had otherwise done much for the University through his support for the establishment of the Zoological Museum.

Jacobsen and the new theatre director, Edv. Fallesen, made personal contact in 1882, and the Brewer got his busts into place at last. In the meantime they had been standing at Carlsberg breeding – for they increased in number to thirteen when Jacobsen had his heart of hearts, Mrs Heiberg, added to the little group of immortals. In the play „En Sjæl efter døden" (A Soul after Death), the lady's husband, Johan Ludvig Heiberg, former director of the theatre, has the Soul meeting a dying actor, who has nothing against dying, „for I hope that the management will be kind enough to honour my memory with obsequies for the departed and to have a garland woven for my bust, and that many people will be annoyed when they see my portrait hanging in our foyer". In the matter of the bust his prayer was heard, and Jacobsen for his part had experienced once again the truth that to make gifts is hard.

J.C. Jacobsen's patronage culminated during the late 1870s in the establishment of the Carlsberg Foundation in 1876 and of the Frederiksborg Museum in 1878. Behind these donations lay the respect for research which he cherished all his life and the desire to use history for the service of the nation. But other, more personal motives were concealed behind these, as we shall see later. They had to do with the question of the continuance of the Carlsberg breweries after his death.

Jacobsen distinguished sharply between tasks undertaken for the public good and charitable works. He was active in both spheres throughout his life, but he always exercised charity anonymously; whenever his actions in this respect could not be hidden, he would ask the recipient to keep his identity secret. Innumerable charitable collections and many individuals received assistance from him, ranging from victims of the fire at Valby and war victims both in Denmark and elsewhere, including French prisoners of war after the Franco-Prussian War of 1870-71, to educational journeys and study tours for researchers and artists.

Among the artists was one person who was in a class of her own, a lady on whom Jacobsen quite frankly showered his munificence and whose acquaintance he was proud of and valued above all others. He had a portrait of the lady standing on his desk. This was the actress Johanne Luise Heiberg. The portrait was actually a New Year's present from Mrs Heiberg to Laura. Laura thanked her most sincerely for it: „You have shown us little ladies such an infinity of the beautiful and the noble, both on stage and in real life, that we must pray God to grant you many happy years in which to go on acting," she wrote in her letter of thanks.

Bodil Wamberg recently remarked in her biography of Johanne Luise Heiberg that in her personal life and in her capacity as a sensual actress, the lady focused exclusively on men at the expense of her own sex. „She loved to invite only gentlemen to her parties and shine before the admiring crowd." „She was the centre point for these men, often their secret erotic dream, and the shirt-fronts merged together before her eyes to form – even at home – the field of attention that stimulated her to display her qualities." She spoke scornfully of the insignificant wives of significant men, „the missuses" as she called them in her letters to A.F. Krieger, the only confidant she had. „Johanne Luise Heiberg never performed the psychological somersault that would have been necessary in order to comprehend these other women's intellectual resources – which, when they remained unused, developed into depressions and frustrations, hatred and grief." What was remarkable was that the „missuses", who knew very well her opinion of them, meekly put up with it, like Amalie Meldahl: „It never occurred to me to be envious or offended: I was all too sensible of my inferiority."

Jacobsen had no reservations about Mrs Heiberg either. He came into close contact with her during 1868/69, when they were both in their late fifties. The Brewer led off by channelling assistance through her to a young opera singer. Coquettishly she called him her „youngest friend" – in fact she had also done this with Krieger when she first got to know him in 1862 – and Jacobsen overwhelmed her with attentions great and small, ranging from a Florentine painting of birds, his own portrait medallion, books and engravings to P.S. Krøyer's picture of a guitar-playing gypsy girl. Jacobsen was otherwise no great fan of Krøyer, but obviously the gypsy girl was the boldest advance he dared to make. He paid for the lady's lengthy holiday trip to Switzerland and Italy accompanied by her daughters, helped her with a new residence when she had to vacate her villa in Rosenvænget, and assisted with her rent. And Mrs Heiberg accepted, not without an element of calculation.

Her problem was how to avoid too great a debt of gratitude to Jacobsen. „Sometimes I shudder to think of the great debt of gratitude I owe to the good Jacobsen," she wrote to Krieger. „I do not feel I am sufficiently fond of him to accept what he has lavished on me this year. I shame to say that my gratitude must either be too cold or else warmer than I can feel, to tell you the absolute truth." Her admiration for Jacobsen related primarily to his practical abilities, resembling somewhat her similar sentiment towards the Norwegian businessman Peter Simonsen, another of her friends. And she also admired Jacobsen for his exertions on behalf of Denmark. „You are the only man in this country who, now here, now there, remembers the votaries of art by your generosity."

Once in a while Laura was included in Mrs Heiberg's invitations. This occurred on the occasion of her daughters' confirmation, for example. Of Carl she entertained no high opinion. Whereas the father's impulses were grand and bore the hallmark of genius, she called the son „a monkey".

While J.C. Jacobsen always kept a certain distance in his relation to the world around him and always followed his own judgment independently of others, Johanne Luise Heiberg formed the exception. In his New Year's greeting to her in January 1878 he wrote: „On the whole I must admit that I am insufficiently receptive to the judgment of others concerning my actions; but nevertheless there are some, and you more than anybody are one of these, whose approval I regard as an enviable felicity, even though I admit that this felicity is greater than I deserve, yet for this very reason I must be doubly grateful to you." The role did not really become Jacobsen.

The light of knowledge

Justus Liebig's chemical theory of fermentation of 1839 took the work on the fermentation processes into a blind alley, where it remained stationary for twenty years. The way Jacobsen expressed it was that science left the brewer „completely in the lurch". All that it offered was vague hypotheses and more or less hazy conceptions unsupported by exact investigations. In this field, absolutely crucial to all brewing, the brewers were still groping in the dark. Effective command and quality control in the fermenting cellars were still blocked. However, there was a breakthrough after the middle of the century.

Fundamental theoretical advances in chemistry, biology and physiology, arising out of the problems of practical life in a very direct way, accumulated during the decades from 1860 onwards. Many of these were associated with the fermenting industries in fact, and in the fashionable conceptual terminology of our day they can be called paradigmatic. New disciplines, summarised under the contemporary heading of zymotechnology, emerged during this period. The tone of the specialist literature was pioneering, often polemical: there was a fight for trophies going on. Today's brewery, winemaking and distillery rest on a foundation laid during these decades, and the technique of sterilisation on which the 20th century preserving industry has been built was likewise established at this time. One of the biggest growth industries of our own day, the medicine and enzyme industry, is indebted to researchers such as Louis Pasteur of Paris, Robert Koch of Berlin and Emil Christian Hansen of Copenhagen. For example, one of Dr Hansen's basic methods, his so-called reconstitution experiments, achieved general dissemination during the 1940s as an important tool in the genetic analysis of micro-organisms.

Pasteur was the pioneer who ended up as sacrosanct in the eyes of brewers. Around the middle of the century he held a post in Lille, the northern French centre for the production of vinegar, wine, beer and spirits, where numerous cases of tainted wine and beer were referred to him by producers, so that he found himself thrust into the mysteries of fermentation. He subsequently continued his studies on the subject in Paris at the École Normale Supérieur, where he became director, and then at the Sorbonne University, where he held the chair in chemistry.

In 1863 the Emperor Napoleon III personally requested him to investigate the causes of disease in wine. Wine and viniculture constituted one of the pillars on which the French economy formerly rested, and the crisis in this sector could well be called national in scope.

The result appeared three years later in the work „Études sur le vin". Pasteur's method consisted of heating the wine to between 60 and 70 degrees Celsius in order to improve the product's keeping qualities. Having first patented his heating method of „pasteurisation" – honour being the fairest tree in the forest – he made it available gratis for anyone who wished to use it. It was soon extended to the treatment of a range of other foodstuffs.

While Pasteur strongly advocated the heat treatment of wine, he was hesitant over the similar treatment of beer. Immediately after the publication of „Études sur le vin", his fellow-countryman Eugène Velten, the Marseilles brewer, with whom Jacobsen had established contact during his tour of France in 1865, began to heat-treat his beer by the Pasteur method, though at lower temperatures than those recommended by Pasteur for wine. Despite numerous difficulties the pasteurisation of beer spread rapidly, especially where the beer was destined for export. This was particularly so in Germany, where heat treatment was widely practised in Bavaria during the 1870s. Pasteurisation experiments soon got under way in Danish breweries too. From 1874 onwards, after previous trials at the Alliance bottling establishment, Jacobsen had Carlsberg's bottled beer for export pasteurised, first with hot air, then in a water bath. The King's Brew-House introduced the pasteurisation of malt extract in 1875-76. Here the bottles were dipped in a water bath, and at Tuborg from 1870 onwards most of the bottled beer began to be pasteurised, not only for export but for the home market as well.

One of the reasons for the pasteurisation of beer for the Danish home market was that Tuborg decided early on to go in for bottling at the brewery itself, direct from the barrels; although there were beer-bottling establishments which were equal to anything the breweries

Part of Copenhagen's new botanical gardens with the greenhouses from 1872.

▶

Jacobsen's investments in the breweries and his patronage of science and the arts ran side by side and seldom came into collision. But there were difficulties in the early 1880s. The building-up of the Frederiksborg Museum was a very demanding task, coinciding with the clash with Carl and the latter's demand for capital assets, which had to be honoured. For once Jacobsen decided to postpone parts of a planned renovation at the breweries, viz. the installation of electric lighting. It was started in 1881-82 and continued the following season. Not until 1888-89 was an electricity generating station installed to supply the breweries' entire requirements. Part of the plant was illuminated by Professor Jürgensen's dynamos and arc lamps, while another part used equipment supplied by the firm of Siemens & Halske of Berlin. Eventually Swan lightbulbs were used in the storage cellars. In the picture, taken from the "Illustreret Tidende" in 1884, the light is coming from the lighthouse erected the year before, which along with a porter's lodge guarded the main entrance from Alliance Way (now Pasteur's Way).

amle Carlsberg.

Foyer of the Royal Theatre. Unsigned, from 1896.

Johanne Luise Heiberg, 1872. ▶

could achieve in terms of cleanliness, nevertheless there were also a number of smaller plants where the necessary standards with respect to the cleaning of bottles and the handling of the beer were far from being met. In any case the beer first had to be racked off from the beer barrels to smaller casks, and the latter would then be transported to the bottlers. At every tapping there was a risk of contamination.

In the long run pasteurisation signalled an undermining of the bottlers' position, since they were unable to absorb the cost of the requisite plant. At Tuborg bottling was done in a long passageway – the front cellar – which ran along the front end of all the storage cellars, and in the closing years of the century there were no fewer than seven beer filling and hand-corking machines in operation here. In fact it was something of a revolution that took place at the end of the 19th century as it gradually became clear that the future belonged to brewery-bottled, pasteurised beer, which brought quite different marketing conditions to the beer industry.

Jacobsen himself conducted studies of fermentation, mostly of a practical character, in part under the inspiration of Pasteur's work but also on the basis of a brief paper entitled „On the active principle in fermentation and the transmission of certain kinds of disease," by Professor C.E. Fenger, a physician and politician. In a letter to Carl at the beginning of 1868 Jacobsen refers to the fact that while working on his paper Fenger had borrowed his, Jacobsen's, copy of „Études sur le vin". „There are," he says, „a number of very important observations by Pasteur and others which I have a great desire to repeat and check, for there are still many aspects of fermentation phenomena which are obscure and call for continued careful observations."

After the humiliating defeat of the Franco-Prussian War of 1870-71, Louis Pasteur began his studies inside the French brewery industry itself. The patriotic goal before his eyes was to make the French brewery industry more competitive. German beer had made inroads in France, notably in Paris, where it had caught the public's fancy. French beer, on the other hand, could not tolerate being exported. He published the results of his studies in 1876 under the title „Études sur la bière". In this work, which rapidly became the brewer's bible – it was not by chance that both J.C. and Carl Jacobsen had their portraits painted with Pasteur's book lying before them – the author demonstrated very convincingly that the yeast then in use for the production of beer, wine, alcohol and bread contained impurities in the form of vinegar and milk, various forms of mould and fungi, green penicillium and various types of wild yeast.

Pasteur gave particulars of a purification procedure which favoured the growth of the desired yeast. The treatment of a culture with tartaric acid and alcohol reduced the bacterial flora, which preferred basic conditions. He also discovered that top yeast in such a tartaric acid solution was killed at 50 degrees Celsius, and this fact could be exploited to determine whether a culture of top yeast was pure or not.

Jacobsen had always experimented with the processes in his efforts to control the various phases of beer-brewing. There is a direct line of descent from his experiments with bottom fermentation in Brolæggerstræde to his interest in the mysteries of fermentation during the late 1860s and early 1870s. His head brewer took part as well. P.A. Vogelius carried out tests in the 1850s connected with Balling's work on the doctrine of attenuation. These brewers constituted a small forum of specialists who followed the technical literature attentively and continuously, and who checked the researchers' reports critically in their breweries.

In 1871 Jacobsen established a small laboratory at Carlsberg for his continuing experiments and for control tests. It was not a production laboratory in the modern sense – not until 1886 was one of these established – but accommodation fitted out with the necessary equipment. The following year, on the recommendation of Professor Barfoed, whom he frequently consulted, he engaged G.S. Faye, a graduate in chemistry, to assist him. It was difficult for Jacobsen to find the time to deal with everything himself. Only a year later, however, Faye secured a post at the botanical gardens in Paris, and Jacobsen did not appoint a successor immediately.

For it was now clear to him that if he was going to get anywhere at all, he must put his studies on a more systematic basis. He was acquainted from his travels with several foreign laboratories and experimental stations in brewery technique, but the work being conducted in Munich, for example, did not satisfy his need to dig more deeply into the problems. He also had a hunch that developments in the field of zymotechnology were about to accelerate. If he wanted to be involved in them – and the inquisitiveness which had always driven him was nudging him on – there would have to be some mechanism by which interaction between zymotechnological science and brewery could be secured. What was required was a more solid organisation. He grasped the point that industrialists could not be serviced by public institutions of learning: the latter could not permit themselves such specialisation. He likewise understood that research was time-consuming and demanded an environment in which it was possible to concentrate on problems undistracted by the daily routines of practical work. Finally, he realised that the research carried out must be so rewarded that its practitioners would be independent of other earnings.

On 1 May 1875, acting on Barfoed's advice, Jacobsen engaged the services of J. Kjeldahl, a technical graduate and Barfoed's assistant at the laboratory of the Royal Veterinary and Agricultural College. Kjeldahl was employed expressly in order to assume a managerial position in a new, larger laboratory for zymotechnological work which Jacobsen intended to open in the near future and of which for the time being he regarded himself as the head. In that same autumn Kjeldahl made a start on the fitting out of his department. The plan was to establish a laboratory with two departments: a chemistry department, of which Kjeldahl was to be head, and a physiology department, of which Rasmus Pedersen, a graduate in medicine, was appointed head on 1 July the following year.

Jacobsen had not only consulted Barfoed but had also discussed his plans in conversations with his friend Japetus Steenstrup. The pattern which finally crystallised from these discussions comprised a laboratory placed under the aegis of the Royal Danish Academy of Sciences and Letters and having in addition a special department, independent of the laboratory, to promote science in general in the fields of interest covered by the Academy.

By the turn of the year 1875/76 matters had advanced to the point where Jacobsen revealed his plan to the „friend of his heart" – Johanne Luise Heiberg. He sent her a note on 9 January ending with the words: „Moreover I shall ask you – as of course I forgot to do today – not to mention the projected establishment of a scientific institute, because it will not be possible to submit the plan for it to the Royal

Academy of Sciences and Letters for some time."

Jacobsen was prepared to finance the project in such a way as to put it on a permanent footing. His only condition was that the Academy should agree never to separate the laboratory from his brewery. He brought in his legal adviser, supreme court advocate Gustav Brock, to formulate a practical deed of gift to the Academy and the necessary statutes. The name of the laboratory was to be the Carlsberg Laboratory, and the scientific institute or trust he called „The Carlsberg Foundation".

Once everything was in place he initiated the venerable president of the Academy, the 72 year-old J.N. Madvig, into the scheme. In a letter to Steenstrup dated 17 September, Jacobsen describes his first conversation with Madvig thus:

„I had a visit the other day from Madvig, who was very satisfied with the plan as far as he knew it. His only real misgivings concerned the relationship between the laboratory and the brewery when these should fall into other hands sometime in the future. I fully agreed with him about this, but told him that the difficulty would disappear when I bequeathed the entire brewery to the Carlsberg Foundation on my death, as I intended to do. He was very pleased at this news; I told him that you knew this to be my intention but that I had asked you not to say anything about it."

Jacobsen's ideas with regard to the brewery's future were maturing during these years, when his relationship with his son was coming to a head. Madvig's hesitations were understandable enough in a way. The Brewer's deed of gift stipulated that the laboratory was never to be separated from the Carlsberg property. The problem might be solved in the manner outlined by Jacobsen, viz. through the Carlsberg Foundation's ultimately taking over the brewery – but to Madvig this only created a new and much bigger problem. Would a scientific foundation be able to cope with the practical task of being a brewery proprietor? For the moment, however, he could push the problem to one side and console himself with the reflection that this responsibility would not fall on the Academy but on the board of an independent foundation. The Academy had no responsibility for dispositions made by the foundation.

In the same month, on 27 September, Jacobsen sent the Academy his deed of gift along with the charter and statutes. These were accompanied by a covering letter asking the Academy to accept the gift. In this letter he mentioned his personal relationship to H.C. Ørsted from the time of his youth. His gift was a tribute to Ørsted's work of enlightenment. He hoped that his new institution would be sustained by the spirit and suffused by the light emanating from the sciences generally, „and since this light has been a source of happiness and well-being for me, my heart feels it to be some repayment of my debt if I also make a contribution to the advancement of science as a whole".

The documents specify that the Carlsberg Foundation firstly shall continue and extend the activities of the Carlsberg Laboratory established by Jacobsen in 1875, and secondly shall foster the various natural sciences along with mathematics, philosophy, history and philology. The financial footing is provided by Jacobsen's donating to the Foundation a capital sum of one million kroner secured by a mortgage on the Carlsberg property at Valby. The capital is to yield interest at the rate of 5% per annum, but the full rate of interest is not to be paid to the Foundation until the decease of Jacobsen and his wife; until then the Foundation will receive 2% per annum in two half-yearly instalments. The income is to be used primarily to defray the cost of running the Laboratory, any surplus being applied to the other purposes. The Foundation is to be governed by a board of directors consisting of 5 members elected by the Royal Danish Academy of Sciences and Letters from its own ranks. The board is to direct the activities of the Foundation, manage its finances, draw up budgets and allocate funds as well as to compile a report on these matters once a year to be presented to the Academy, accompanied by an income and expenditure account and balance sheet. Jacobsen wishes the Foundation to be assured of continuity of management, as he calls it. He proposes that election to the board of directors should be for 10 years, re-election being permitted. He also wishes the status of the Foundation to be as independent as possible. This indeed is the reason for bringing the Academy of Sciences and Letters into the picture as being in his eyes the only institution in the fortunate position of standing independently of extraneous, non-scientific concerns and influences. In addition, the Foundation's board of directors are to have control over the statutes in the future, inasmuch as these may be altered only by a unanimous vote of the directors approved by the Academy.

The statutes spell out the Laboratory's tasks in great detail. The study of the processes of malting, brewing and fermentation constitutes the main item. Two laboratory heads of professorial status are to be in charge of the work, and it is emphasised that the Laboratory is to function as a scientific institution, not as a school of brewery or an establishment for teaching students. The laboratory heads are accordingly permitted to develop their abilities by undertaking other tasks as well. For example, they are to keep abreast of research in other countries by travelling. The Laboratory is to make its activities known abroad as a testimony that Denmark „is taking an honourable part in scientific progress". Indeed, research findings are to be published in both Danish and foreign journals. No result of the activities of the Laboratory which is of practical or theoretical value may be kept secret. Overall responsibility for the Laboratory is placed in the hands of a governing body consisting of the three scientific members of the Carlsberg Foundation and one or two adjunct members with brewery or laboratory expertise nominated by the Academy from outside its own ranks.

The statutes contain a number of provisions specifying the Foundation's obligations towards science and letters generally, of which the following may be cited: the awarding of travel grants to older scientists and scholars for visits abroad of longer or shorter duration; temporary honoraria for younger scientists desirous of qualifying for a subsequent career in the public service, stipends for exceptionally eminent researchers to enable them to work as free scientists independently of any public appointment. The circle of recipients is to be wide, both members and non-members of the Academy being eligible for consideration.

As we have already noted, Jacobsen's letter to Madvig acknowledged his debt to Ørsted. On the same day as the deed of gift was promulgated, a statue of the physicist, to the cost of which Jacobsen had contributed, was unveiled at a commemorative ceremony held in the Ørsted Park. The Carlsberg Foundation was to stand similarly as a monument and testimony to the brewer's appreciation of Ørsted and the latter's seminal influence. Thus, the day for promulgation of the charter, statutes and deed of gift had been selected with care.

The Royal Danish Academy of Sciences and Letters accepted the gift unanimously at its meeting of 29 September. The charter and deed of gift received the royal assent on 18 October, and on 27 October of the same year the Academy appointed the Foundation's first board of directors. It consisted of the philologist J.N. Madvig as chairman, the historian Edvard Holm, the physiologist P.L. Panum, the zoologist Japetus Steenstrup and the chemist C.T. Barfoed. Thus two of Jacobsen's close friends came on to the first board of the Foundation. The members of the board of trustees of the Carlsberg Laboratory were appointed soon afterwards. Those selected were the three scientific members of the Foundation plus the two adjunct members: the Academy nominated Jacobsen himself and Kogsbølle to fill the latter positions.

At the beginning of October Jacobsen received word confidentially that the King intended to pay him a visit at Carlsberg. „I am therefore compelled to be at home and to be properly attired in my everyday clothes, but am not in a position to take part in the work," he wrote to Japetus Steenstrup when sending him some corrections of the text of the Foundation's statutes, which were in course of being printed. He regarded the visit as a sort of compensation for the King's being unable to „make me anything" (i.e. award him an honour) and wanting to get out of it „with this bargain".

After a couple of days of waiting in vain for the royal guest, Christian IX turned up one Tuesday afternoon, in civilian attire and accompanied by an adjutant. He came in his capacity as patron of the Royal Danish Academy of Sciences and Letters and thanked Jacobsen for the establishment of the Carlsberg Foundation. He did this in „a straightforward, friendly manner ... after having conversed with me about the size of my brewery, about exports to China etc., about my art collection etc., about Fredriksborg and so on, I begged leave to present my family to him, with whom he then spent some time, after which I showed him the conservatory, the terrace, the bowery walk and Pompeii. Then we returned to the rooms, where he took his leave after a short conversation with my ladies. Since he did not ask about the laboratory or the brewery establishment, I made no move for him to visit them." A little disappointing, this, for Jacobsen liked nothing better than to show off his brewery and the new laboratory. Mrs Heiberg and her daughters had been given the complete tour when they paid a visit earlier in the year.

His Majesty made his farewell. „At his departure I took the opportunity – which I had almost forgotten – of begging a favour, viz. to be allowed to hoist a swallow-tailed flag at Carlsberg, which he granted in the most flattering terms as a special grace, and some moments later, while he was still within sight of the brewery, the flag was raised," relates Jacobsen of the visit in another letter to his friend Japetus. The entire episode lasted three quarters of an hour.

The Carlsberg Foundation set the seal on the impressive record of Jacobsen's patronage. Two years later he added a third dimension by placing the newly-established Museum of National History at Frederiksborg under the Foundation's umbrella and securing the Foundation's finances with further donations. Both Foundation and Laboratory rapidly became known outside Denmark and helped to reinforce respect for the name and activities of the Brewer.

In the historical context, the establishment of a foundation and a laboratory is unusual. The Carlsberg Foundation's status is unique, in the literal sense of the word, among foundations and trusts. The Foundation was launched very early on, between a quarter and half a century before the great foundation-creating era began in earnest in the rest of the world. As regards the Laboratory, this formed one of the nineteenth century's rare exceptions where an entrepreneur deliberately invested in research, employing his own researchers in order to acquire insight into the scientific basis of the production processes and in this way drawing practical utility from the new knowledge for the benefit of his firm.

Today it is quite natural. We all consider it imperative that part of the production effort should be earmarked for research having regard to the appropriate utilisation of resources, innovation, planning, coordination, product development, quality control and so forth, both on the macro and on the micro plane. In this context we often speak of basic or pure research aiming at the acquisition of new knowledge without any specific use for it in view, and research, which seeks new knowledge for a particular purpose. Both these elements have their place in the programme framed by Jacobsen and his advisers for the Carlsberg Laboratory and set forth in the statutes in 1876. In retrospect, the statutes and the laboratory concept were farsighted. The Carlsberg Laboratory is still active today as the nucleus of a great research centre, and its statutes are still in force. Jacobsen's overall design, including the Foundation and its activities, has stood the test of time.

Pasteur had been the vital inspiration for the establishment of the Carlsberg Laboratory. Shortly after it came into existence Jacobsen set about acquiring a work of art to honour and commemorate Pasteur. He had originally had it in mind for Léon Bonnat to paint the French scientist's portrait, but when he learned that Bonnat's fee for such a work was 30,000 francs he abandoned the idea and decided on a bust instead. He chose the French sculptor Paul Dubois and obtained Pasteur's consent to the project. The bust was subsequently mounted in the Laboratory's new building. However, Jacobsen could not quite get Bonnat out of his head. Before he died he managed to get the French artist to paint a portrait of Pasteur with his grandchild beside him. This picture hangs today in the Pasteur Institute in Paris.

The fire

The night was just like any other, filled with the routines of work. The brewing season had ended on 4 April, and the men had been busy on cleaning duties for the past couple of days. Everything had been washed and polished and was now spotlessly clean. At knocking-off time they threw their wet and dirty clothing into the warm loft above the steam boiler and went home. At one o'clock in the morning the duty maltster, Mario, started turning over the malt kilns. At a little after half past three the draymen arrived from their homes in Valby. They passed through the brewery and went down to the storage cellar, where they started preparing to barrel the casks, the orders for 6 April 1867, ready for driving out to the customers in town during the morning.

Suddenly at four o'clock Mario noticed smoke. He traced it to the boiler and engine shop and discovered that a fire had broken out. He summoned the rest of the men, who at once awakened Kogsbølle in his living quarters adjacent to the brewery office. One of the workers ran down the hill to the main building and shouted for Jacobsen.

Kogsbølle rushed up to the loft above the mill to open the fire hydrant, but the smoke was so thick that he was unable to reach the water tank.

Jacobsen could see from his house in the half-darkness of dawn a great column of smoke billowing from the roof along the entire length of the brewery wing, and as he hurried to the brewery an intense glare from the window of the loft above the steam boiler assaulted his eyes. He dashed into the engine shop to get the steam engine and its water-pump into action. There was still some pressure in the boiler and it proved possible to raise this quickly, but the planking of the loft was already ablaze and huge flaming fragments were raining down on the machinery, which Jacobsen found impossible to start. However, he did manage to lift the safety valve and open a test cock on the boiler and an intermediate cock on the water pipe, so enabling him to make use of the water pressure from the upper tank.

He aimed a jet of water into the burning loft through the east window while ordering the men with the brewery's fire engine over to the west side, whence they were able to direct another jet through the opposite window. A few moments later a mass of roofing tiles crashed around his ears; he ducked, and then when he looked up again a great gout of flame shot upwards through the roof directly above the staircase of the mill.

At this point Jacobsen realised that all hope of nipping the fire in the bud had gone.

Meanwhile Kogsbølle had got steam up in the tubular boiler in the garden grounds, and the pumps began working. At first they played water directly on to the fire, then they supplied it to the two large fire engines which had arrived from Copenhagen and Valby and were parked in the inner yard. In this fashion they managed to save both of the brewery's warehouses with their wooden cornices and – more important – their stocks of lager beer. The cellars were full, and the market was thus assured of supplies for the summer.

When Jacobsen saw that the fire was spreading to both sides of the roof, he made an attempt to fight it from the corn store, but neither from the upper loft of the latter nor from the next one could he get in for the smoke. When he went back through the first chamber of the malt house he discovered that the fire had begun creeping down by the office stairs on the second floor. He ordered some men up with fire buckets to save the staircase. This likewise failed. The fire raced through the stair well and set the ground floor alight. Kogsbølle managed to save only a part of his belongings from his rooms. By about 7 o'clock the entire complex of buildings was a single sea of flame. One hour later, everything had burnt down.

The fire got into the huge stockpiles of malt, some 5000 or 6000 barrels in all. The burning malt ran down the steps to the storage cellars. The wooden walls enclosing the steps caught fire, and the malt was able to run freely into cellars A and B, where 8 fermentation vats with their supports were consumed. The actual cellar vaults, on the other hand, were undamaged. The malt went on burning all that day, all the following night and on into the next day before it was finally quenched.

The brewery premises were vaulted with very flat arches, only 1/2 a cobble in thickness and of English perforated stone. These were found to have withstood both the fire raging above them and the pressure from fallen joists and beams. These arches saved all the equipment and machinery in the brewery premises. The vaulted chambers in the kilns did the same and were in serviceable condition after the fire.

Some of the outer walls, such as those of the two cooling houses and the corn store, remained standing. All that remained of the malt house was the cellar walls up to ground level. The rest of the masonry had to be demolished. The stabling and Jacobsen's own dwelling-house were untouched by the fire. The fire was thought to have started by spontaneous combustion in a sack of cotton waste used for cleaning machinery, or else through the workmen's dirty clothing catching fire in the warm loft. It may have been caused by a forgotten pipe, a cigar butt or a „friction stick", so called, an old-fashioned type of match officially banned at the brewery, where only Swedish safety matches were issued to the workers. Further than this Jacobsen could not get with his investigation.

Early in the afternoon Jacobsen sat down at his desk and wrote an account of the accident to Carl. „I shall suffer a considerable loss from this fire, since the new corn store and all the new iron water tanks, steeping tanks etc. were uninsured, but I can stand this loss, heavy as it is. I am completely composed and in good heart. My presence of mind has not deserted me for an instant. I do not wish you to make the slightest alteration in your travel plans but ask you to continue your activities as though nothing had happened. Your mother is extremely well after being reassured about my having been exposed to some danger in the hours following the fire, though not very much in fact." Jacobsen felt that his energies would measure up to the strain. „Intense activity always has an animating effect on me and increases my resilience."

Jacobsen asked his son, who at this time was in Paris en route for Marseilles, to remain in the city and lend assistance by expediting a number of orders which he was in process of placing for materials for the rebuilding. On the very day that the brewery burned down he was giving orders to Kayser the master carpenter to rebuild the corn store, the masonry of which was largely intact. Over the next two days he pondered the question of how much fireproof construction to use in rebuilding the devastated plant, with French iron girders, brick floors and lofts. He decided to employ this construction everywhere and to construct all roofs exclusively of iron, apart from the corn store, the girders and roof of which would be replicas of the old.

The orders went off one by one. On 8 April Dupont & Dreyfus in Paris received orders for all the iron girders for the malt house; by 20 April Jacobsen had detailed plans ready for the other buildings, and orders were placed with the firm accordingly. Finally, the order for iron girders and rafters was despatched on 9 May. The deliveries were accomplished very promptly, the first consignment leaving the French ironworks as early as 28 April and arriving on 11 May though it could not be cleared until three days later because of an unseasonal snowstorm. Screws and angles were prepared beforehand from models. The laying of the first tier of girders over the malt cellar was already put in hand on 16 May.

At the same time the clearing of broken masonry, scrap and rubble was nearly completed, and excavation of the cisterns and various foundations had reached the stage where it was possible to make a start on the brickwork. Jacobsen divided the laying of girders between the firms of Burmeister (malt house) and Hüttemeier (brewery and cooling house wings).

Jacobsen had seen the iron construction with brick floors in Paris and elsewhere during his travels in France in 1865. He ordered French hollow bricks to be sent by steamer. The building procedure was to make the floor as soon as the girders had been laid, thus „closing" the storey. At the same time as the next storey was being built, machinery, fixtures and fittings etc. were brought into the covered storey and the workspace was made ready. Not even two strikes by the journeymen bricklayers or a very rainy month of July caused any serious hitches in the tight schedule which Jacobsen had worked out in close collaboration with Kogsbølle. It was true that the bricklayers' strikes meant that in the case of the malt house the floors could not be laid until the entire iron framework, including the roof girders, had been got into place. Because of the rain Jacobsen decided to begin here by laying the top floor, which he covered with a thick plastered layer of Portland cement under whose protection completion of the floors beneath could proceed „dry-shod" and undisturbed. „Somewhat daring" was his own comment on this extraordinary procedure. But it worked. Nevertheless the ground floor was not finished in time to dry out sufficiently for Kogsbølle to live there during the winter.

The rebuilt plant could boast another innovation. During his sojourn in France Jacobsen had become a sworn devotee of steam boiling, and in order to apply steam boiling to the maximum extent he needed a third steam boiler. So as to concentrate all the hearths at the malt kilns, the brew-house and the drying chambers had to be moved, which involved extra work and put a strain on the timetable. But this operation succeeded as well. The target he had set himself was to be ready for the new brewing season on 1 September, his be-all and end-all being to avert any interruption of his deliveries. On that very day he carried out the first brewing at the new Carlsberg and – as he wrote in his journal – „the brewing went along undisturbed ever after". It sounds almost like the end of a fairy tale.

The brewing went on, while the finishing work on the roof proceeded towards the gradual completion of its covering of tiles. This took until the end of September. The topping-out ceremony was held under the roof on 28 September.

„Even before the fire was properly extinguished, this energetic man was standing at the drawing-board sketching out designs for all the new plant, as though by the light of the flames." Thus was the drama depicted by the sculptor Th. Stein in his memoirs. And indeed the rebuilding of Carlsberg in 1867 forms a cogent example of the inner resources Jacobsen could draw on in extremity.

He had a fair inkling of this himself. In the days immediately after the fire there were many who visited Carlsberg to demonstrate their sympathy, friends and acquaintances with whom Jacobsen worked in his public and business life. He appreciated these visits. „What pleased me most about them was the faith they showed in my steadfastness and energy, which I really feel to be stronger than ever before." He noticed but little in the way of fatigue, and in a letter to his son assured him that he was sleeping soundly at night.

It is of a piece with all this that Jacobsen and Kogsbølle did not rest on their oars but in September 1867 formed the decision to resume the task, suspended after the fire, of fitting out the last storage cellars (nos. 17 and 18) with ice-containers along with a cooper's shop and tar room. J. Larsen was contracted to reopen the abandoned excavations. The spoil was used to make the ornamental „hills" in the northern section of Jacobsen's garden layout. Cement foundations were laid and a start was made on the masonry work until frost forced a stop. In 1868 an underground cellar was specially made for the experiments with top-fermented beer. In addition an underground passageway was constructed from the fermenting cellar to the southern ware-house, and here the so-called fermenting cellar E was established „in order to conduct fermentation slowly and in cool conditions, in the Schwekat manner". The decision is yet another proof of the priority which Jacobsen accorded to product development even in difficult times. He noted in his diary: „With this, the plant is complete, and the brewery at Carlsberg is thereby considered to be finished." But such did not prove to be the case. J.C. Jacobsen never did finish building his Carlsberg.

The estrangement

J.C. Jacobsen's fundamental approach to his business was that the brewery ought not to be too large for him – or his works manager – to be able to oversee and personally direct operations. This was the only way in which the responsibility for a high level of quality could be fixed and unambiguously placed. He regarded the Carlsberg which he had erected after the fire of 1867 as a finished and complete establishment. In the following year he took Erhardt Kogsbølle into partnership. For his son he built an independent brewery, the Annexe brewery alongside Carlsberg. It was ready in 1871, and Carl took it over as tenant, without any real agreement being made on detailed terms. No proper tenancy contract was established between them; everything depended on a word-of-mouth agreement, and Carl managed the new brewery for his own account except for new investments in fixed plant. A study had been made of the market before the plant was built. The conclusion was that there was no room in Copenhagen for more Bavarian beer breweries; Jacobsen advised Carl instead to work up the production of improved top-fermented English-type beers in his brand-new plant, partly for the home market and partly for export.

The prognosis was made under the impress of the recession in the second half of the 1860s. In the event it did not hold good. On the contrary, a boom gathered momentum in the early 1870s and in a few short years completely altered the structure of the brewery industry, first in Copenhagen and then in the provinces. Both consumption and production rose very steeply during the next twenty years concurrently with a swing of consumption away from ale and towards Bavarian beer. In the ten years from 1871 to 1881 production of Bavarian beer in the Danish capital rose from 71,000 to over 300,000 barrels per annum, and the share of the total market taken by this beer exploded from less than a third to over a half. Bavarian beer continued its advance in the 1880s, though at a more controlled pace, from about 332,000 barrels in 1881 to about 426,000 in 1887, when a temporary

The fire at Carlsberg, 6 April 1867. Contemporary drawing by P. Hauberg.

J. C. Jacobsen's first export advertisement for Carlsberg beer and English beer types, 1870.

The New Carlsberg Brewery, 1884. Carl Jacobsen's residence, Bakke-gaarden, can be seen at the extreme right.

Frederiksborg rises again. Drawing by A. Schovelin, 1861.

saturation point was reached on the Copenhagen market.

The growing sales of Bavarian beer to the inhabitants of Copen-hagen and the flagging market conditions for the top-fermented types created disquiet among the large, old ale breweries, the biggest of which had been fitted out as modern steam-beer breweries during the 1860s. Rabeshave on Langebrogade at Christianshavns Vold, and A. Vogelius' brewery in Rahbeks Allé, which J.C. Jacobsen had helped him to construct, were examples. These felt themselves compelled to go in for producing Bavarian beer. Over a period of only four years, from 1879 to 1882, Marstrand, Tvede, Rabeshave, Vogelius, Ravns-borg and finally the King's Brew-House started up this production. By virtue of these massive new investments an over-capacity was created in the branch that brought a return to exceedingly keen competition once more.

The background to this switch from cheap ale to expensive Bavarian beer was, as noted, rapid population growth and higher wages result-ing in new patterns of consumption, of which one element was that the people of Copenhagen acquired the habit of a daily consumption of Bavarian beer. Producers had great difficulty in satisfying this strongly rising demand during the 1870s. The Tuborg factories built around the newly-established harbour at Hellerup not only manufac-tured fertilisers and phosphates but also included an export-beer brewery designed to sell strong bottled beer to countries overseas. It had been thought at the time the brewery was built that there was no room for a Bavarian beer brewery alongside the Carlsberg breweries; but Tuborg too had considerably underestimated the vigour of the Bavarian beer boom. By the spring of 1876 it was clear to the Tuborg management that the strategy must be revised. They turned away from a loss-making export business and looked to the home market, where the future lay. Production was converted to lager beer of the Carlsberg type in cask, and sales trebled from 10,000 barrels in 1876 to 27,000 in 1877. This made the business profitable at a stroke.

J.C. Jacobsen had his problems in coping with this surprisingly heavy pressure of demand. He endeavoured to exercise a restraining influence after having transferred entire categories of customer – first his provincial customers, then the Copenhagen suburbs – to his son, who had given up the improved English beers in favour of lager beer early in 1871. Jacobsen also tried to ration his deliveries to the beer-bottlers, which meant that in reality he was helping to tempt others to fill the vacuum thus created. Finally, he sought by every means to increase his production within the given framework. He established new storage cellars. He installed new improved coppers and later started up an entirely new boiler house. He added an extra malt house and increased the height of the old warehouse by an extra storey, along with many other measures.

In 1879 Jacobsen converted the oldest malt house to pneumatic malting, which sent production shooting up from 80 to 120 barrels of barley per day, and in the same year two Linde cooling apparatuses were installed at Carlsberg. As we have seen, the cooling of the storage cellars had long preoccupied the thoughts of the brewery industry. The system of ice cellars was capricious. It was vulnerable not only in very hot summers but also in mild winters, when home supplies of natural ice could fail and imports of expensive ice, from Norway for example, become necessary. Jacobsen experienced this himself in the mild winter of 1874, when Norwegian ice became an article of speculation. In June 1873 Dr Carl von Linde gave a lecture at the brewery congress in Vienna held in conjunction with the world exhibition in that city. Jacobsen, who had a seat on the praesidium of the congress, was deeply engrossed by it. „At the congress on Thursday morning we first heard an interesting introductory lecture by Dr Linde on the principles of manufacturing artificial ice, after which Windhausen gave a long and boring lecture which drove most of the audience away, and continuation of the discussion was then postponed until next day," he relates in a letter to Carl.

There were several competing cooling systems on the drawing board, but Sedlmayr invited Linde to design an experimental machine for him in Munich. It was ready two years later and looked promising. The following year, in 1876, Linde extended the application of his machine by using it for cooling the fermenting cellar at Anton Dreher's brewery in Trieste. Linde received an order for his system from Feltmann, the Rotterdam brewer. Jacobsen himself waited until he was able to study the various types of cooling apparatus and see them in action at the Paris exhibition in 1878. Here he took his final decision and chose Linde's system. The cooling plant took up a lot of space;

the big machines had to be installed in the closest possible proximity to the fermenting cellars, which involved much rebuilding. The coppers for Carlsberg's new steam-boiler plant were brought from abroad as well – in fact from the same exhibition – and were installed at the same time. But the new pneumatic malt house had the advantage of taking up only a quarter of the space occupied by the old one; this saving of space was utilised for new malt storehouses.

With the aid of these and other measures of modernisation J.C. Jacobsen was able to push his production to the heights. His output at the end of the 1860s was between 25,000 and 27,000 barrels annually, reaching 31,000 barrels in 1870/71 and 46,000 in 1872/73; in 1874/75 it was up to 58,000 barrels and in 1876/77 to 71,000, and by the end of the decade it passed the 80,000 mark to reach over 93,000 in 1881/82. He could not now go any further with the then available space and infrastructure.

When he had got his last storage cellars ready, he felt for a short time that he could „breathe freely" again. Now he could give his beer the storage time that he wanted, and he established an unbreakable rule that Carlsberg beer must never be sold at less than this storage norm. This landed him in a new dilemma, however, which he tried to escape from by refusing to accept new customers while at the same time putting his draymen under stricter supervision; they were not allowed to sell to anyone outside the old-established circle of customers without his knowledge. During the winter of 1880, however, demand from these established customers broke the bounds of his production again, and his answer was to dismiss customers and ration his deliveries. This did not make him popular with the beer-bottlers, but Jacobsen was inflexible and got through the rest of the year. History repeated itself the following winter. He tried to weather the storm by brewing on Sundays, but in the spring he had to dismiss customers again. In addition he prolonged the brewing season into the warmer weather by three weeks.

Whereas Jacobsen felt that the advance towards large-scale operations in the brewery industry threatened the maintenance of quality in the overheated business conditions of the late 1870s, his son did not have the same qualms. He stored his beer more briefly, without in his own eyes doing any harm to the quality, and Carl was thus able to push his plant's productive capacity to the skies. Where his father reckoned 40,000 barrels of storage space for annual sales of double that amount, Carl, with a storage cellar capacity of only 14,000 barrels, had driven his annual turnover up to more than 100,000 barrels in the course of the decade. He had surpassed his father's sales at the beginning of the 1880s and was marketing under the Carlsberg name lager beer which J.C. Jacobsen refused to acknowledge. The father's unshakable conviction was that an expansion of production could not be accomplished by a reduction of storage time, which could only risk losing the product's place as the industry's leading brand. He cited for example the unpleasant experience Tuborg had had at the end of the 1870s from selling inadequately stored beer. Similarly, several of the ale breweries whose „conversion" to Bavarian beer had only been halfheartedly done dumped second-rate products on the market and harmed the reputation of lager beer.

Father and son were in deep disagreement. Jacobsen Senior had no feeling for marketing. For example, when he was offered the chance of either a part share or outright purchase of the „Alliance" bottling and exporting business, he declined with the remark that „a commercial business such as this is something for which I have neither the aptitude nor the desire, and which I should therefore be unable to manage properly". On the other hand, however, it was not for nothing that Jacobsen Junior had spent some of his years of training in England, where he had become familiar with both the power of advertising and the tied house system. The breweries sold the bulk of their production via public houses and hotels which they owned themselves. And the method of promotions and special offers had got into his blood. While in Strasbourg with the Hatt family he had observed the popularity of the lighter short-storage types of lager beer, but his father rejected them with the words: „I do not approve of the way they have started delivering half-stored beer all the year round in many places in Germany and in Strasbourg, for by so doing you accustom the public to be satisfied with what is cheaper and less good, and once on that slippery slope there is no stopping until you get to the cheapest and worst, which is the very new, rough beer that is brewed today and drunk the day after tomorrow." He remembered the days of the brewery industry's great slump, which had formed the background to his own life's work. It was the Bavarian method that had restored the reputation of beer, and this was not to be put in jeopardy now.

Despite all his exertions, J.C. found himself in a cleft stick. His customers' demands on him were more than he could honour. His son was striving energetically to occupy the ground which the father was losing by his restraint. What Carl wanted, as he put it, was to use the materials at his disposal „commensurately with the requirements of the manufacture and the business in order to ensure the best possible conditions for a good beer". Set this against the objects clause drafted by his father for the statutes of the Carlsberg Foundation – „regardless of immediate profit, to develop the art of making beer to the highest possible degree of perfection" – and two diametrically opposed business approaches are in stark confrontation.

There was another aspect that disturbed the father. His son was also beginning to show himself a chip off the old block by encroaching on J.C.'s territory as a patron of the arts, with donations to the Academy of Art for the purchase of sculptures, with the establishment of the „Albertina" trust in 1879 for acquiring classical sculptures to be placed in public institutions, and with private purchases including modern French works, which were not to the old man's taste.

The sales situation demanded that the Brewer should keep pace with the market and supply his product so as to reap the maximum benefit from the uniquely favourable business conditions. But the Brewer for his part would not deviate from his standard, and moreover he was obsessed with the *idé fixe* that his establishment ought not to be made any larger than he could manage personally – a not uncommon idea, indeed, among other founders of firms. However, Jacobsen was in course of adjusting himself to the idea that he must eat his own words. It was a hard decision. After a period of „much doubt and deliberation and sleeplessness" he brought himself to recognise „that the irresistible march of events, despite all my obstinacy and resistance going beyond the limits of what is sensible – indeed even acceptable", made an enlargement of his brewery „an inescapable necessity". He was, he wrote in a letter to Michael Lunn in July 1881, „in the strictest sense of the word a helpless tool" of market forces. But he was also a victim of his own ambition to be the top man of his calling, not only in terms of technology and product development but also as market leader in Copenhagen.

The most obvious thing to do, of course, was to bring the Annexe brewery under his own management and production, letting his son start up on his own – all the more so because Jacobsen, thanks to his huge donations and large-scale new investment at Old Carlsberg, found himself in a tight situation as regards liquidity. Jacobsen had defrayed the cost of building the Annexe brewery, and of expanding it during the 1870s, out of his own funds; in fact he owned it, but his son ran it and had made a lot of money out of it because he had got it on specially favourable family terms. Carl had taken it over at 30 years of age and in ten years had made himself a fortune worthy of a patron of the arts. Precisely because the agreement between father and son had been so loose and imprecise, Carl quickly identified himself with New Carlsberg, as the Annexe was called in day-to-day parlance. There still remained a relationship of dependence between them inasmuch as all enlargements of the Annexe brewery were dependent on the father's sanction; and too late J.C. realised that on his son's return from abroad he ought to have furnished him with the funds and let him try his strength and talents completely on his own.

J.C.'s temporising attitude to expansion at New Carlsberg, which was also dictated by the cautious entrepreneur's awareness that he might land in a situation of excess capacity, irritated his son exceedingly. Neither of them had the other's confidence: they did not discuss their day-to-day business affairs with each another. It was therefore easy for Carl to have his fling in the sales boom with a product which was swept along by the Carlsberg name but was not lager beer of the original quality. The father's old mistrust of his son flared up. The problem was not only to sever the link with Carl but also to find a solution which would guarantee that Jacobsen's life's work would not fall into his son's hands after his death. The answer to that side of the question was provided by the foundation model. That left the purely personal side, the family.

There is no reason to doubt J.C. Jacobsen's love for his son even though his strategy as mentor had undeniably miscarried. In his bleaker moments he regarded his son by turns as a rich man's spoilt child or as a representative of the ungrateful younger generation that worshipped other gods than his own.

Jacobsen knew full well that his wife was on the son's side; a breach with his son would place a strain on the father in his marriage, and a strain on the mother too. Her psychosomatic disposition presented a risk that made him apprehensive. He suspected that Laura was rooted in the conviction that there was not the smallest particle of love for his son left in him. In the crisis situation that shaped itself, she acted with greater composure than might have been expected. And with respect to the daughter-in-law, Ottilia, J.C. nourished a high regard for her but was clear in his mind that she stood totally on her husband's side. This held firm. Ottilia declared to one of her friends that „there is not going to be another unhappy marriage at Carlsberg".

Finally, the clash was coloured by the diametrically opposed temperaments of father and son. Both of them made use of advisers, but with the important difference that the father instructed his advisers as to what he wanted. The son, on the other hand, had need of advice. A specially indispensable support to him was Michael Lunn, the friend of his youth, who endeavoured sedulously to steer Carl's highly impulsive temperament and many unconsidered utterances away from the injurious and into more fruitful channels. Michael would explain to Carl, for example, that he ought to keep agreements once entered into rather than seek to get round them. Lunn knew and respected both parties. He admired Jacobsen, and the latter in fact begged Lunn not to abandon Carl, who really needed his help. Lunn frequently had to tell Carl truths which were ill received, yet the friendship held for the present. When Carl for a while started dropping hints that J.C. Jacobsen was now so old that he had become absentminded and not fully in possession of his faculties, not even shrinking in moments of exasperation from describing his father as mentally deranged, his friend entreated him at last not to underestimate the old gentleman's judgment and capacity for action. On the contrary, the son might well take a lesson or two from his father: „Your father will go on running rings round you until you get some real practice in distinguishing between the essential and the inessential and in considering your chess-moves as thoroughly and surely as he does before you put them into effect. Your father understands the art of waiting when waiting will be to his advantage, and how to take a swift decision to make a sacrifice even, in cases where by sacrificing a few pieces he can improve his own position or weaken yours, so that the sacrifice becomes not a loss but a gain. Only when you have learnt that art from him will the battle perhaps begin to be dangerous for him."

The battle was fierce. At stake were both the plant itself and the Carlsberg brand name. Carl was not going to yield up voluntarily the goose which had so recently filled his basket with golden eggs. He suggested to his father that the latter could easily set himself up elsewhere, and was even cool enough to suggest the Hamburger site adjacent to Vestre Kirkegaard, the churchyard. The beer label was equally crucial, and here the son got the New Carlsberg name legally recognised. The Carlsberg Foundation, which was to inherit Jacobsen Senior's estate, tried to keep out of the family conflict but was drawn in from both sides de facto. The Foundation had difficulty in deciding where it stood, partly because the chairman, the venerable Madvig, did not comprehend very much of the underlying financial realities that fed the flames of war. The outcome was that the Captain got his way.

The move which he decided on after thorough deliberation – while Laura watched him with fearful forebodings because Jacobsen shut himself away – was a mild one. He would try to force Carl to accept long storage of the beer as a condition either of outright or partial sale to him of the Annexe brewery or of the establishment of a formal lease; with the proviso in either event that production at the Annexe brewery should be limited to 40,000 barrels of beer annually. The idea of selling was motivated by the need in 1878/79 to raise liquid capital for such purposes as extensive new investment. Jacobsen proposed to his son an agreement that would enable the latter to acquire the brewery and entire property over the course of some years. He estimated that Carl's copious income would enable him to repay the sum at which the property stood in the books over a period of three or four years. In 1878 this was reckoned to come to over 1.5 million kroner, representing J.C.'s aggregate investments in New Carlsberg. He had amassed this from his own profits and from his working capital.

If a sale agreement could not be reached, then Jacobsen was ready to raise a mortgage loan on New Carlsberg or borrow money from the Handelsbank by promissory notes or cash credit of the order of at least 600,000 kroner.

Carl became very agitated and felt that his father now wanted to disinherit him. J.C. next focused on the idea of a tenancy agreement, which as well as limiting production at the plant contained a demand for the name of the brewery and its products to be changed. Carl again refused outright, although Michael Lunn tried to make him realise that his father's terms were far from unreasonable. Juridically speaking a proprietor did have the right to impose such a requirement in a lease. „If you really feel you cannot accept this, you know, then you must go into liquidation and then either go out of the brewery business for the time being and occupy yourself in some other way or else get yourself another brewery – either by building one yourself or by buying one," he wrote on 13 October 1879 in his comments on J.C.'s draft tenancy agreement. Lunn's advice to Carl was to reconsider buying the Annexe brewery. „Suggest to your father that you buy it from him by contract of sale for the value of the plant, paying off the entire sum over 4 years. The cellaring question, i.e. the storage of the beer, does not matter so much here, because after all you have to be cautious for your own sake not to expand too much before you have seen how the beer goes under your brewery's own name. Disinheritance is a chimera, I believe, which only has any prospect of becoming a reality if you leave Carlsberg."

Carl was still not to be reasoned with. He was dissatisfied both with the limitation of production and with the change of name. His mother put pressure on him and remonstrated with him over his unbending attitude towards his father. „When you look at Ottilia and me, as a rule you show your wonderful smile, which becomes you so well, but to others you often appear very cold and impatient, it does not become you, it does not come from anything good but from an implacable disposition which is destroying all the gentleness and humility in your soul and which little by little is gaining a hard and ruthless hold over your disposition." Frants Djørup, as uncle and doctor, explained to him that the strained situation between father and son was having an upsetting effect on his mother's nervous system and ruining her health. He also tried to convince Carl that underneath his father's sternness and intransigence was concealed a tender and loving father's heart, and ended by urging upon him his duty as a son. „Towards his father a son is always in the wrong!"

The avalanche had started to roll. The family quarrel was not to be stopped, because underlying it there was a world of realities which could not be conjured away by fine words about peace of mind and filial devotion. On 27 November J.C. Jacobsen came up with a new idea: he proposed that his son should build a new brewery with his own money close by the leased brewery and run the whole enterprise as his own responsibility while at the same time leasing the Annexe brewery. Jacobsen insisted that the Annexe brewery's production should be limited and that the name of Carl's beer, both there and at the new brewery, should not be related to the Carlsberg name. Carl accepted this. In the evening they dined together at the Meldahls' but did not discuss the matter. Next morning Carl came over to his father and confirmed his acceptance. He started at once on the planning of his new plant, to be built on a site acquired from Bakkegaarden.

The idyll seemed to have been restored. Under the influence of the milder atmosphere between the parties Carl suggested that an oral agreement between father and son would suffice as far as the Annexe brewery was concerned, but on 9 February 1880 J.C. appeared at Michael Lunn's office on Købmagergade and asked for the contract to be formalised. Of this meeting Lunn wrote to Carl: „ ... as you know he is constantly revolving thoughts of his death and imagines this to be considerably nearer than we would hope it to be. Having in mind this idea that he could soon be called from us, he wishes to see all his various affairs put into complete order as far as possible."

The lease was signed that same month. The Annexe brewery was to be renamed „Albertina". The trademark was to be a red Maltese cross on a white ground, replacing the New Carlsberg swastika logo. Carl was to change the markings on his bottles and barrels during the month of April. By a later addendum to the lease, on 1 April 1881, Jacobsen Senior consented to the name „Valby Brewery" being given to the brewery establishment because Carl wanted it for his new brewery under construction on the neighbouring site. The lease was terminable at one year's notice from either side, with vacant possession on 30 September, the last day of the accounting year.

J.C. Jacobsen was in full swing making his testamentary dispositions. Even when he established the Carlsberg Foundation in 1876 he had stated that he was considering bequeathing his brewery to the Foundation at his death. A couple of months after the setting-up of the Foundation, Carl understood from a remark made by J.C. at a party at Carlsberg one Sunday that his father's decision was already taken. In a letter the next morning he expressed his great disappointment that his father had not discussed it with him beforehand: „ … this action of yours, which testifies so strongly to your civic sense, will be accompanied for me by the memory of a slight seldom inflicted on a son by his father, however small the day-to-day intimacy between their minds might be in other respects. You have certainly enhanced my view of you as an historical personality, but not in the same degree as a father." Now, three and a half years later, in a letter of 6 January 1880, J.C. Jacobsen placed the draft of a will before the Foundation and asked for the directors' comments.

Madvig, chairman of the board of directors, gave vent to his misgivings „that it could not be considered advisable to couple an institution such as the Carlsberg Foundation with ownership of real property and a specifically prescribed industrial enterprise", but with the others' help he got a grip on the idea that the very reason Jacobsen wanted the Carlsberg Foundation was as a guarantee that his firm would be carried on in accordance with his principles after his death. The board of directors grasped clearly that this was a cardinal point for the old brewer, and they complied with his wishes.

But what about the Annexe brewery, which J.C. Jacobsen also owned but which his son had just leased? To Michael Lunn's great chagrin, Carl could not refrain from trying to circumvent the agreement on the change of name. He played petty tricks with wordings and tried to create the impression that his beer was still Carlsberg beer, with the result that J.C. Jacobsen bade compromise – and patience – goodbye. On 25 July, through his lawyer, supreme court advocate Anton Klubien, he gave his son notice to quit. He wished to have disposition of the brewery himself and bring it under Carlsberg, thus also transferring it to the Carlsberg Foundation on his death. With a full year's notice and with Carl's new brewery nearing completion he knew that his son would be able to manage.

The latter, who had counted on the Annexe brewery, especially its brew-house, when fitting up his new brewery, could now see – a bare month before the topping-out – that he would have to expand in order to offset the loss of the Annexe brewery. „You speak so prettily about my gratitude as a son. You cannot bring it up any more, Johannes, for it has been drawn on so many times that it was used up long ago, and there is even a large deficit," he wrote to Johs. Steenstrup on 5 August. The disinheritance chimera raised its head again. „When my father, after having given away Old Carlsberg, now robs me of the former New Carlsberg, he is virtually disinheriting me, for whether he leaves me little money or much is only of secondary value to me, and I simply do not enquire about it." To Klubien he said: „If my father laid all the money he liked on the table, millions, it would mean nothing to me when he robs me of New Carlsberg." He and Ottilia felt that they were being evicted from their home at the Annexe brewery.

Laura reacted in unusual fashion. Without telling J.C. she visited both Klubien and Lunn in order to prevent the Annexe brewery from being taken from her son. To her mind Jacobsen's attitude on this point was sick: he saw only malice and incompetence in Carl. But the two lawyers had to tell her that only by prevailing upon the directors of the Carlsberg Foundation to decline to accept the Annexe brewery could it be secured for Carl. She then mobilised the circle of friends, appealing to Japetus Steenstrup, and to Madvig as well, to do something to keep Jacobsen's behaviour within bounds. Carl too appealed to the directors. He wrote to Madvig on the matter and ventilated the possibility of a lawsuit if the Carlsberg Foundation accepted the Annexe brewery.

The topping-out ceremony at Carl's brewery took place on Sunday, 14 August. It began at half past two in the afternoon with divine service at the brewery, then at 4 o'clock came the topping-out itself, with red wine and fancy cakes. To commemorate the day Carl had established a number of bursaries for his employees. At 5.30 there was dinner at Bakkegaarden for the master builders and suppliers. The only friends present were Lunn, the merchant Møller and Johannes Steenstrup. At Laura's instigation pastor Ewaldsen had contrived for Carl to send an invitation to his father, but J.C. did not come – he went off

to Frederiksborg – thereby demonstrating openly that the estrange-
ment between father and son was a fact. But Laura was present.

Carl protested against the notice to quit, threatened legal action and
would not move „until the bailiffs put me out of the brewery next
year". His wrath against his father found spontaneous outlets. He
sent back the gifts he had received over the years accompanied by a
letter which he forgot to copy in the heat of the moment but jotted
down on a piece of paper from memory afterwards. „Since my father's
behaviour, which is regarded by his wife as unjust and by those who
hold him dearest as deranged, cannot be an example to my children, I
consider it important that they should be reminded of his existence as
little as possible. I am therefore sending back those objects which
might particularly evoke such recollection in so far as they have not
been disposed of by other means." He refused to received the Laboratory's publications from the Carlsberg Foundation, which he vitu-
perated as a helpless tool in his father's war against him. Verbal
cannonades were followed by more tangible pranks. The son had the
gate between New and Old Carlsberg barred, so that his parents were
unable to drive to and from town by their accustomed route. The road
separating the two breweries also became an object of strife. Carl
called it „Pasteurs Vej" while his father favoured the name „Alliance
Vej". „These two crazy people are each putting up signboards bigger
than the other's down there," remarked Emil Chr. Hansen, „because
each of them is trying to cover the other's street-name. They are
making themselves objects of derision even to the workers, and the
scandal has found its way into several newspapers, even in the provinces."

At the same time as he was blowing off steam in these ways, Carl
was working unremittingly to secure the name „New Carlsberg" for
himself. He applied to the Ministry of Justice for permission to
change his name, for himself and his family, from „Carl Jacobsen" to
„Carl Jacobsen Ny Carlsberg" – Carl Jacobsen of New Carlsberg
– reflecting an ancient peasant custom as in his grandfather's name,
Chresten Jacobsen of Nørkjær. But the Ministry refused. He had
better luck in getting the name attached to his new residence. Ottilia
had prevailed on her father-in-law to accept it when the young people
called their new home at Bakkegaarden „New Carlsberg". Carl got

the name extended by a declaration on the title deed to cover all parcels of land under the Bakkegaarden estate, including the one where his own brewery was under construction. When on top of this he applied to the Ministry of Home Affairs for the name to be officially authorised, the Ministry replied to the effect that this was not necessary in view of the declaration pertaining to the land.

J.C. Jacobsen submitted objections to the Ministry in the matter, contending that by recognising the New Carlsberg name as Carl's, a property with a brewery established on it was being given the same name as his own branch brewery which had been functioning for 11 years. He contended that the name Carlsberg was indisputably his own and ought not to be allowed to be appropriated by others, even with such additions as „new", „little", „great" or the like. In fact he had never previously considered it necessary to safeguard the name given in 1847 for himself and his properties. His appeal was not upheld, however. Carl had captured the name New Carlsberg.

At the Carlsberg Foundation the mood was uneasy. Carl insisted in a letter to Madvig that the Annexe brewery was part of his inheritance which his father, by terminating the lease, was now wanting to bequeath to the Foundation. Did they really want to be involved in a lawsuit? The question tormented the board of directors. Two days later came J.C. Jacobsen's counterstroke in the shape of a letter to Professor Holm concerning the Frederiksborg Museum's financial difficulties. The Museum needed another 25,000 kroner a year for running expenses; Department B, comprising funds freely disposable for research, ought to have another 15,000; and Department A, the Laboratory, required another 10,000. He intended to donate the sum of one million kroner, representing the capitalised value of these revenues, to the Foundation on its anniversary on 25 September. The Foundation's mortgages on his property would then amount to 2.2 million kroner altogether, which was more or less equivalent to the book value of Old Carlsberg after an annual amortisation of 3% on the invested capital. Holm suggested that he should refrain from executing a deed of gift with a mortgage, but Jacobsen replied that this form was chosen precisely so that the gift which his will was to include would not be larger than he was entitled to make according to law, „without the need for anyone else's consent". Thereupon the directors resolved, at their meeting of 15 September, to express their thanks to the Captain for the gift.

Madvig, who was still nursing his misgivings at the idea of the Carlsberg Foundation's one day ending up as a brewery proprietor, came to realise after a thorough coaching that for reasons of competition, the Annexe brewery would be absorbed into Old Carlsberg; but this only aggravated his worries. At the beginning of October he sent J.C. Jacobsen a letter, extremely verbose and woolly, in which, after a solemn march-past of his array of misgivings, he concluded by suggesting to Captain Jacobsen that his son Carl ought to take over the breweries by redeeming in stages the mortgages held by the Carlsberg Foundation. He signed off the letter with his „sincerest regards" and remained „Yours very truly and respectfully, J.N. Madvig".

It seems safe to say that such a letter at such a moment missed its mark. Jacobsen was firmly resolved to make over his breweries, including the Annexe brewery, to the Carlsberg Foundation in his will, and to get his son to accept this. Failing that, he intended as an alternative to convey his breweries into the Foundation's ownership forthwith. To this end he called a conference with the Foundation's board of directors and concluded a letter to his friend Japetus Steenstrup with the words: „Since I live in constant anxiety in case something should happen to me before I have steered Carlsberg into the safest possible harbour, I earnestly desire that this matter may be settled as quickly as possible." The recognition of Carl's right to the „New Carlsberg" name had made him angry and impatient. Now he wanted the business finished with.

In his counter-move Carl tried to draw his mother into the battle. He got her signature to a declaration that read: „My mother has told my father, as well as Madvig and Steenstrup, that it was unjust to take New Carlsberg from me – but she has said that I ought to tolerate this with patience and charity. Written at my mother's dictation, 22 November 1881, C. Jacobsen Junior, and countersigned by Laura Jacobsen."

To his question whether she could really put her signature to a will which she considered unfair, she replied „that she dared not assume such a responsibility, but if it came to the point – she would go to Madvig and seek his advice". In a letter to Madvig on 1 December Carl accordingly expressed confidence that Madvig would not be a party to the basing of the Carlsberg Foundation's future on an injustice.

With this Carl had overstepped the mark. Madvig sent him a reply admonishing him in vigorous terms for having brought his mother into the affair by means of the written statement, which he begged Carl to destroy. He urged Carl to take a „cheerful, manly decision to cease all attempts at resistance, to yield to the father to whom you owe a respected name and who, by giving you a profession and working capital, laid the foundation of your wealth and well-being".

The Carlsberg Foundation insisted on Carl Jacobsen's giving his father's will his endorsement: the board did not want Carlsberg conveyed to the Foundation during Jacobsen's lifetime. At last, on 17 January 1882, the two parties signed an agreement whereby J.C. Jacobsen handed a patrimony of one third of his fortune to his son immediately – it amounted to a tidy million kroner – in return for Carl's renunciation, on behalf of himself and his descendants, of any legacy from his father. The latter for his part consented to Carl's new brewery being named „New Carlsberg" from 1 October 1882 and for as long as it was owned by his son and his descendants. Jacobsen himself would henceforth call his breweries „Old Carlsberg". Carl was enjoined to avoid possible confusion between the firms and the marking of their goods arising from the similarity of names; and finally Carl furnished the required renunciation of inheritance and engaged to furnish his written assent to his father's will, which was drafted and submitted for signature a couple of days later.

The litigation was over, but the wounds refused to heal. Bitterness sat deep in both the parties. The father closed the mirrored shutters in his dining salon so as to hide the view of his son's new brewery. Battles followed in the wake of the agreement, over Carl's labels for example, which J.C. watched carefully and felt to resemble his own so closely that confusion was possible. He instituted proceedings. Carl's export lager labels were the ones concerned, being in his father's opinion too similar to the labels for his own export beer. Since Old Carlsberg's export beer was also marketed at home this was a breach of the agreement. Carl's lawyers, Michael Lunn and Charles Shaw, took no pleasure in their task. Shaw recommended a „decent" settlement to get the matter „done with", but Michael Lunn was instruct-

Laura Jacobsen. Bust by L. Brandstrup, 1896.

◄

Aug. Jerndorff's painting of 1886 is the only portrait of J. C. Jacobsen painted from life, the year prior to the Brewer's death. Jacobsen is standing in his greenhouse at Carlsberg, known as "Pompeii". The language of symbols is speaking to us here. The microscope, flasks and Pasteur's "Études sur la bière" on the table in front of him tell the story of his implicit faith in product development through insight into the laws and processes of Nature.

Carl Bloch painted a portrait of J. C. Jacobsen in 1868. It was exhibited at Charlottenborg, but its whereabouts today are unknown.

►

The battle of the labels at Carlsberg is an episode from the infancy of trade marks. When Carl, shortly after the agreement with his father, changed his square lager beer label (top left) to the red oval (bottom left) his father sued him in the jurisdiction known as Hof- og Stadsretten, since he considered that its resemblance to his own export beer label (bottom right) could lead to confusion. The court refused to rule on the similarity of labels (a matter which fell under the jurisdiction of the police and criminal court) and acquitted Carl on the ground that each of the two labels referred to its own market, home and export respectively, each with its own beer type, thus precluding confusion in practice. To strengthen his argument before the supreme court – where the father won the case – J. C. Jacobsen inserted the announcement reproduced overleaf in order to make clear that his export beer also had a public at home.

The model for J. C. Jacobsen's export label was Scottish, viz. Wm. Younger's India Pale Ale label (top left). In a letter to his mother Carl relates that he showed his father this label in Burton-on-Trent in 1869. They agreed that it was "almost the ideal label". J. C. Jacobsen decided to adapt it, and to Carl's question about the requisite differentiation his father replied that "if the trademark and the handwriting are different, that is difference enough". The oldest surviving lager beer label with J. C. Jacobsen's signature and the beer-bottler's name printed on it is shown for further comparison (top right).

In 1885 Carl registered a lager beer label at the Trade Marks Office (bottom left). It complied with the stipulation in the agreement that he must only use the "New Carlsberg" name and his trade mark – the swastika – on the label, but not his own name nor that of his firm. The breweries abandoned the swastika as a trade mark when the Nazis subsequently adopted it on their flags.

In 1904 Carl commissioned the artist Thorvald Bindesbøll to design the now-classic Carlsberg Hof label for the new "pilsner" beer which was now in process of conquering the market (bottom right).

Old Carlsberg 1887. When J. C. Jacobsen died the surroundings of Old Carlsberg were still rural. Ad. Kittendorff painted a water-colour in that

year from where the West Prison is now situated.

The French sculptor Paul Dubois' bust of Louis Pasteur. As a thank-you for the honour Pasteur dedicated his dissertation "Examen critique d'un écrit posthume de Claude Bernard sur la fermentation", Paris 1879, to Jacobsen.

ed to fight on at all costs. The supreme court handed down its verdict on 3 April 1884, giving victory to the father. Carl was to cease using the labels within 8 weeks after the verdict.

The New Carlsberg establishment was ready in all its pomp and glory by the summer of 1883. Lunn suggested to his friend that he should get off to a flying start by holding a week's open house for the public, followed by refreshments in the storage cellars. In order to prevent „all the ne'er-do-wells in town" from swarming in he recommended Carl to send out admission tickets with names obtained from the office in Brolæggerstræde. Representatives of the press should be invited a few days beforehand to a special showing with a buffet afterwards in one of the brewery's most interesting rooms. „You must do the honours yourself, but you should be accompanied by reliable aides who can relate what you yourself cannot, viz. your earlier tribulations. See to it that there is also beer from the Annexe brewery for comparison. That is an advertisement which none of your competitors can imitate. But since I do not really believe that beating the big bass drum comes naturally to you, speak to Fraenkel, who knows to a T how to look after this kind of rabble." Such was Lunn's recipe for an opening party. „I should really have liked to be there, since I think that with luck I could have sneaked a few vermin into the journalists' furs, but it will hardly be possible to arrange that before I get back."

A couple of months later J.C. Jacobsen likewise presented his combined establishment to a circle of friends with an interest in Carlsberg. The date he chose was 25 September, the anniversary of the establishment of the Carlsberg Foundation; and in his invitation he declared that this was the culmination of his life's work. At two o'clock in the afternoon Pompeii was the point of assembly for about 30 gentlemen, viz. the Carlsberg Foundation's board of directors (Madvig, Holm, Steenstrup, Panum and Barfoed), the governors of Frederiksborg (Worsaae, Meldahl, Heinr. Hansen), past and present colleagues at Carlsberg, including Vogelius, Kogsbølle, Blad, Emil Chr. Hansen, Kjeldahl – although Kühle, who was now the day-to-day manager of the business after Kogsbølle, was absent on a journey abroad. The manufacturers and tradesmen who had worked at Carlsberg were also invited, Hellerung, Hüttemeier, Professor Jørgensen,

Kayser, Oxelberg, Schmiegelow and the architects Bønecke and Thomsen, and finally artists such as Carl Bloch and Laurits Tuxen, along with supreme court advocate Klubien and others.

Jacobsen gave his guests a historical survey of his work, from Ørsted's lectures and the experiments in his mother's wash-tub on Brolæggerstræde to the present modernised, combined plant, which produced more than 120,000 barrels annually but could easily expand to between 150,000 and 180,000. He himself now had only a few more years to live, but his life's work was safely anchored to the Carlsberg Foundation. Knowing this, he was at peace.

Next came a conducted tour of the breweries, then at half past five dinner with Jacobsen himself in the main building, with one speech after another and the 72 year-old gentleman at the centre. The industrial historian Camillus Nyrop, whom Jacobsen wanted to interest in the history of Carlsberg, was one of the guests, and Jacobsen showed him Pompeii's display of the six busts of H.C. Ørsted, L.N. Hvidt and Thorvaldsen, Homer, Pericles and Scipio Africanus, „the men" – reports Nyrop – who according to his words to me have had decisive influence on his life. He told me on the same occasion that instead of fairy tales he had told his son the story of Achilles and the siege of Troy, which possibly had influenced his character 'so far as it has developed up to now'."

The war in the brewery industry went on. As a preliminary to the planned reconquest of his share of the market, J.C. Jacobsen had already reduced his wholesale price for lager beer from 20 kroner per barrel to 18 in May 1881. This had caused uproar among a number of his competitors, who tried unsuccessfully to form themselves into a brewery association to maintain the former prices. It can be stated without exaggeration that Jacobsen's success in the years prior to his death in 1887 was massive. Old Carlsberg swept over the Copenhagen market, stopping sales short for all other breweries of significance. By 1887 Old Carlsberg's sales had reached more than 150,000 barrels annually, while New Carlsberg was marking time with sales at about the same level as in 1881, viz. around 114,000 barrels.

The scientist and the brewer

The times of tribulation were not over. After Jacobsen had at long last managed to arrange for incorporation of the Annexe brewery, end the bitter war with his son and secure the latter's signature to the agreement and assent to his father's will, a new problem cropped up, striking a blow at the most sensitive stage of Jacobsen's production process, the fermenting cellar, the focus of his professional pride.

Despite the use of Pasteur's „pure" yeast, breweries in many places still received unpleasant surprises. It had to be admitted reluctantly that the tartaric acid method was not infallible. If a brew once failed it was no use pasteurising it after it was drawn off. Breweries thus affected had to suspend production and try to resolve the dilemma in the traditional way, i.e. by scrupulously cleaning out all the fermenting vats and everything else with which the beer came into contact, then obtaining fresh pitching yeast from a non-infected brewery and hoping for better luck next time.

In the spring of 1882 the beer at Tuborg went bad. Philip Heymann, who shortly before had been endeavouring to mobilise the Copenhagen lager beer manufacturers to fight J.C. Jacobsen because of his price reduction, sent the Brewer a friendly letter appealing to him for help. „Give me some good advice." Jacobsen's generosity in the technical field was well known. For example, Th. Schiøtz, the Albani brewer of Odense, told G.A. Hagemann the engineer in 1876 of Jacobsen's readiness to help him when as a young man he wanted to build a Bavarian beer brewery in Schleswig. Jacobsen initiated him into „his brewery's wisdom in the wholly open manner of a gentleman". Heymann was not left in the lurch either.

Jacobsen inspected the Tuborg installations in May and recommended various alterations in the fermenting cellar and other procedures. The most important thing he did was to offer at the same time to supply Tuborg with yeast from Carlsberg. Valby delivered yeast three times a week to Hellerup. At the end of six weeks, renewal of the stock of yeast was complete, and the results did not fail to materialise. At a board meeting in August 1882 the chairman of Tuborg was able to report „that the quality of the beer after using the Old Carlsberg yeast had become significantly better, so that we have latterly been free from the appalling complaints, which had reached enormous dimensions". The bad beer had cost Tuborg many customers, but now they began to come back.

Great was the consternation when, early in the autumn season of the following year, Old Carlsberg found its beer beginning to manifest an unpleasant, bitter taste and a disagreeable smell. It was true that fluctuations in the quality of beer were not unknown from previous experience, but as a rule these had been short-lived and without market consequences. Jacobsen quite justly used to emphasise the uniqueness of the fact that he had not changed the yeast in his brewery since 1845, when he had obtained his pitching yeast from Gabriel Sedlmayr's brewery in Munich. Jacobsen took part in the investigations personally. He ordered the big English microscope to be sent up from the Laboratory and spent weeks peering into it for bacteria, with no result other than a spoilt lens. The reduced keeping properties of the beer that also disclosed themselves upset him to the point where he sent instructions to his manager, van der Aa Kühle, who was travelling abroad, to obtain new yeast from Munich. Jacobsen wrote to Kühle on 7 September: „Dr Hansen has examined the sediment in the bottled beer under the microscope and found that it contains wild yeast, which he is now starting to study by the ascospore-formation method. Dr Hansen wants to try to isolate pure *saccharomyces cerevisiae* from our own existing yeast, which will be very interesting, but it will take such a long time before he can produce sufficient for pitching that I do not dare to wait until then to obtain yeast." He followed this up a week later: „If Hansen succeeds in isolating *saccharomyces cerevisiae* from the yeast contaminated by wild yeast forms – the contamination is now beyond doubt – in sufficient quantities for practical use, this will be a great honour for the Laboratory and of great importance to the breweries."

Hansen did succeed. On 12 November pure yeast was used for the first time in the brewing of beer at Old Carlsberg. The brewery's total beer production of the following year, viz. 200,000 hectoliter, was already based on pure strains of yeast. The same applied to the neighbouring brewery of New Carlsberg. The new method spread like wildfire from the Valby breweries to other breweries both in Denmark and beyond. A few years later the use of pure strains of yeast was the normal procedure in the manufacture of bottom-fermented beer at all major breweries throughout the world.

Behind this achievement was concealed an entirely new understanding of the physiology and morphology of alcohol fungi. It had now become possible to penetrate and chart yeast cultures in earnest, and in so doing to devise a method bringing substantial improvements into the entire technology of fermentation. At last there was an effective cure for beer disease. This new understanding was due to Emil Christian Hansen, who showed that yeast is not a homogeneous substance but can be broken down into a number of strains of which only a few are usable in brewing. The strains suitable for brewing Hansen called cultured or pure yeasts, the others wild yeasts. Even as early as his reading of „Études sur la bière", which Hansen received for review, doubt had formed in his mind. In the margin of the chapter on the pure yeast and tartaric acid method he noted: „It is possible that the question is much more complicated, and that it is a matter not of a single yeast but of several strains of yeast surviving the treatment in question." Pasteur's purification method was certainly capable of improving a yeast culture in the short run inasmuch as the bacteria were killed, but it did not produce an absolutely pure culture of top yeast, bottom yeast or wine yeast.

Emil Christian Hansen was appointed to the physiology department of the Carlsberg Laboratory on 1 January 1878, and this introduced into Jacobsen's life a personality who not only brought to his firm a know-how which, at the most critical moment of Jacobsen's professional life, raised Carlsberg to a position of absolute international leadership in the fermentation field, but whose work also enhanced the financial strength of the firm in the highest degree by opening the road at last to the kind of quality control towards which generations of fumbling effort had been devoted without success. „Wind and weather are capricious, and they play a vital role in this trade," the earlier-mentioned Th. Schiøtz had informed Hagemann in 1873, when the latter was seeking guidance on setting up a new brewery.

Liberation from these extraneous factors was now possible.

Hansen's studies at the Carlsberg Laboratory were not conducted without friction. The problem was that the results of the scientist's researches would not allow him to avoid having to correct the great Pasteur, and this was something which Jacobsen would not tolerate. It culminated in a confrontation between the two of them, the scientist and the brewer. Matters were not made any easier by the fact that Hansen was critical at many points of Jacobsen's close friend and adviser in matters of research policy, Japetus Steenstrup. The latter had recommended Hansen's appointment to the Laboratory, and Jacobsen had followed Hansen's work attentively from the first day; while doing so he had discovered that Hansen nourished a certain suspicion of his associates and a fantasy that he was being watched. „As people of his origins usually do," explained the Brewer to Steenstrup. In itself the observation was quite correct: a very vital part of Hansen's personality was shaped during his growing up.

Emil Chr. Hansen never doubted his high abilities any more than he doubted his calling to be a scientist. But the calling was difficult for him to pursue. The world of reality had been harsh and cruel. Actually Emil Chr. Hansen could be termed a proletarian child among 19th century Danish scientists. He came from circumstances scarcely dreamed of by most of his professional colleagues.

His childhood home was in the Jutland town of Ribe. His father, who was a painter, found it difficult, especially during and after the First Schleswig War of 1848-50, to feed and maintain his family, which numbered five children of whom Emil, born in 1842, was the eldest. Increasingly it became the mother who, after the hard childbearing years were over, kept the family afloat and out of the dreaded poorhouse. While the father resigned himself to dreams of great men and deeds or pottered over never-to-be-realised projects, his helpmeet slaved away as a washerwoman or occasional cook. In her son's words, she was one of that hardy breed of women found in West Jutland in those days, with tongues like razors and a stern approach, both physical and moral, to everything.

There were wide differences of station in the cathedral city of Ribe. In his uncompleted memoirs, Hansen writes of the unbridgeable chasm separating the upper crust, consisting of bishop, prefect and city merchants, from the lower orders to which the painter and his family belonged. As a boy he had borrowed Hans Christian Andersen's Memoirs from the lending library and devoured them by candlelight around the family table. As an old man he confessed that he had not been born with the gentle, childlike disposition of the celebrated storyteller. He would not be applauded or petted by the mighty. „If you have no taste for fine company you may as well stay at home. The world only judges by appearances anyway," was one of his maxims, formulated in fact in a letter to Hagemann when the latter was urging him to have his portrait painted for inclusion in Krøyer's picture of „Men of Industry".

Forced to make shift with his own resources, Hansen soon developed a mature awareness of his own worth. But he was vulnerable by temperament, sensitive to criticism and rigidly on guard against the outside world all through his life. To conceive ideas was one thing, but to prove them and get them accepted was another. It demanded toil and struggle. Struggle was a central concept of Hansen's world – struggle for existence, for an education, for recognition.

Since there was no money for the grammar school, Emil found himself receiving a business education, which did not appeal to him; he was then trained to his father's trade, and at the age of eighteen he left home as a journeyman painter.

In the ensuing period he lived an unsettled, almost vagabond existence, in which hunger, cold and illness were some of the enemies with which he did battle. The turning point came in 1862. Replying to an advertisement, he obtained an appointment as private tutor to the children of the dairy lessee and steward of the manor of Holsteinborg. The landgrave himself helped him financially to spend three months in Copenhagen, where he took the schoolteachers' examination. There followed a further period of private tutoring while simultaneously preparing himself for the school-leaving certificate and studying natural science, especially zoology and botany. In 1866 Hansen received a scholarship from the Ministry of Cultural Affairs for the „Monrad Course", as it was called, at the Technical University of Denmark. One of the lecturers whom he met there was the zoologist J.C. Schiødte, who had himself come up the hard way and who conceived a great interest in the young Hansen. The latter completed his course of education there in 1869, then made his living for a time by coaching veterinary and medical students and by teaching at the Schneekloth School.

In 1871 he became a student, took his first-year undergraduate propaedeutic examination and was at last able to begin his studies at the University of Copenhagen. For a brief spell he assisted Japetus Steenstrup with his studies of bog geology and made one discovery which overturned the established chronology; but he felt insecure with Steenstrup, whom he suspected of wanting to „keep him down" and prevent publication of his discovery under his own name; he also believed that a dispute between Steenstrup and Schiødte was having unfavourable repercussions on himself.

Steenstrup remained his pet aversion all through his life. „The worst, the most insufferable and I may add the most dangerous thing about that old scoundrel is the meek way he always puts his head on one side and wraps himself in gentle goodness overlaid with a varnish of piety." Such was the wrathful student's assessment of his professor in 1875. A short generation later, at Steenstrup's funeral in 1897, this was the obituary scribbled by Hansen on the back of the black-edged printed notice of the funeral: „He was specially fond of those scientific studies where the researcher does not have to face up to life with sharp decisions but where there is always plenty of scope for the play of possibilities and probabilities. Really exact science was far beyond him, however great his interest in scientific research generally."

Otherwise Hansen divided scientific researchers into two categories. The first was characterised by the possession of more audacity than shrewdness. „Accordingly they express ideas which are half-considered and often quite untested; they excite attention, give many impulses, but on the whole they produce as much confusion as real enlightenment. The uncritical multitude will always be dazzled by them." The second group, on the other hand, curbed audacity with shrewdness. „They keep to themselves what is half-considered and incomplete. They are proud personalities who shun publicity, and their work is frequently more intensive than extensive." And he added: „As a rule they maintain a certain cool distance from the multitude." This neat self-portrait was delivered in the course of a conversation with J.C. Jacobsen and was a palpable dig at Japetus Steenstrup.

For the rest, Emil Chr. Hansen devoted his study time to Darwin, whose „Voyage Round the World" he translated into Danish in collaboration with Alfred Jørgensen. It was published by Salmonsen of Copenhagen in 1876. This was also the year in which Hansen received the University's gold medal for a work on Danish manure fungi. This brought him closer to the field in which he was to find his main focus of interest. Encouraged and guided by Professor P.L. Panum, he grappled with the physiology of fermentation, and this led to the award of his doctor's degree in 1879 for his dissertation „Om Organismer i Øl og Ølurt" (On Organisms in Beer and Beer-Wort). The studies for the latter were started at Panum's department and completed at the Carlsberg Laboratory, where Hansen was appointed on 1 January 1878 to fill a vacancy occasioned by the retirement of the botanist Rasmus Pedersen. Six months previously – also on the recommendation of Japetus Steenstrup in fact – Carl Jacobsen had engaged him to work at the small New Carlsberg production laboratory, but he let him go to his father when the research post fell vacant in the physiology department of the two year-old Laboratory.

There were problems in obtaining sanction for Hansen to defend his dissertation. He had no bachelor's degree, and a majority of the University Academic Council voted not to grant exemption. The Ministry did so, however. When Emil Chr. Hansen sent his doctoral dissertation to his new employer, J.C. Jacobsen, he referred in a covering letter to what he saw as the hostile attitude of the University. Jacobsen defended the University in his letter of thanks, adding an expression of unease over „the evident bitterness with which the presumed wrong has filled your mind and the somewhat too strong (exalted) expressions of conceit and self-assertiveness into which this feeling has tempted you (the comparison to Pasteur)".

Hansen hastened to assure Jacobsen of his esteem for Pasteur: „My work is trifling by comparison with masterpieces such as Pasteur's, but I do believe that regarded as a doctoral dissertation it is good, and this opinion I still hold. It could be compared most nearly to Salomonsen's dissertation on the putrefaction of blood." Hansen was referring here to the physician and bacteriologist Carl Julius Salomonsen, whose studies of the putrefaction of blood were published in the same year. He could not resist pointing out, however, that such distinguished scientists as Julius Thomsen, C.T. Barfoed, Japetus Steenstrup and J.C. Schiødte had not written doctoral dissertations: two of them (Thomsen and Barfoed) did not have a school-leaving certificate; Steenstrup had taken this examination only but no university degree; Schiødte had no formal qualifications at all. Jacobsen attended Hansen's defence of his dissertation, and according to Eugen Warming, who acted as one of the official opponents, the Brewer took a good deal of interest in the proceedings. Every now and then he made his presence somewhat noisily felt from his place in the auditorium, greatly to the amusement of those present.

These little exchanges are symptomatic of the subsequent period of Hansen's scientific career, the revolutionary years from 1879 to 1884 when his fundamental theoretical and practical work would be done but when Pasteur would stand like a Moloch between him and Jacobsen.

It was difficult to manoeuvre on the Carlsberg terrain at all as it became more and more thoroughly sown with mines. The atmosphere was poisonous, and the quarrel between father and son cast its shadow in the Laboratory too. Hansen genuinely understood the son's situation, but he nevertheless resisted Carl's repeated invitations to him to change his place of work and have a large research laboratory placed at his disposal at New Carlsberg along with a better salary and settled pension rights. The latter was something he desired fervently. However, despite many points of irritation Hansen considered the old brewer to be an extraordinarily gifted man whose interest in his business and in science set him apart from others and commanded respect. „He looks on the breweries more idealistically than any other brewer I know." When something needed nurturing he spent freely, whether for the brewery, the Carlsberg Foundation or the Frederiksborg Museum.

The other side of the coin was Jacobsen's restlessness and capricious spirit. „The Captain never rests, always building and scheming, knowing nothing of Sundays and holidays. On he goes, his activity prodigious, but disjointed and more or less planless." Surrounded as he was by „a swarm of admirers and sycophantic petty thieves", it was difficult, in Hansen's opinion, for the 70 year-old brewer to get sound advice from anyone. Much work was wasted. „An administration in which everyone has his own territory to look after, with clear authority and corresponding responsibility, is unknown here. We suffer the same way in the Laboratory. Here too he wants to do as he likes according to his whims. He does not let Kjeldahl and me really act as heads of department."

Such was the view from where Hansen stood in 1882, when the struggle between father and son was reaching its climax.

Just when the difficulties in the fermenting cellar had been solved in purely practical terms thanks to Hansen's discoveries and everyone could breathe freely again, a crisis blew up between the scientist and the brewer. At issue were the actual interpretation of the results and the mode of presenting the epoch-making reform in Denmark and abroad. J.C. Jacobsen, returned from a trip abroad in September 1882, told Hansen of the praise he had received from German colleagues for his investigations, which had been published in the Proceedings of the Carlsberg Laboratory. He asked to be kept up to date on the studies of yeast. „He pressed me urgently to publish, as soon as my studies permitted it, a series of popular pamphlets in German, with an abundance of illustrations and everything couched in easily-intelligible form, recounting the essential points from my studies promulgated in the Carlsberg reports and so making them accessible to the entire brewing world," runs the aide-mémoire which Hansen wrote on the conversation.

It was in this phase, the information phase as we may call it, that the two chief actors came into collision with one another. The Brewer, who enjoyed the position of Nestor among his European colleagues, had his own ideas about how to present the matter. He was the expert on this. Furthermore, he was the founder and proprietor. It was his beer and his yeast that were involved. He wanted to introduce the news, which did not mean that he was trying to exclude Emil Chr. Hansen's name from the reform. He was not trying to deprive Hansen of the credit for his studies. What was more serious was that Jacobsen would not allow Pasteur's authority to be shaken. Hansen's theory was to be harmonised with Pasteur's teaching and fitted into it. One could even go so far as to say that J.C. Jacobsen never really understood the theory behind Hansen's reform. The result was a clash between two personalities of high principle and strong will. The sparks flew.

Hansen was exhausted after a very intensive spell of work during which he had had other tasks imposed on him besides his yeast studies. For example, at Jacobsen's request he had had to tackle an analysis of Copenhagen's drinking water, which was infected by algae. Professor Panum sent Christian Hansen, subsequently founder of the Christian Hansen Laboratory, to consult his namesake, and had also asked for one of the senior lecturers from Lund University to be given a course in bacteriology. Emil Chr. Hansen became bitter towards J.C. Jacobsen and never forgave him. The Brewer also crossed him over another matter. Jacobsen refused point-blank to establish a yeast institute from which the sale of yeast could take place. At a party given by Jacobsen in his home at which a number of brewers and technical people were present, Jacobsen spoke in strong terms against doing business in yeast; they ought to give it to each other without recompense. One of the guests, Dr W. Schultze, director of the Liesinger Brewery in Vienna, replied: „Ja, Herr Kapitän, Sie haben die Millionen, die wir suchen!" (Yes, Captain, you have the millions that we are seeking!)

It hurt Hansen when the wealthy brewer rejected the proposal for marketing the reform. It vexed him when the idea was put into practice by others, such as Alfred Jørgensen's laboratory of fermentation physiology in Denmark and the Heineken yeast institute in Holland. Moreover, these were people whom Hansen, at the request of Jacobsen and the Laboratory board of trustees had trained on the courses in fermentation physiology which had been rapidly established with participants from near and far. Finally, he felt it was mean on Jacobsen's part not to give him a substantial increase in salary in recognition of the great financial benefits derived by the brewery from his yeast reform. When he compared – as he did – his own remuneration with that of the administrative director, he considered the disproportion to be quite unfair.

The conflict came to a head in the spring of 1884. At the invitation of Professor Julius Thausing, Hansen had written an article, read and corrected by Jacobsen, for the Austrian journal *Allgemeine Zeitschrift für Brauerei*. The article was received with thanks by the editor and sent for printing. But Jacobsen, on a visit to Vienna and not quite satisfied with the presentation, forced Fassbender, the editor, to send the manuscript back to Copenhagen saying that it could not be published. And that was not all. While in Vienna Jacobsen wrote his own version, which was printed in a special issue prepared by the editors for a German brewers' congress about to take place in Berlin. Hansen's counter-move was to send the rejected paper to *Zeitschrift für das gesammte Brauerwesen* in Munich, Professor Lindtner's illustrious journal, which promptly published it.

On Jacobsen's returning to Copenhagen, Hansen sent him a letter in which he wrote: „I am deeply saddened that you could inflict this injustice on me, and my grief is the greater because downright errors have found their way into your revision. I am not thinking here at all about the question of Pasteur's importance but only of what I actually said in my work and what is not said there." He went on: „My youth is behind me; every moment is valuable and too precious to waste in unnecessary conflict; therefore I beg you for peace, and in order to get it I will make all the concessions to you that my conscience and my honour as a scientist will permit." The letter ends by expressing the wish for improved conditions of work in the physiology department, to which Jacobsen assented with the words: „I believe that consideration for the Laboratory requires that all further discussion of the Zeitschrift article, which is now a *fait accompli,* should now come to an end."

Final and decisive recognition was not long in coming, however. A fortnight later, the household god descended upon Copenhagen. The great Pasteur arrived in the city in order to take part in the international medical congress at the beginning of August. Jacobsen was ready and had rolled the red carpet out.

The Brewer had been on one of his very long journeys during the summer that included not only Cracow and Vienna, where he „arranged" Emil Chr. Hansen's article and also met the architect Theophilus Hansen, but also the great international electrical exhibition in Turin, taking a route via the Tyrol and Verona, where he had enjoyed himself revisiting old haunts after 40 years; it had been a thoroughly strenuous „Jacobsen tour" on which he discovered to his satisfaction that his powers were still unimpaired. On the way home he cut Rotterdam out of the programme in order to be prepared for Pasteur's arrival in Copenhagen. He had invited Pasteur to stay at the Hotel d'Angleterre as his guest, with a suite on the first floor overlooking the square and comprising drawing-room, study and bedroom with dressing-room.

The Hotel d'Angleterre had been purchased in 1872 by A/S Det københavnske Byggeselskab, the Copenhagen Building Company Ltd, in which J.C. Jacobsen was an active shareholder. The old building had been pulled down and rebuilt in 1873-75 from drawings by the architects Vilhelm Dahlerup and G.E.W. Møller. The Brewer gave much of his mind to its fitting up, making various studies on the site in August 1874, for example. In a letter to Agnes Berthelsen from Paris he described how the Grand Hotel was fitted up. He had taken a suite on the first floor with a view over the Place de l'Opéra and the boulevard. He wanted to see how the new d'Angleterre might be fitted up and was a little self-conscious at being surrounded by so much luxury, but he had pulled himself together quickly and registered under the name „J.C. Jacobsen de Carlsberg, Capitain". „Since I have thus become a man of rank, I straighten my bent back as far as possible and swagger about to the best of my ability with a distinguished and condescending air!"

Pasteur made visits to Old Carlsberg and to the Carlsberg Laboratory during the congress. And with this the days of struggle on the home front were at an end for Emil Chr. Hansen. He has left us a report of this event in his diary:

„It was on a Saturday morning that I met Pasteur for the first time. The celebrated Englishmen Paget and Archland had been at the Laboratory in the morning, and they made a particularly pleasant impression. There was a streak of coldness in Pasteur's politeness. Captain Jacobsen came walking down with him from the main building, and we greeted one another outside the Laboratory. While we others all took our hats off when we got inside, including the old Captain, who otherwise usually keeps it on in fact, Pasteur sat down with his tall black hat on his head, quite unembarrassed. I expressed my regret that I could not speak French and asked his permission to speak in either English or German. He replied that the only language he understood was French. Since he speaks slowly and clearly, it is fairly easy to understand him. Our conversation revolved around my new yeast studies, and what concerned him most about these was to demonstrate how in his opinion they stemmed firstly from his own work and secondly from his disciples such as Gajou. When I brought up the question whether in his culture trials with pathogenic bacteria Pasteur had induced temporary or constant physiological changes, he tried to assert that new physiological varieties had actually been formed, but he landed in contradiction here, and I got the impression that the profounder significance of this question was beyond him. For as a rule Pasteur's studies stop there, where their practical interest comes to an end. He invited me to visit him in Arbois and in Paris, and urged me to study pathogenic micro-organisms. We parted a little coolly.

„The next day, Sunday afternoon, more of the French doctors came to the Laboratory. Pasteur stood at Kjeldahl's door out to the hall, with Kjeldahl, the aforementioned and myself having grouped ourselves around him on both sides. It was to Dr Bourquoy in particular that Pasteur addressed himself. Everyone stood with heads bared, listening attentively and respect-fully, Pasteur alone having kept his tall black hat on. A great star glittered at his breast, and the little man swaggered and spoke with much energy. He held a discourse on top and bottom fermentation and wove a compliment to me into it. When six o'clock came, we went to the Captain's, where a very fine dinner was provided. Verneuil sat beside Captain Jacobsen, Pasteur directly opposite. Madvig presided at the end of the table with old Mrs Pasteur. Captain Jacobsen made a somewhat high-flown speech in Pasteur's honour. The latter thanked him by praising Jacobsen equally, and also spoke with appreciation of the progress which I had made possible in the fermenta-tion industries. Dr Hornemann, who was also there, referred to this later in his *Hygiejnisk Tidskrift* (Journal of Hygiene)."

So much for Emil Chr. Hansen. As to Laura, she was not present at the dinner. She was away at a health resort. But Jacobsen had mobilis-ed his other ladies, who inter alia had been set the task of studying French under the direction of Agnes Berthelsen. One day the Brewer had the horses harnessed and drove into town with Mrs von der Aa Kühle – né Johanne Wibroe, now the wife of Jacobsen's works manager – to choose a dinner dress for her to wear on the big evening. The one chosen was in light green brocade. Mrs Meldahl was asked to act as hostess. „You can imagine my horror when our host said that I should have Pasteur at the table," she wrote in a letter to her daughter. „However, it went extremely well. I had the bright idea of pulling the Germans to pieces, and as it always does, common hate proved a stronger bond than common love."

As to the food, the dessert on the menu was a no less homely Danish summertime speciality than „rødgrød med fløde" (a fruit jelly served with cream).

Pasteur repeated his invitation to Hansen when they were taking leave of one another at the railway station and thus by degrees showed a friendlier side of himself. During his sojourn in Copenhagen he was positively worshipped, and the Germans were brushed aside all through the congress. Koch and a number of other prominent German researchers did not attend.

Emil Chr. Hansen accepted Pasteur's invitation and travelled to Paris in the spring of 1885. The Gallic spirit was alien to him; he was Gothic, without much feeling for the Romanesque, but he lost his heart to the French capital in the end.

Pasteur was kind and attentive, escorting him personally round the laboratories in Paris and receiving him at the experimental station outside the city where the work on rabies, which was now the main focus of Pasteur's research, was being conducted. As is well known, Pasteur's genius spanned an extremely wide range, and by this time he had left industrial microbiology behind him long ago.

Pasteur had arranged a memorable experience for the Danish scientist by inviting him to the dinner celebrating the admission of Ferdinand, viscomte de Lesseps, to the far-famed French Academy. A vast concourse of ladies and gentlemen in gala dress, the flower of France's notabilities, was assembled for the ceremony. The guest of honour, the creator of the Suez Canal, was attended by old Victor Hugo. After de Lesseps had delivered his introductory address, Ernest Renan replied with a witty discourse. The ever sharply observant Hansen, for whom no detail was insignificant even on a festive occasion, noted in his diary that the ladies were heavily made up, and added: „I have also found it striking to observe how common it is in Paris to see women with actually quite heavily developed beards, especially moustaches."

Hansen was twice invited to dinner with the Pasteurs *en famille*, on one of these occasions along with the Finnish painter Edelfeldt, who was working on a portrait of the host. The conversation was lively – „there was a lot of chatting at the table" – there was music and singing afterwards and a good deal of merriment, but it was hard for Hansen to keep up with the voluble Frenchmen, and their arrogance irritated him. Among the exchanges of repartee he thought he caught Pasteur's characterisation of the Dane: „A quiet, serious people who don't understand jokes and always have a headache." In truth it has to be said that the Danish guest lived up to the description. Hansen positively pestered his host with his personal worries. He talked to him in detail about unsatisfactory conditions of employment and the strained relationship with Jacobsen. However, Louis Pasteur urged him most strongly to remain at the Carlsberg Laboratory. On this point he had written in a letter prior to the visit: „Je vous estime beaucoup et j'ai d'autrepart une sorte de culte pour les grandes quali-tes de M. Jacobsen." (I hold you in great esteem, and moreover I adore the great qualities of Mr Jacobsen). Pasteur lived up to these words handsomely as far as Hansen was concerned when he caused the gold medal of La Société d'Encouragement pour l'Industrie natio-nale to be awarded to the Danish scientist in 1886, an honour which attracted much notice internationally and inaugurated the long series of marks of distinction conferred in time upon Emil Chr. Hansen.

In 1901 Hansen summed up his work in a popular article in the periodical *Frem* (Forward), in words which can appropriately stand as an epitaph on his endeavours, and into which, characteristically, the name of Pasteur has been woven: „Theoretical and practical currents are combined in my work, which contributes as much to fermentation technology and chemistry as to bacteriology. Since its purpose is to bring about reform, it was bound to be fraught with contention for long periods, but it has also brought me that joy of the researcher of which Pasteur says: 'There is nothing more fulfilling to the research scientist than to make new discoveries; his pleasure is doubled, how-ever, when he sees direct use being made of them in practical life.'" J.C. Jacobsen also gave Hansen the credit for the reform in yeast research and the fermenting cellar in his lecture to the Technical Association in 1884. It eased matters. Generally speaking the tone between the two combatants became milder during the later years. In March 1885 they discussed plans for a new laboratory building, for which Emil Chr. Hansen had supplied a sketch of the physiology department. „He almost urged me to enlarge my demands," says the diary, „and in general showed me much consideration and great kindness. On such occasions there is something amiable and good-natured about the old man. A pity it has not always been the case."

The castle of dreams

The Romanticists had a passion for ruins and old castles, and Frederiksborg was the dream castle of the Danish Romanticists. Here nature and history were fused together in a cocktail to intoxicate the imagination while evoking the nostalgic moods to which it was a delight to abandon oneself.

In 1812 the great portrait collection of Danish kings and queens and others of Denmark's prominent men and women had been removed from the Royal Chamber of Art and placed in the Castle. The presence of this Pantheon reinforced the Castle's character as a stronghold of historical memory and at the same time nourished fantasies of an Aladdin's cave behind its moat and thick walls. Writers and poets competed in paying homage to Frederiksborg. Adam Oehlenschläger loved the setting as it appeared at sundown: „How wistful against the tranquil waves the ancient pile in evening red!" Others preferred the clarity of daylight, and others again the magic of night-time. Painters too felt the enchantment of the place. The Norwegian J.C. Dahl, who had come to Copenhagen from his home in Bergen to study painting at the Academy of Fine Arts, was the first to introduce romantic Frederiksborg to the visual arts. Of one of Dahl's pictures, a night piece which was exhibited at Charlottenborg, the reviewer Peter Hjort wrote: „There stands the ancient castle gleaming in the moonlight, bearing faithful witness to the exploits of the ages from which its existence derives." Next followed the Danish artists in force, thanks especially to the art historian Professor L.N. Høyen, who drew the attention of his pupils at the Academy to the inexhaustible material for drawings and paintings afforded by the setting. From the early 1830s onwards the artists streamed out to set up their easels: P.C. Skovgaard, Johan Thomas Lundbye, Christen Købke, Jørgen Roed and many others.

Prints and lithographs made many of the scenes part of the national heritage. A visit to the Castle was a popular outing for many Copenhageners in the first half of the nineteenth century. J.C. Jacobsen went there with his parents as a child and continued the tradition throughout his life with excursions to North Zealand by wagonette.

Until 1848 Frederiksborg was really a Sleeping Beauty's Palace. It had not been used as a residence for over 100 years, and awoke from its trance only when the absolutist kings had themselves anointed in the castle chapel. Christian VIII evinced some partiality for Frederiksborg, as for example during the royal hunt, when he used to stay at the Castle for a couple of weeks; now and then he would also show off the Castle to his guests. The Swedish royal family stayed there during the summer of 1846, on which occasion Johanne Luise Heiberg along with other royal actors performed on a temporary stage erected in the Audience Chamber. King Wilhelm IV of Prussia had the opportunity of seeing the historic royal stronghold during the same year.

The town of Hillerød, which had been ravaged by a great fire in 1834, appealed to Christian VIII to make use of the Castle as a residence again. This would not only restore the town's former prestige but would also invigorate its trade. But the king refused: he could not „cut himself off", as he wrote, from the business of government. His successor Frederik VII, however, brought life to the Castle at last. He decided to make Fredriksborg his main residence. Frederik was uncomfortable in the atmosphere of Copenhagen, where not only the old court circle and the aristocracy but also the citizenry and many of the politicians showed their distaste for his relationship with Louise Rasmussen, subsequently Countess Danner. He used the Castle mainly as a winter residence, arriving in October or November and staying there until well into the spring. That he began using a castle nearly 250 years old at precisely the time of year for firing entailed a distinct fire risk – to which, however, no particular attention was paid, although about 75 tile stoves and 15 open fireplaces were being lit and stoked in the main castle building every day.

On the night of 16/17 December 1859 disaster struck. Winter had arrived early, it was a cold December night with 8-10 degrees Celsius of frost, and the lake around the Castle as already frozen over. The main building of the Castle burned down, only the chapel and the Audience Chamber being relatively unscathed. Frederik VII and his consort left Fredriksborg early in the afternoon of 17 December and travelled to Copenhagen. The main castle was then a smoking ruin, and fire was still blazing underneath the king's and princess's wing. At the meeting of the Lower House the same day the speaker read out a Ministry of Home Affairs announcement concerning the fire, and the House passed a resolution charging him to convey its sympathy to His Majesty.

The issue became political straight away. Were the ruins to be left as a romantic relic, or should the Castle be rebuilt? Experience showed that castle-building was an expensive business. During Denmark's Age of Absolutism prior to 1849 the opposition had endeavoured to resist the building projects of splendour-loving monarchs, which had weighed heavily on the public finances. The young democracy was no less critical and much less restrained of speech. Many National Liberals were strongly opposed to the idea of rebuilding the Castle and recommended using the money for railway construction instead. Their newspaper „Fædrelandet" likewise took a negative stance. There was a surprising intervention here from the pen of L.N. Høyen, who scouted the idea of rebuilding on aesthetic grounds. The exterior of Frederiksborg exhibited an arbitrary, incoherent, sometimes tasteless and meaningless mélange of earlier German and Italian building styles. It was true that, viewed as a whole, it had produced „a lively and picturesque effect", but the architecture represented „a by no means happy era in the evolution of art", Høyen assured his readers. It was not worth recreating.

However, reactions after the fire were unmistakable, especially outside the capital. Over the course of the 19th century the castle at Hillerød had attained an unusual status in the consciousness of many. Along with the Viking cairn and the flag it stood as a symbol of the nation, and its destruction by fire was considered a national catastrophe. Collections for the rebuilding of Frederiksborg started up quite spontaneously in a number of towns – in Odense as early as 20 October and in Hillerød the following day. On 9 January the King appointed the „Committee for the collection of voluntary contributions to the restoration of Frederiksborg Castle". Its chairman was Count A.W. Moltke of Bregentved, the first prime minister under the free constitution, and its other members were C.A. Broberg (merchant), L.P. Holmblad (manufacturer), V.F. Johnsen (departmental manager) H. Koefoed (supreme court judge and judge advocate general), J.P. Trap (private secretary to the King) and J.J.A. Worsaae (archaeologist), the last-named in his capacity as inspector of Denmark's antiquarian monuments, all-powerful director of museums and also curator of the Rosenborg Collection (the assemblage of objets d'art accumulated by the royal family over successive generations and kept in the Rosenborg Palace). The Committee wrote to all county governors and parsons asking them to assist by arranging local collections. This proved to be a very effective system. One county governor excused himself, however: this was Orla Lehmann, the National Liberal leader, who sat for the Vejle constituency at this time. The landed interest also failed. The Committee tried a special appeal to the big landed proprietors, but the response from that quarter was poor. Count Frijs of Frijsenborg, the greatest landed magnate in the country, sent the Committee a very affable letter but gave nothing, while the merchant A.N. Hansen, one of the leading figures of the business community, refused to contribute.

At Trap's suggestion, Frederik VII led the way with a donation of 100,000 rix-dollars. Countess Danner also wanted to be involved, but with an earmarked contribution. She wanted to give an organ to the chapel, and this offer split the Committee; after much deliberation it declined to accept the donation for this specific purpose but asked that the money should be donated unconditionally. This was tantamount to treading on the King's toes and effectively closed the door to further contributions from members of the royal family. The Rigsdag voted a sum for the restoration of the chapel itself. The chapel was in fact a parish church and as such unrelated to the politically sensitive issue of rebuilding a royal residence.

If there was to be rebuilding, there had to be an architect. The one chosen was the 32 year-old Ferdinand Meldahl. He was a man of action; a few days after the fire he travelled from Aarhus, where he was engaged in enlarging the mental hospital, to Copenhagen for a talk with Trap, his next-door neighbour. A week later he was granted the title of professor, and after the appointment of the Committee he wrote a piece for the newspaper „Berlingske Tidende" refuting Høyen and at the same time asserting that the fantasy sums being bandied about as the cost of rebuilding were more or less shots in the dark. His own estimate was 600,000 rix-dollars. On 16 January he entered into private negotiations with Worsaae concerning the iron construction which he considered ought to be used, and a month later it was resolved that he should direct the rebuilding, which meant that the responsibility was removed from the royal surveyor of buildings; the latter had to be content with keeping Fredensborg and Kronborg. Prior to this Meldahl had unsuccessfully sought an audience with Frederik VII; on the other hand he had spent half an hour talking to the Countess, whom he found very intelligent. The day after the appointment his fatherly friend C.E. Fenger became Minister of Finance. In short: everything worked out for Meldahl, who had an astounding capacity both for knowing the right people at the right time and for getting others to do as he wanted. Malicious tongues said of him later that his motto might well be: „Out of the way, boy, here comes Ferdinand."

Matters moved swiftly. The topping-out ceremony was held at Frederiksborg on the King's birthday in October 1861, and Meldahl was made a knight of the Dannebrog. By then the chapel wing had been roofed, the two spires facing the castle lake had been erected and the roof trusses of the other two wings raised. Parallel with this, work had been done on the chapel interior. Many of the fittings had been saved from the fire, but there were still extensive repairs to be made. Amidst war and defeat the chapel was completed and consecrated by Bishop Martensen on 28 August 1864, the sermon being delivered by the poet-priest C. Hostrup. The royal family were present. The guests noticed the very youthful Princess Dagmar, aged 16 and still attired as an immature little girl in a round hat, making a final appearance one month prior to her engagement to the Russian heir apparent. Meldahl was not invited, but he was not forgotten. A new decoration was conferred on him. Along with two other members of the Committee, Holmblad and Broberg, he was awarded the Silver Cross of the Order of the Dannebrog. Meldahl's second in command and good friend Heinrich Hansen, the painter, who had played a large role in the restoration of the chapel and had made many studies at Frederiksborg prior to the fire, became a professor. Now the Castle was no longer a ruin.

Heinrich Hansen was also active in another matter concerning the Castle. A group of artists and businessmen had founded the Kunstflidslotteri, the „Arts and Crafts Lottery", in 1860. As well as Heinrich Hansen and Meldahl, its management board included J.P. Trap, the sculptor C.C. Peters and the ivory and bone turner I.A. Schwartz. The middle of the 19th century was the epoch of the great international exhibitions of arts and industries. Many of the objects which were executed for the Lottery, from sets of furniture right down to small items of silver, porcelain and the bisque ware so beloved of the age, were entered in the exhibitions and were frequently awarded medals. A good deal of skilfully designed furniture in the „historicist" styles of which Heinrich Hansen was fond was disseminated via the Lottery. The profits made from the Lottery went towards the restoration of Frederiksborg.

The first task on which the Lottery focused was the reconstruction of the royal oratories. The king's and queen's oratories had both been destroyed in the fire. They stood like a gaping hole under the organ. Since the Lottery believed itself to have sufficient funds available, it applied for and was granted ministerial permission to undertake the rebuilding of the King's Oratory independently. J.C. Jacobsen, who from the very beginning had been one of the most active contributors to the Castle cause generally, had already taken the initiative before the consecration of the chapel by organising a competition for the reconstruction of the room. Heinrich Hansen, who was an architectural painter, was the only entrant, and both the prizes offered were awarded to him by a judging panel on which L.N. Høyen also now sat. Moreover in July 1864, Jacobsen, acting on his own account, had commissioned from the painter Carl Bloch 23 religious paintings depicting themes from the New Testament. They were to be painted on copper and in exactly the same format as those which had been lost. Bloch was to start by painting a subject of his own choosing and to execute the work in Rome, whither he accordingly betook himself.

When the result appeared in 1861 Jacobsen was overjoyed. Bloch had demonstrated that his artistic ideal was Raphael, a master after the Brewer's own heart. And on another occasion Jacobsen declared that the spirit of Correggio lay over Bloch. This was in a letter to his son in 1868. The series progressed slowly. When the Oratory was ready in 1871, a number of Bloch's pictures were still awaited. The last of them was delivered in 1885, so that Jacobsen was able to see the end-result of this very large donation. Two of Bloch's pictures were sent to the World Exhibition in Paris in 1878 along with one of the doors to the Oratory with C. Rønne's marquetry after Heinrich Hansen's drawing; the door was awarded a gold medal.

The Oratory at Frederiksborg is described by the art historian Mette Bligaard as the finest chamber, in terms of craftsmanship, created during the entire restoration of the Castle. It is dominated by dark woods such as ebony and nutmeg, which lend an appearance of mystery to the westward-facing chamber, thus enhancing the effect of Bloch's paintings, where the scenes and miraculous events of Christ's life are presented as visions with the aid of a brilliant surrealistic whitish light but otherwise characterised by Bloch's portrayals of Italian life and manners. Another art historian of our day, Mogens Bencard, has called the series an outright masterpiece in the history of painting.

J.C. Jacobsen's donation to the Oratory was the start of his really deep involvement with Frederiksborg. It emerged that neither the Restoration Committee nor the Lottery disposed of sufficient funds to proceed to the fitting up of the interior of the Castle. The problems entailed in the residence question had not been solved, and popular interest was beginning to evaporate. As well as the chapel there were two other large chambers at Frederiksborg which there might be hope of conjuring forth again after the fire, viz. the Banqueting Hall and the Rose Room. The best card in the hand was the Rose Room, where there were remains of stucco decorations and other items, while the Banqueting Hall had been depicted shortly before the fire in one of Heinrich Hansen's paintings. The interior restoration work was now concentrated on these two tasks.

The Restoration Committee held meetings now and then to which persons were invited who had shown particular interest in the cause. On one of these occasions, after viewing Frederiksborg, those attending drove to the Railway Hotel at Fredensborg, where a modest dinner had been arranged. Worsaae, Holmblad, Broberg, Trap, Meldahl, Heinrich Hansen, Peters and J.C. Jacobsen were present with a number of others. The conversation revolved around the general question of how the Castle interior could be completed. Meldahl spoke strongly for an all-or-nothing policy. He would not accept a compromise; the job should only be tackled if it was done properly and the interior fitted out as a genuine royal palace. To be content with merely laying floors and cleaning walls and ceilings, thus postponing the fitting out for posterity to grapple with, was not a course he would agree to.

This was when Meldahl and Jacobsen for the first time got down to a detailed discussion with one another about the rebuilding of the Castle. In Meldahl's „Recollections of my collaboration with Captain J.C. Jacobsen, Brewer", he writes that since 1860 Jacobsen had shown him more and more friendliness, „but from this day forward there existed between him and me a relationship of trust and friendship which constantly grew". It lasted until Jacobsen's death. The chemistry between the two gentlemen functioned well.

The idea of a restoration of the Castle's interior was beginning to engage, not to say haunt, Jacobsen's mind, while in other quarters there seemed to be greater and greater expectations that he would take over the various tasks. This was going on pari passu with the slow but sure drying-up of the former sources of money.

On a subsequent occasion Meldahl and Jacobsen visited the Fakse quarries together for the purpose of examining the new Fakse stone, in which they were both interested as a suitable and completely novel local building material. They found themselves having dinner again, their host this time being Garde, who was the proprietor of the quarries. Jacobsen suddenly said: „What would it cost to restore the Banqueting Hall?" Meldahl plucked a figure out of the air and answered: „About 100,000 rix-dollars." „How much of that can the Lottery find?" „About half" – also an inspired guess. „A half: I see. All right then, I'll give the other half."

No further hints were dropped about the Castle during the rest of the meal, but afterwards – during the cigar stage – Jacobsen came over to Meldahl and said: „That was not just the dinnertime spirit running away with me. I am asking you now to start the business moving and put in an application to the Ministry along the lines we discussed. I shall give a half."

The Lottery then requested ministerial permission to make a start on the Banqueting Hall in 1874 and the Rose Room the following year, both under the direction of Heinrich Hansen and Meldahl. In the case of the Banqueting Hall it was a long job. Over a period of six years, from 1874 to 1880, the hall was recreated with its marble floor and its carved, painted wooden ceiling; but there was other work that went on even into our own century. The restoration presented many difficulties. For example, it was impossible to reconstruct Karl van Mander's lost tapestries in full, since not all their main themes were known. In addition to this, the money did not suffice to procure real tapestries, which were very costly. Meldahl suggested imitation tapestries, painted instead of woven, with an eye to their replacement with the expensive woven ones when these could be afforded. A decorative painter named Overgaard could make a test painting. Jacobsen turned the proposal over in his mind; it appealed to his urge to get Frederiksborg „dressed up" so that the past could be brought vividly to life – as quickly as possible for preference. In the middle of Kongens Nytorv one day he chanced to meet Meldahl on his way to dine at Court and stopped him with the words: „Go ahead with the test: I shall give the thousand or two that it costs. But have the whole southern end wall of the Banqueting Hall with supporting columns done right away."

Meldahl, who was going away next day, gave orders the same evening for the work to commence. This gave rise afterwards to much fuss with the Ministry, whose sanction ought to have been obtained first. When the test work was approved, Meldahl travelled to Paris to obtain a tender for the entire consignment. But the French were unable to execute the commission much more cheaply than the Danes, and Jacobsen resolved to have it carried out in Denmark so as to give young decorative painters encouragement and something to exercise themselves on.

Jacobsen kept his eye on everything, often even the minutest details. His passion for architects and materials had free rein here. He had set his heart on filling the Banqueting Hall exclusively with objects relating to the era of Christian IV, but he did not get his way. Meldahl did not go along with him in everything, and there were others who had their ideas too.

Following the precedent of the Vasa Hall at Gripsholm, which served for J.C. Jacobsen as a prototype along with Versailles, the Brewer wanted to hang full-length portraits of European princes contemporary with Christian IV in the Banqueting Hall. As early as

1830 Høyen had suggested having such portraits there, in full court dress. Meldahl accepted the full-length idea but wanted portraits of the present royal family, i.e. the house of Glücksborg. The question was topical in a sense. These were the „Fredensborg days", when Christian IX, the father-in-law of Europe's crowned heads, and Queen Louise often gathered all their six children around them at Fredensborg, along with their husbands and wives. Laurits Tuxen was chosen for the commission, but it was not until many years later that the Glücksborg portrait series was completed.

The restoration of the Banqueting Hall at Frederiksborg has been called an exploit carried out with incredible audacity. Both this restoration and the later ones in the rest of the Castle made Worsaae furious. It was the design of the ceilings that irritated him especially. They were not authentic, and they were not typical of their time, he contended. Before Worsaae died in 1885 he disclaimed responsibility for what had been done at Frederiksborg in this respect. Harsh polemical attacks on Meldahl followed from other quarters. He defended himself with the argument that it would have been scandalous if the vast sums which had been made available had been used in order to abide by the low standards most commonly found in works from the time of Christian IV. He was really invoking one of Høyen's old postulates here. The critical pot has been kept simmering at varying degrees of fierceness right up to our own day, but there is ground for agreeing with the late Povl Eller, former curator of the Museum, that Meldahl stands head and shoulders above his many detractors as the man who cut to the heart of the problem and saw it as posterity later came to see it:

„When you have an old house and want to use something new in it, there is no point in cobbling up something artificially old; you must be aware of your own time and do the work as best you actually can. This is what Meldahl did in Renaissance forms, rather like the modern architect who selects the colours and shapes which seem best to him, which give the best totality for his time and taste. Historical styles are those which were once modern to contemporaries."

Jacobsen was easily able to go along with Meldahl in this respect and generally speaking had much faith in him. When the Brewer, because of disagreement over the purpose to which the foyer of the Royal Theatre should be put, suddenly withdrew his proposed gift, Meldahl, who was chairman of the theatre building commission, was worried over how this would affect their otherwise good relationship. But according to Meldahl's memoirs, Jacobsen visited him and said: „What shall I do with the 20,000 kroner which I am now saving? Can you make use of the money for Frederiksborg? I think you said you could finish the Rose Room for that amount. Think it over: I'll give you the money for that purpose.“

The collaboration became even closer later on. One day Jacobsen turned up at Meldahl's residence at Charlottenborg and launched on a discussion of the interior fitting up of the „King's Wing“. Jacobsen developed his plan in detail: „ ... the Castle ought to be fitted out as a museum of national history.“ He asked Meldahl when he thought the King's Wing could be made ready, and whether in fact he would want to take part in the work. Meldahl would, but there were relationships which would have to be clarified first, viz. with the royal family – would they be willing to relinquish their hold on Fredriksborg at all? – and with the other museums – how was a new museum at Hillerød to fit in with the existing ones in terms of its theme?

Through the mediation of Trap, the King's secretary, both the King and the Ministry quickly acceded to the idea of a museum, but Worsaae was hesitant if not totally unsympathetic. There would be a collision with Denmark's other museums, he thought. In consideration of this Jacobsen amended his project so as to place Worsaae, in his capacity as director of museums for all Denmark, on the governing body of the new museum. He would be ex officio chairman. By this means, the Brewer felt, any collision would be avoided. Meldahl arranged an improvised „meeting“ between himself, Worsaae and Holmblad in a corner during one of the large royal audiences at Christiansborg, and put the pressure on Worsaae. Holmblad argued that it would be indefensible to refuse such a huge gift. The upshot was that Worsaae gave the plan his support and undertook to assist in formulating an application to the government.

Next, Meldahl started drafting a plan for fitting out the King's Wing, while Jacobsen submitted his official offer to the Castle Committee. It was for a sum of 200,000 kroner (100,000 rix-dollars reckoned in the old currency) for the restoration work, conditional upon the Committee's being willing to accept his plan for establishing a museum. The museum was to be a home for the cultivation of Denmark's past, a place where the sense of history would be awakened, refined and educated. Denmark had its part to play in the broad cultural progress of mankind. Awareness of this would buttress the nation's self-esteem and moral strength. There was a need for it. As regards the remoter reaches of history, from which only a few relics survived, Jacobsen felt that the aid of the artist must be invoked. With respect to later periods he hoped for assistance from both public and private sectors in procuring exhibits for the museum. The remains of the former portrait collection from Frederiksborg, which had ended up in the Rosenborg Collection after the fire, would form a nucleus which it might be possible to supplement with originals and copies from elsewhere.

Here Jacobsen miscalculated. He had advanced into hostile territory innocent of the Acquisitive Principle which decrees that the museum curator has not been born who will voluntarily relinquish what he has once acquired. Any question of returning the royal portrait collection to Frederiksborg was far from Worsaae's thoughts. In his application to the Ministry, therefore, he laid it down that the new museum would not compete with or intrude upon the work of the other museums. In addition, Frederiksborg was situated in a somewhat out-of-the-way place. Translated into Worsaae's officialese this came out as an expression of mild disquiet over the idea of transferring historical objects to „a less appropriate location for their general appreciation by the public". The museum might be able to manage with copies, „ideal representations", and for the rest with whatever was to be found in the state's collections of major pictures, busts and the like that had been rescued from the Castle fire. Finally, he drew attention to the fact that the royal family wished to retain access to the museum as a place for holding festivities on special ceremonial occasions. The application was approved by the King on 25 June, subject to the condition that „no obligation to make pecuniary sacrifices in this connection" would fall upon the state.

These more or less camouflaged reservations took Jacobsen by surprise. It was now clear to him that he would have to enter into direct negotiation with the fire-eating dragon guarding the entrance to the cave. He had a number of conferences with Worsaae during the spring, in the course of which he received another big surprise: the portraits rescued from Frederiksborg were no longer deposited at Rosenborg temporarily; Worsaae had quietly obtained the King's signature to an ordinance incorporating them into the Rosenborg Collection. They could no longer be given back again at all: they belonged to Rosenborg. This put a spoke in the wheel without a doubt, but it was not the only one. At another meeting which Jacobsen had with Worsaae, this time at the Old Norse Museum, Worsaae explained to the Brewer that in fact there were very few pieces there which could be said to belong to Frederiksborg. Jacobsen made an intensive effort to persuade Worsaae to replace Christian IV's celebrated silver altar from the King's Oratory in its original location, and was able to do so with all the more justification since the Oratory was now restored, but Worsaae was not to be moved.

Jacobsen tried making a gift to Worsaae. Unsolicited, he offered to pay for a marble floor long desired by Rosenborg in Christian IV's audience chamber. Worsaae accepted the donation but still did not budge. Now the two gentlemen each knew where the other stood, and the horsetrading could begin. One day early in November Worsaae was at Carlsberg to thank the Brewer for the flagged floor at Rosenborg; while there he mentioned that he would like to put to him „the plan and drawings in the Frederiksborg business for further discussion".

The Carlsberg Foundation became drawn into the plan by virtue of the fact that it was to finance the museum's future operation. Jacobsen wanted the Foundation to act as intermediary in the museum scheme, contributing an annual subvention of 10,000 kroner, and for this purpose he endowed the Foundation with the equivalent capitalised value, viz. 200,000 kroner. With regard to the museum's management he proposed a board of governors consisting of three members: one nominated by the King to represent the royal family's interest (Meldahl was appointed); next, as chairman, the curator of the Danish Crown's chronological collection at Rosenborg (this was Worsaae); and finally, a member of the board of the Carlsberg Foundation nominated by the Royal Danish Academy of Sciences and Letters (Professor Edvard Holm, the historian, was selected). The Foundation and The Royal Danish Academy assented to the plan, whereafter a royal ordinance establishing the Museum was promulgated on 5 April 1878. The Museum's statutes were drafted by the chairman, Worsaae, but underwent a number of alterations at the hands of both Professor Holm and J.C. Jacobsen. They were ratified by the King on 7 October of the same year.

The establishment of the Museum had a political sequel in the Rigsdag. When the Finance Act for the year 1879-80 came up for debate, the Finance Committee demanded information from Home Affairs Minister Skeel concerning the way in which the Museum had come into existence. During the discussion that followed the Committee divided itself into three minorities. The largest of them, headed by Chresten Berg and Viggo Hørup, thought that the government had lacked constitutional power to dispose of Frederiksborg without the consent of the Rigsdag. The national collection taken up to restore the Castle had made it a property of the people rather than a mere item among the state's assets. The other faction of the Venstre (Farmers') party, which had split in 1872 over the question of the provisional Finance Act, was represented by Frede Bøjsen, a folk high school figure, and Count Holstein of Ledreborg. They were not opposed but regretted that the matter had not been discussed beforehand by the two chambers. A third minority led by Jacob Scavenius and editor C.St.A. Bille from Højre (the Conservatives) contended that there was nothing to be dissatisfied about.

In the Lower House it turned into a major debate. The Minister of Home Affairs argued that he had had every right to act by virtue of the very fact that the state had stipulated that no demand should be made on it for any form of subvention for the Museum. Holstein for his part acknowledged Jacobsen's extensive donations but reproached the government for its handling of the matter. For him the question of the Rigsdag's authority to grant funds in conjunction with the unresolved struggle over the Finance Act constituted the crucial factor. Chresten Berg on the other hand did not pull his punches. The whole affair was fishy, a step back to the days of absolutism: everything had been carried through with the connivance of the government and the court,

J. C. Jacobsen as seen by Otto Bache. Preliminary study for the coronation picture. ▶

History painting at Frederiksborg. Detail from Otto Bache's great picture of Christian IV's coronation procession in 1887. Count Rantzau is walking at the extreme left. His right hand points towards the painter, who is mingling with the crowd. F. Meldahl can be seen obliquely behind, and the artist has placed J. C. Jacobsen and his wife at the window. The art critic Emil Hannover had very mixed feelings about the picture, which he felt was a lavishly-mounted play stuffed with tinsel. It lacked the unity and vibrancy of a true work of art.

◀ *Carl Jacobsen with his son Alf. Detail from a photograph of Carl and his employees at New Carlsberg, 1885.*

Laura Jacobsen in the summer of 1887 on the island of Fanø. From left, seated: Laura, Paula (grandchild) and Ottilia (daughter-in-law). From left, standing: Theodora (grandchild), Agnes Berthelsen and Helge (grandchild).

fuelled by the wish to puff up the glory of the royal family. The proceedings culminated in a grand confrontation on the floor of the House between Berg and Bille. Once that was over and done with, the affair ran into the sand. No proposal for a vote was put.

There was another sequel which occurred after Worsaae's death and turned out differently. It touched on posterity and reputation. In 1886 one of the staff at Rosenborg made public the notes on the Rosenborg Collection which had been left by Worsaae. In them Worsaae had written that in 1878 he had had to resist a fierce attack on the Collection when an attempt was made to claim both historical portraits and furniture from Rosenborg for the new Museum at Frederiksborg, and even to have all the medieval and renaissance relics from the Old Norse Museum transferred to Frederiksborg. But „my firm resistance caused the plans for the Frederiksborg Museum to be changed so that it would not compete with the three already-existing historical museums in the capital". Naturally J.C. Jacobsen was hurt to read these baseless attacks. He rebutted them in vigorous terms in a letter to the Ministry of Home Affairs. He thought that Worsaae's memorandum must have been written at a moment when relations between them were tense. Jacobsen did not want his demurrer to be made public, but he asked for it to be deposited in the Ministry.

During an audience with Christian IX in August 1880, Jacobsen offered to donate the same amount for the fitting up of the Princess Wing as he had for the King's, viz. 200,000 kroner, and on the same terms, i.e. that the Wing should be made over to the Museum. After some negotiations the formalities were completed. In November of the same year a royal decree was issued giving effect to the extension, and Meldahl buckled to with his accustomed energy. The architect, his artists and craftsmen finished the work four years later.

The 25th anniversary of the fire fell on 17 September 1884, and this was the day chosen for the inauguration of the now-complete Castle and Museum. In his capacity as royal surveyor of buildings Meldahl handed over Frederiksborg to the Ministry of Home Affairs, which in turn placed it in the care of the Museum's board of governors. The day was celebrated with a great banquet at Hillerød to which were invited not only notabilities by the dozen but also the multitude of artists, craftsmen-designers and craftsmen who had been involved.

For Ferdinand Meldahl, the Frederiksborg building project as a whole had had several aims. The first had been to save whatever could be saved of the original complex, the next to create the framework of a museum while at the same time providing fitting surroundings for royal entertaining at the Castle. This was the remaining vestige of the residential privilege. Frederik VII had declared immediately after the fire that he intended to return and use Frederiksborg as his residence again, but as time went on the royal family realised that the residence idea was dead.

After the Restoration Committee and the Lottery had reached the end of their tether, Jacobsen became the real builder and father of the Museum. His dream was a symbiosis in which Castle and Museum would coalesce to form a centre with activities all arranged on a historico-didactic principle. The visualisation of the past was Jacobsen's aim. Like Meldahl he wanted to give historical paintings a prominent place in the Museum. Whereas the architect thought on decorative lines and wanted historical wall-paintings that fitted into the room's overall scheme of interior decoration, this objective was a subordinate one in the eyes of a public-spirited personality like Jacobsen. He wanted a historical picture-book for people to leaf through, and when transmitted relics failed, imagination must in a sense take over. He wanted to invite the Danish people to come inside and survey the great historical drama so that they might shake off the defeatist psychosis that was the legacy of 1864 and regenerate their sense of self-esteem.

Worsaae's ideal of a museum was of a different kind. For him the systematising museum with its collection of exhibits was the be-all and end-all. Holm, as a professional historian, had to distance himself from portraits or sculptures of persons of whom there were no authentic likenesses. Neither of the two was able, with the best will in the world, to approve the Museum's becoming a picture-book with idealised portraits or sculptures to bring to life the famous and notable personalities of the past, even though another of Denmark's great castles, Christiansborg, was populated by an abundance of such representations. The views of Worsaae and Holm gained ground swiftly after Jacobsen's death. The critical school triumphed over the imaginative as it also triumphed in the historical world, and the epoch of historical art ended abruptly with the rise of new art movements. Paradoxically enough it is our own generation that in certain respects is more in tune with the idea of arousing and sharpening the public's interest through visualisation. The panoramas and the passion for waxworks of the past have their counterparts today in the scanoramas, video presentations and other forms of museum technology which play an ever-growing role in an age where the exhibition has become the centrepiece. The systematised museum, ponderous with its collections, has not disappeared, of course, but presentation to the public occupies a fairly prominent place, one reason being the justifying of grants, because it draws visitors; and more and more practitioners of the historical profession are beginning to acknowledge the power of both the TV series and the comic strip – Asterix being one example – as stimulants of the appetite which can pave the way for a more intimate interest in the past.

Jacobsen and Meldahl made good partners; they had an electrifying effect on each other. They both travelled abroad; Meldahl to Germany, where a number of museums around the middle of the century had drawn inspiration from castle collections. One of these was the Bavarian National Museum in Munich, founded by Maximilian II of Bavaria in 1855. Jacobsen had different models. Gripsholm Castle in Sweden was one of them. Since the end of the 18th century Gripsholm had been the home of a great portrait collection which was rapidly enlarged during the 19th century. The Castle functioned in Jacobsen's time as the national portrait gallery of the Swedish state; it was a museum, open to the public, housed in a castle with a great historical past. Jacobsen had visited Gripsholm many times and made extensive notes on it, as he always did when travelling. There were other collections which attracted him too. He had visited the recently-founded Nordic Museum in Stockholm. One of the reasons for its renown was the success achieved by its panoramic exhibitions, mounted by the Swedish museum official Artur Hazelius, at the World Exhibition in Paris in 1878. The following year at the Exhibition of Arts and Industries in Copenhagen, the director of Copenhagen's Tivoli Gardens, the illustrator and collector Bernhard Olsen, exhibited some of the results of his own extensive collecting (which became the embryo of the Danish folk museum), and both

Meldahl and Jacobsen let themselves be carried away by the opportunity they saw here. They discussed the idea of fitting out folklore interiors at Frederiksborg. Nothing came of it except for the acquisition of a room with decorations and articles from Ditmarsken (Friesland) which has since been dismantled.

And then of course there was Versailles, which Jacobsen visited for the first time in 1855. This was the museum of historical paintings par excellence. Maximilian II of Bavaria had fallen under the spell of the French royal palace during his visit in 1846 and had taken it as a model. Generally speaking Louis Philippe's museum can be said to have been one of the biggest box-office draws of its day, and Napoleon III continued the programme with chronologically-arranged battle scenes, the Galerie des Batailles, as it was called. But the Franco-Prussian War of 1870-71, ending in catastrophic defeat and the fall of the Second Empire, put an abrupt end to this mode of glorifying the past. And the Napoleonic allegories vanished.

Thus there were many factors combining to bring the conceptions underlying the Frederiksborg Museum under early debate by the Museum's board of governors. The latter had invited J.C. Jacobsen, as it was empowered to do by the statutes, to join it as an „adjunct member having voting rights with respect to the procurement of art works". The difficulties were quite considerable. Whereas normally the building-up of a museum begins with an assemblage of objects and then proceeds to the acquisition of exhibition premises, in this case it was the other way round. A royal castle had been fitted up and a framework created for a museum which did not exist and whose collection of exhibits was more or less an unknown quantity.

The only point which was clear was that the collection would be arranged chronologically. There were tensions from the very first moment. While Jacobsen and Meldahl stood for the imaginative dramatic principle, authenticity was the watchword of Worsaae and Holm. Worsaae had undermined Frederiksborg from the start by effectively blocking the return both of the portrait collection and of pieces individually stored and very well worth seeing, such as Christian IV's silver altar: he therefore bore a heavy share of the responsibility for the fact that the cupboard was completely bare at the Museum's inception. He recommended making a start with copies and with the transfer to Frederiksborg of more peripheral types of piece, while Jacobsen was pressing for his visualisation concept to be realised.

Jacobsen was in a hurry. He felt that the sands of time were running out, and he wanted to see some result from his massive donations before closing his eyes for the last time. An attempt was made to combine the hypothetical with the authentic by providing the Museum with casts of objects and so, for example, illustrating Gorm the Ancient and Thyra's period of rule by means of statues of the royal couple, whose appearance was unknown, along with casts of the Jellinge stones, monuments to Gorm and Thyra, set by their son. Meldahl was not enthusiastic about this; archaeology and reproductions of tombstones did not suit his beautiful rooms. Moreover, he thought they were extremely dull and boring to look at. But he did accept a mass of arms and armour assembled on his own initiative by Jacobsen, who had either purchased them personally or had them acquired on his behalf in Stockholm, Vienna, Munich and Turin. Some of them were copies of the armour of famous Danish noblemen while others were anonymous. Such a collection belonged in a castle – Meldahl and Jacobsen were united on that – and it was exhibited on the ground floor of the King's Wing, where its function was purely decorative. According to the Museum's first printed guidebook the Rose Room was decorated with what was termed „mercenary soldiers' armour". Holm was strongly opposed to this arrangement. „An ironmonger's shop," he snapped. Holm felt something of a supernumerary; of course it was always the Brewer who decided off his own bat to procure things for the Museum without consulting the board of governors.

Jacobsen did not criticise his colleagues out loud, and his respect for them was great, but he did press them, with varying success. The commissioning of paintings was one of the sensitive issues. On this he lost patience and tried at one point to arrange a meeting at Frederiksborg with a group of artists – his group of artists, including his „Roman" friends – to which he invited the rest of the board. Now he would get some system into the business. But both Worsaae and Holm excused themselves.

Then in 1880 Jacobsen brought off a *tour de force*. He placed before the board a plan, drafted by himself, for decorating all the rooms at

Frederiksborg. Now the people's illustrated history of Denmark would become a reality. His plan has been called a monumental translation into museum terms of Adam Fabricius' popular history book of the same name from 1854/55. Particularly with regard to the Middle Ages, Jacobsen's plan follows the history book and contains fantasies side by side with representations of archaeological finds and topographical material. Another popular history book, A.D. Jørgensen's „Forty Tales of the History of the Fatherland", which was published in 1882, during the Museum's inaugural phase, reflects Jacobsen's faith in the role of history as a national educative force. Using Meldahl as intermediary, Krieger had helped the Brewer to make contact with the author. The work was aimed at the North Schleswigers particularly. The forty tales, like the eighty themes which he envisaged being depicted in paintings on the Frederiksborg walls, are a selection of instructive aspects of Denmark's history. Edvard Holm was the only member of the board of governors to examine Jacobsen's proposal in any sort of detail. He recommended that „discreditable affairs" such as the battle of Hemmingstedt, when the Danish army was bitterly defeated, and „infamies" such as the „Stockholm Massacre" (the judicial murder of leading Swedish nobles by the Danish King Christian II in 1520) should be struck from the list, and also pointed out that subjects from cultural life had been completely omitted from Jacobsen's list. Holm asked: „Cannot Ludvig Holberg serve as a theme, for example?"

The board accepted Jacobsen's proposal, though with amendments, and it was decided to implement the plan gradually as the Museum's funds allowed. However, circumstances developed differently from the way Jacobsen had outlined in his great plan. It soon became evident that the very rigid and formalised elements in his proposal were impracticable; the overall conception itself was never brought to realisation.

Despite these differences of opinion the board of governors, in collaboration with Jacobsen, was nonetheless able in the course of a surprisingly few years to procure a very large number of pieces, many of which were of really high quality. Worsaae was active in the purchase of a significant collection of monumental Renaissance furniture, chests with armorial bearings, carved cupboards and a number of tables. When purchases had proceeded far enough to make it possible to begin an exhibition in the rooms of the Museum, it became clear to the committee that there was nevertheless insufficient material in hand to fill the walls, which would emphasise the emptiness of the rooms. In order to overcome this it was decided to use Danish graphic portrait exhibitions – especially the important Halwegh engravings after Abraham Wuchter's and Karel van Mander's portraits – as decorations in the window recesses and on the walls. And a quite unique collection had been acquired at the end of the 1870s. Carl Schiøtz, a hospital doctor of Roskilde and the owner of one of the biggest and best collections of copper engravings in Denmark, had died leaving a collection which had been started by his father-in-law, Rasmus Borck, manager of the Orphanage. It comprised nearly 7000 sheets, many of which were unique. It was J.C. Jacobsen who heard about this, and he passed the word to Worsaae. The Museum managed to acquire the entire collection, and some of the portraits were hung, others kept in folders. Today this collection is an aid very much in demand by historians and art historians.

Little by little some of the large paintings commissioned were completed and could be hung. Some of them became great successes with the public, e.g. „The Meeting of Otto Krag and Hans Nansen at the Castle Bridge in Copenhagen", „Christian IV at Niels Kaas' Deathbed" and „Svantevits and Arkona's Fall".

Lastly, there is the picture which, more than any other, typifies the historical paintings of Frederiksborg, Otto Bache's „The Conspirators of Finderup Grange Riding Away after the Murder of Erik Glipping in 1286". It was painted in 1882 as a commissioned work for the Museum. Mrs Meldahl noticed a sketch for the picture at a party given by the artist and told her husband about it. He wrote to Jacobsen about the „priceless composition"; the picture was „extraordinarily charged with atmosphere". Jacobsen asked the question which for him was central: „Is it a historical portrayal for the public?" When he saw the sketch he was convinced of it, and Bache was able to make a start.

J.C. Jacobsen's interest in Frederiksborg did not end with the Museum. It lasted until his death. He thought constantly about the embellishment of Frederiksborg as a whole and of restoring the ruins to their original condition. The Swedish savant Dr Böttiger discovered in 1864 that Adriaen de Vries' bronze figures from the Neptune fountain, which the Swedes had carried off from Frederiksborg in 1659, was still at Drottningholm Castle outside Stockholm. Jacobsen at once set about getting the big fountain in the outer castle courtyard reconstructed. As always he collaborated with Meldahl on the task and through the intervention of Minister Brostrøm obtained permission from King Oscar of Sweden to have casts taken at Drottningholm by the sculptor Johan Börjeson. Jacobsen travelled to Stockholm and assured himself that the work was going according to plan. An attempt by Börjeson to get the originals sent to Frederiksborg while Drottningholm retained the copies did not succeed. Heinrich Hansen was commissioned to design the architectonic part of the fountain. Jacobsen himself was very much preoccupied with the problem of how the fountain was to be made to function satisfactorily. He wrestled with complex calculations of the paths of the jets, 90 in all, which had to land inside the basin around the fountain – no easy matter. And he made a test assembly at Carlsberg, which Meldahl looked at. In a brief letter to Professor Holm dated 28 November 1886 the historian Johannes Steenstrup wrote: „Uncle Jacobsen is around and about as you know, but just now he is the jet-master as well. He is extremely busy with his fountain for Frederiksborg and is trying out the jets in all possible ways. Two figures and pedestals etc. still seem to be missing."

There was one other great project which, shortly before his death, Jacobsen offered to launch at Frederiksborg, viz. the installation of a peal of bells in the church tower. He placed the necessary funds at the disposal of the Museum to enable a start to be made. However, he did not see the task completed, nor that of the fountain.

It has been said of his relationship to Frederiksborg by Jacobsen's critics that in this phase he allowed himself to be overpowered by the royal incense billowing around the Castle, and it is true that it brought him into close contact with the royal family. But this always took place via intermediaries, chiefly Worsaae and Meldahl, who had regular access to the court. Jacobsen did not make any attempt himself to reap any reward, in the form of honours and the like, for his efforts on behalf of Frederiksborg. On the contrary, what is remarkable is the degree of aloofness shown towards him in this respect in official quarters considering the open-handedness with which other entrepreneurs and patrons of the arts during this age – C.F. Tietgen for example – were treated. From beginning to end what drove the work forward was undoubtedly the old romantic spirit in Jacobsen, who had had an experience during his youth that fixed itself in his mind and partook of the quality of those rare and vivid dreams of which reality can sometimes be built. Towards the end of his life he confided in Meldahl that „it is that summer when as a young boy I first heard from Jægerbakken (Hunter's Hill) the Castle bells ringing out over the lake in the still of night that has particularly fascinated me with the place and imbued me with enthusiasm for the Castle all my life."

It was the dream of the fairy-tale castle in North Zealand.

The eternal city

Jacobsen celebrated his last birthday alone. He had travelled to Sweden, one reason being in order to arrange matters with regard to the casts of Adriaen de Vries' figures for the Neptune fountain. On the day itself he made an excursion to his beloved Gripsholm. He set off early in the morning and returned to his hotel at 8 in the evening, then sat at the writing desk to send a report on his day out, written „on the loveliest summer evening, concluding an exceedingly beautiful day", to Laura, who was holidaying at Holtegaard.

The voyage on Lake Mälaren had been long – 3 1/2 hours – but strikingly beautiful. On arrival he sat himself down in the restaurant in Mariefred and enjoyed a modest three-course menu. To celebrate the day he ordered, quite unusually for him, half a bottle of champagne, then toasted family and friends at home in absentia.

„I was then in excellent form for enjoying my visit and studying this splendid castle, where as always I remembered our first visit to it twenty-odd years ago, shortly after the Frederiksborg fire, when I was first struck by the thought which I expressed, that such a museum of national history as this was perhaps what Frederiksborg could and should become for Denmark one day. But at that time it was only a pious hope. For Frederik VII was still alive then, and he wanted to reside in the Castle with the countess after it had been rebuilt. That this obstacle would vanish so swiftly one could not have guessed, and still less could I have guessed that my civic activities would develop to such a degree that I should become the instrument for making this patriotic idea a reality!"

It was the hour for leave-taking and the settling of accounts, and Jacobsen was grateful for the final figure. He had gone far, both as a brewer and as a citizen. To only a few was it granted to accomplish so much. „In the brief span of time which is all that can be left to me, I dare not count on being able to accomplish very much more, but I can take solace in the reflection that everything suggested by my own and my excellent advisers' reason and insight has been done to secure the future preservation and progress of what I have created, so that it will not die with me but with God's help will also bear fruit in the years to come," he wrote to his wife. Then he went to bed. It was 11 o'clock and he was tired. Next morning he sealed up the letter and then tackled a series of arranged meetings. The following day he travelled to Gothenburg and from there by boat to Copenhagen.

A month later the family quarrel was composed. On 4 October 1886 – his confirmation day – Carl went across to his father. They talked together as though there had never been a bitter word between them. The first sign of a thaw in the cold war between father and son had manifested itself the previous year at Easter time; Ottilia and Carl had sent their eldest daughter, Theodora, over to Old Carlsberg with a bouquet of flowers, which J.C. had hastened to acknowledge with a thank-you note in which, to Carl, he interpreted the Easter greeting as „a promise that for me too, the long hour of pain may be followed by a resurrection into a new and better life here on earth". With this as consolation he could echo the line from Oehlenschläger's song „The Hermit": „Teach me, o forest, to wither away with gladness!" „Good Friday was a bitter day, but beautiful was Easter morn!" Now, a year and a half later, Carl went the whole way. He knew that only thus could the reconciliation be consummated fully. The son must come to the father, and the father's door stood open.

Two days later was the weekly at-home day at New Carlsberg. Ottilia summoned her friends hastily: „Come out to us this afternoon: the old people are coming."

It was a happy winter. Johannes Steenstrup gives the news of the reconciliation in a letter to Professor Edvard Holm at the Carlsberg Foundation: „I was at Old Carlsberg on Friday, and the young Jacobsens, the Kogsbølles and a few others were there. Not for a long time indeed has the big dining salon witnessed anything like the quiet joy bursting out, the convivial tones and gay chatter; it has rejuvenated Uncle Jacobsen exceedingly. Jerndorff has painted a good portrait of Jacobsen – I have not seen it – and I have heard that Mrs Jacobsen has ordered a similar one for Carl Jacobsen, and that the Dutch brewer who came up here immediately the reconciliation had taken

place has also ordered a third. But I did not get this from the family."
The Dutch brewer was W. Feltmann of Heineken.

In the same letter Steenstrup mentioned that J.C. Jacobsen was thinking of a grand Italian tour as soon as spring should arrive. Carl for his part had decided to invite a small group of artists and scholars on an archaeological trip to Greece. Ottilia would go with them. J.C. would have his wife with him as well. The two families would spend some days together in Rome before the younger group carried on to Greece with their friends.

Laura asked to be allowed to stay at home. For her Rome had always been something unattainable, indeed almost presumptuous to think about. Had not the poet Goldschmidt said that no one ought to travel to Rome without having been „christened" – i.e., without having acquired a knowledge of Rome's history from the earliest times and a good grasp of art? These things she lacked. She was an unschooled housewife and had not done her homework. She felt thoroughly unhappy at the idea of going along, she said; but another fear was lurking under the surface. Jacobsen was in the habit of travelling alone and had always returned from his many tours safe and sound. Now he suddenly wanted her with him. She felt a distinct foreboding that something was going to happen on this journey, but she kept her anxiety to herself and tried to exorcise it by remaining at home on the pretext of lack of education. „Well, if you are so reluctant to travel, I shall stay at home," he replied. „This time I shall not travel without you, for I shall travel no more."

That decided the matter. They left on Shrove Monday. All the workers stood along the route from the Annexe brewery to the exit at the barrier. They saluted the Jacobsens, and some of them called out, „Have a good journey!"

There were few other places in the world at that time where the romantic could get his fill of ruins and the grandeur of the past as he could in Rome. It was the educated citizen's wish to have visited the world city on the Tiber at least once in his life. Goethe had shown the way to Rome with his *Italienische Reise*. The encounter with the antique landscape and the cultural monuments of Italy brought him close to the life of the ideal of harmony and unity which he had dreamed of in his youth. The spiritual effect of this meeting was for him nothing less than a rebirth.

The road to the classical humanist ideal lay via Rome, even for those who, visiting there many years later and not sharing this ideal with Goethe, hoped that as a result of the journey they might find themselves and realise themselves – what one would nowadays call the difficult art of achieving a balanced personality. J.C. Jacobsen, of the mercurial, rational, achievement-driven temperament, Jacobsen the ever-active and restless, knew pain deep within himself in spite of his many triumphs. Only once did he experience the rare, strange moment. It was not in Rome, but at Sorrento, „the only place of sojourn where I have not felt the urge to work and have been able to give myself over wholly to pleasure," he confided to Johanne Luise Heiberg. The word „pleasure" in his mouth was not a material but a spiritual dimension. „This place has therefore stood in my memory as an earthly paradise." When Jacobsen next sought his paradise on earth, he did not find it.

The academic middle classes, who set the tone of European society for a large part of the 19th century, were brought up on Antiquity and the classics. *Literis et humanitati* was the motto to be read over the portals of the grammar schools; but those portals also bore an internal inscription which was the one the disciples had before their eyes every day: Knowledge is Power. Both mottoes had their application in the golden age of the middle class.

Roman history was an obligatory subject. Jacobsen loved it and knew it to the tips of his fingers. Many of the best-sellers of the age dealt with Rome's greatness and decline, such as Edward Gibbon's great work of that name – „The Decline and Fall of the Roman Empire" – whose author flattered himself that it lay on the educated woman's night-table. During the course of the century archaeologists started making serious excavations in Rome, and their finds and results lent extra excitement to a sojourn in the city. The 1860s brought many sensations. Systematic excavations were begun in the ancient port of Ostia, at the mouth of the Tiber. Pope Pius IX honoured the archaeologists with his presence in 1866. The finds made within the walls also attracted attention. During the demolition of an old building in Trastevere a Roman store of marble was found with a splendid assortment of stones, testifying to the large scale of imports into the city during Antiquity. One of the most beautiful stones was given to the Jesuit Il Gesù church; an altar plate was made from it. The barracks of one of the fire and police corps of ancient Rome was discovered in another place, the headquarters of the 7th cohort according to the inscription on the wall. Towards the end of the 1860s the Empress Livia's house at Palatium was uncovered, a part of Augustus' residence and outbuildings. The find confirmed what the sources had related concerning the Emperor's simple lifestyle. He preferred to live in a private house such as would have been used by a prosperous citizen rather than build an opulent palace for himself.

Another treasure was revealed to the public for a brief moment. About 1860 the Pope opened the great baroque monument at the summit of the choir of St. Peter's. This was where the Cathedra Petri was kept, the stool of the apostle Peter, an ivory throne with curious inscriptions, which was placed in the basilica for several months with a Swiss honour guard, then hidden away again.

During his sojourn in Rome the Danish author Meïr A. Goldschmidt witnessed in the spring of 1863 what Goethe had dreamed of but never experienced, viz. the bringing up of an antique statue of a historical personage from beneath the ground. There was a rumour in the city that a marvellous antique statue had been found; no one rightly knew where, but Goldschmidt and the Norwegian literary historian Lorenz Dietrichson hired a carriage and followed the crowd out of the town. After a long drive through the Campagna they at last reached the place where the new excavations were going on. The remains of another of Livia's villas had been found, the „Villa ad Gallinas". Here, between fragments of antique water-pipes and bricks and a piece of mosaic floor sticking out from the gravel and sand, people were pushing and shoving their way into a rectangular space still half-covered with earth and flooding with the water oozing down into it. There the statue lay in the semi-darkness. It was the statue of Augustus from Prima Porta, which Livia had had placed in a niche in her villa. A few of the fingers were all that was missing: otherwise everything was there in all its glory, with the finely-wrought reliefs on the breast-armour, the characteristic strong forehead, the imperiously outstretched arm, all so lifelike and dignified.

The Emperor August reborn.

It was also in the 1860s that the Englishman John Henry Parker began the systematic photographing of Rome's antique monuments, the preliminary to a great work on Rome's archaeology and valuable in having been accomplished just prior to the commencement of the massive engineering and urban renewal projects of the 1870s and 1880s which obliterated part of the old Rome.

Another celebrated illustrated work on Rome was by the French literary figure Francis Alphonse Wey, „Rome, Descriptions et Souvenirs", which was published in 1872 with xylographic illustrations in a large format. The xylographs were placed at the disposal of publishers in many countries. One of the national editions was by a Danish traveller to Rome, Vilhelm Bergsøe and was published in 1877 under the title „Rome under Pius the Ninth". The text was Bergsøe's own, and like much other North European literature on Rome it contained an undertone of hostility to the papacy not to be found in the Roman Catholic Wey, who described both the religious life and the papal court in very respectful tones. Bergsøe's work helped to keep the romantic fascination with Rome alive in Denmark right up to our own time. Thus the art historian Christian Elling tells us in his childhood reminiscences of the impression which the work and its pictures made on him. Such books were the ones to be found in the educated citizen's home. Sometimes they were purely decorative, admittedly – coffee table books – but in other homes they were read, leafed through and brought out when travel letters from family and friends circulated for reading aloud in a closed circle.

Then there were the artists. The first half of the century was the golden age. Bertel Thorvaldsen became a fixture in Rome, where he became the Scandinavian colony's Nestor. Contemporaries idolised him, called him the master of classicism, the equal of the Greeks and whatever other superlatives they could hit upon. He made Rome a familiar concept. A long line of painters did the same: C.W. Eckersberg, Constantin Hansen, Jørgen Roed, Christen Købke, Albert Kühler, Wilhelm Marstrand, Carl Bloch and others. Wayside inns and rural scenes, street scenes and portraits; there was a passion for the Roman profile, especially of the female. Dietrichson accompanied Henrik Ibsen – a traveller to Rome in 1864-68 – on a tour in the heat of summer away from the towns and up into the cool mountains around Lake Albani where they took lodgings with a vinegrower. Here they enjoyed life in the rustic surroundings, endured the fleas at night, and admired the three lovely daughters of the house, especially the youngest, Mariette, sweet sixteen, resembling in figure and features an ancient caryatid from Rome's Pantheon. „She made half-simpletons of us all."

Authors made their considerable contribution as well. H.C. Andersen, the aforementioned M.A. Goldschmidt and Vilhelm Topsøe, Ludvig Bødtcher, who spent a full eleven years in Rome and who by founding a library for the little colony created the embryo of a Scandinavian society. Later on in the century came the hangover at last. Holger Drachmann could not stomach the idolatry: he introduced a gust of fresh air in opposition to the conventional tourist enthusiasm when he wrote home in 1876 describing Italy as a deflowered beauty. „I am so tired, so utterly tired of all these ruins," he sighed. *Il dolce far niente* also irritated him: „This flat idleness, this lecherous prowling around the streets and yawning over the coffee, the intellectual exhaustion of trailing around galleries, the continuous pumping of the wells of the past, these pale, slim or fat black-eyed women who look at my three ells (six feet) as if they want to eat up all three ells of meat in one night, these unspeakably formed men, whose conversation is worse and stupider than a harlot's."

The sights of Rome, both the long familiar and the new sensations, generated a tourism that was formed into a system. John Murray's „Red Book" showed the way with a classification of the sights, and the German Karl Baedeker did the same; while in 1868 another Briton, Thomas Cook, set about marketing the standardised tour with the sights threaded on a string and all the practical factors – travel route, hotels, tickets – arranged from home. Europe's highest-spending citizens in the 19th century were the English. English tourists swarmed everywhere, including Rome. J.C. and Carl came across them during their trip in April and May 1862.

Carl describes his encounter with Rome in a letter home to his mother. First the climate and the flora. „We live here in continuous sunshine ... In Florence we already bought tea roses and put them in little bouquets in our buttonholes, and here in Rome we have flowers in all the vases." He has found out that the roses are already in bloom in January. Then come the sights: „The little cloister in the Lateran Church. It is just as Rørby has painted it in the middle gallery," he explains to his mother, „but Rørby has made it somewhat cold; when we went in, the sun was shining warmly in the confined space, and the roses with which the whole garden is filled were in full bloom, fig trees and other southern plants looked down upon the roses, and the ground was covered with the most luxuriant grass. The loveliest cloister in the world. We were completely alone there, and I doubt that we would have torn ourselves away from this little world had not a group of English people with their guides taken possession of it."

On the Wednesday afternoon they decided to go to the Sistine Chapel and hear afternoon mass at half past four, „but the rush of English people is so prodigious that one has to get there as early as two o'clock and stand waiting in line on the steps. We stood there huddled together for two hours, and when it opened, we all dashed up the steps. The soldiers now wanted to hold us back a little, but then a tremendous wrestling match broke out between the English people and the soldiers, and so the latter gave way and let the people pass unhindered. It was a race up the stairs, three long steps at every bound. I was standing among those at the front and flew up as fast as I could with an Englishman just ahead of me. But suddenly – alas – he stumbles and falls, and I, at top speed and literally on his heels, cannot avoid him but get one leg on either side of him and finally land on his back. There I sat. The others rushed past, however, and when he began to move I had to get off and crawl away over him. I said very politely, 'I beg your pardon,' but he did not seem to want to take it in a friendly spirit. I hold this among my most precious memories."

Another of Carl's enjoyable tourist memories from the trip was the visit to Frascati and „the brilliant exhibition" – as he expresses it – which his father gave on a donkey in the square. The son's interest in art had free scope here in Italy. He analyses for his mother an early work from Raphael's youth in the Palazzo Borghese collection. She is familiar with it from one of the prints at Carlsberg: „You found the principal figure on the left the least attractive, and he is certainly the least beautiful, but he is a quite excellent mainstay and is natural in the highest degree, as are his two young helpers. The position of the

Christ figure, especially of the legs, is not beautiful either, but it is natural." It is the next generation's approach to art which is budding here.

For J.C. his stay was an initiation. His enthusiasm for Rome's enormous wealth of historical relics, of art, of natural beauty and street scenes, in which he soaked himself from morning till night, he later sought to pass on to Johanne Luise Heiberg in conjunction with her visit accompanied by her daughters in 1874-75, for which he paid. It was the finest gift he could offer her. But to his great disappointment the lady did not feel happy in the city, with its fever, its dirt and its fleas, not to mention the dull Scandinavians sitting in their club swilling wine.

A couple of letters from the end of 1874 contain Jacobsen's confession of his passion for Rome. The city always retains its hold on him. Some irresistible force drives him to seek and seek for deeper understanding. To be in the city is to become a historian, an archaeologist, an art-lover. And the dirt-ridden streets and narrow alleys „belong once and for all to the old Rome which I love". The absence of modern comforts is something one must learn to accept „with Roman patience" in accordance with the motto that in what one loves, one forgives much. The landscape from Monte Mario, the view from Monte Pincio, the sunset from the ruins of the imperial palaces, the Forum and the Colosseum by moonlight – all is in harmony with the one melody: „It is good to be here".

Later on in the year the despondent Mrs Heiberg livened up a little with the arrival of Bjørnstjerne Bjørnson in the colony, and Jacobsen at once continued his correspondence course with new instructions: „Exchange the plasticity in the marble with the living plasticity in the 'people's' quarters on the Piazza Montenara and the surrounding neighbourhood frequented by the country people, or go to a church festival in Albano or Arrizia and experience the colourful, wonderful spectacle in the trattorie and in the streets." He reveals his own secret at the end:

„The Palatine Hill. When you press forward over the ruins of the imperial palaces, overgrown with bushes and weeds, right out to the edge where the Circus Maximus once was. From some of the points jutting out there between the bushes you have a splendid view over the Tiber valley to the heights on the other side and to St. Peter's, the dome of which particularly is revealed in its most beautiful guise when the sun is about to go down behind it."

To walk around Rome and ponder the fate of the city was no bad thing either. The colossal downfall from the days of empire was proclaimed by the monuments that survived it, a downfall the seed of which was sown, in his opinion, during the republic after the fall of Carthage; it was the necessary consequence of excessive power and wealth. „How much can our own age, indeed all ages, learn from the history of Rome," he concluded his apologia.

Now, twentyfive years later, Jacobsen was on a pilgrimage to Rome. He wanted to see his old love again before he died. His wife was at his side, just as the patricians of old had had themselves depicted in their mausoleums. Sophie Steenstrup and Agnes Berthelsen were invited along as lady's companions.

The journey went excellently, and everyone was stimulated by it. They arrived in Rome on 4 March and were received by Carl and Ottilia. There was much pleasure at the reunion. They celebrated Thorvaldsen's „Roman" birthday together on 8 March. They had always honoured it, and on 13 March the younger Jacobsens went on to Athens in order to meet their travelling companions of archaeologists and artists.

The weather in Rome was disappointingly cold. It rained and blew without cease, and at one point Jacobsen was considering going further south to Naples and Sorrento. However, his inbuilt reluctance to alter a programme once fixed won the day. They remained in the city and invited fellow-Danes to dinner at the Hotel Quirinale, where they were staying, one of these being an old acquaintance from their visit in 1862, Professor Niels Ravnkilde, who lived in Rome and was a prominent and helpful member of the Danish colony.

Early one morning a fortnight later Jacobsen awoke feeling so unwell that he felt he needed assistance. With his Baedeker in hand he left the hotel at 5 o'clock and went looking for a doctor. He found one, who by chance turned out to be the Danish consul's physician.

The diagnosis was a prostate, which required an operation. A long and painful period of illness followed, accompanied by fever. From his sickbed Jacobsen dictated a letter to Heinrich Hansen concerning the fountain at Frederiksborg. It was 10 April, the first day of Easter. He mentioned his illness only in passing: „I am unwell and have to stay in bed, although the illness is not dangerous." But his condition fluctuated back and forth, and towards the end of the month those around him became worried. Letters and telegrams were sent to Athens, but Carl and Ottilia were not in the city. They were away on an excursion with their friends.

Jacobsen's strength began to fail. From his bed he wrote in a trembling hand a pencilled note to Meldahl, who was in North Italy. He thanked his friend for a letter he had received and expressed a wish and a prayer to the architect that he should avoid over-exertion „in order to be able to continue your valuable work as far as possible".

When the young Jacobsens returned to Athens and discovered the news of the father's worsened condition they set off without further ado and travelled day and night to reach the deathbed, where they found the old man lying in a delirium, declining French verbs. He awoke from his coma and recognised them; they were able to say farewell to one another.

J.C. Jacobsen died at midday. It was Saturday, 30 April 1887.

He had arranged his affairs in time and put everything into order for the future, but not his own interment. Assistens churchyard, where his parents lay, had appealed to him, and so had Vestre churchyard directly opposite Carlsberg. Aunt Bertha, alias Agnes Berthelsen, who over the years had become the Brewer's private secretary, with whom he corresponded and to whom he gave instructions while on his travels, believed that „our beloved old darling" would be pleased to rest with Carl and Ottilia and their children. She wrote Carl to this effect during Jacobsen's illness. Carl took over the arrangements for the funeral and wanted the reconciliation between father and son to be made manifest in the ceremonial and the entombment.

The family arranged a service at the Protestant churchyard in Rome. According to Carl's almanac this was held on Tuesday, 3 May. Then came the journey home to Denmark. The coffin arrived at Copenhagen station on Thursday 19 May, and brewery workers from

Old Carlsberg bore it to the hearse, which carried it to Holmens Church chapel; then on the Saturday the coffin was taken on to the residence at Valby, where it was placed in Pompeii and decorated with silver wreaths and flowers. A ceremony was arranged for staff and brewery workers. The actual interment by Mother Church followed on Monday 23 May. The coffin, with Carl Jacobsen and his seven year-old son Alf walking behind, was taken in solemn procession from Pompeii via New Carlsberg Way-Vesterfælledvej-Vesterbrogade-Farimagsgade and Studiestræde to the Cathedral, where Pastor Ewaldsen presided over the church ceremony. The King was present, as were all the illustrious figures in Denmark's academic and art worlds. Among the wreaths covering the coffin was one in silver from Danish North Schleswigers.

After the graveside ceremony the coffin was placed in one of the chapels of the Cathedral, where it remained until Carl's church in Valby, the Church of Jesus, was ready. In 1891 it was conveyed there and placed in the family chapel in the crypt of the church.

It had been a grand affair. „The coffins of Goethe and Schiller in Fürstengeist in Weimar were poor by comparison with the one for this mighty, wealthy brewer," Emil Chr. Hansen confided to his diary concerning the funeral service. As we know, pomp and circumstance were not his cup of tea. As to the summing up, however, he was not in any doubt. „His merit, and it is a great one, is that he did not use his money for luxury and high living but applied it to the furtherance of the interests of mind and spirit." These were words of honour in Hansen's mouth. Fate – and Carl Jacobsen – willed in fact that Emil Chr. Hansen was decidedly not cheated when he was buried in 1909 in Vestre churchyard. He was given a magnificent sarcophagus placed in a rotunda with a view over Carlsberg.

How did J.C. himself view the totality of his work? Two years before he died, he looked back on it in a letter to Johanne Luise Heiberg, who had flatteringly called him a genius. That was a description he definitely disavowed. „The development came of itself, and I have for a long time wished and hoped that it would now cease, because my taste has never been for the big but only for the complete, for which I have had an innate instinct." The urge for the complete was reinforced by another of his instincts: joy in the work itself, „which for me has been and still is the most cherished of pleasures. This turn of mind, which has been the source of my life's happiness and which has created Carlsberg, I have secretly expressed in my motto Work and Frugality." It stood in golden letters to be read under his monogram on the lighthouse at the main entrance to Old Carlsberg. „But," he concluded, „how many will understand and believe that a brewer with a turnover of several millions annually has become 'big' without wanting it – indeed against his will! Frugality is gladly attributed to scientists and to devotees of the arts, because as a rule their selfless dedication to the service of mind and spirit is so conspicuous that no one can be blind to it; but a frugal millionaire! – that is beyond the understanding of the multitude."

Laura's widowhood at Old Carlsberg was a long one: it lasted 24 years. She lived on to see her son Carl donate his brewery to the Carlsberg Foundation in 1902/03 simultaneously with the establishment of the New Carlsberg Foundation. He called it „a reconciliation offering to eradicate every trace of an ancient disharmony between a father and his son". One of the objects of the New Carlsberg Foundation was to secure, in concert with government and municipality, the Glyptothèque inaugurated in 1897, where Carl's objets d'art were housed. This great collection, of world reputation, had already been made over to the public in 1888 through a deed of gift in his own and Ottilia's names. The collection was augmented in 1899 by a new donation through which a large extension building was added to the Glyptothèque.

Ottilia died in the same year that the New Carlsberg Foundation was established, and Laura lived long enough to experience her son's brief and unhappy second marriage to the 40 years younger Lilli von Kohl. It was dissolved in 1908. And at last, in 1911, Laura Jacobsen died at the age of 91 years. She was laid to rest in the family chapel alongside her husband. Her son followed her only three years later.

Postscript

The story is over. All that remains is to list assets and liabilities.

My book is based on a large body of sources, most of them unpublished and consisting mainly of the Jacobsen family papers in the archives of the Carlsberg Foundation. The bulk of this collection was assembled by Vagn Jacobsen, Carl's son and also a brewer, but it has been supplemented over the years by a long succession of minor collections. The actual family archives, where the Steenstrup papers also rest, are somewhat disordered and are currently in course of being arranged more systematically. When this process has been completed it will be sufficient to make reference merely to the letter-writer and the date, and this is what I have done below.

In addition there are numerous private archives in the Danish Record Office and the Royal Library, some of which contain a good deal of Jacobseniana, e.g. the archives of Anthon Meldahl and Johanne Luise Heiberg. Emil Chr. Hansen's archives too are worth while studying. They are housed partly at the Carlsberg Foundation and partly in the Royal Library. As far as these particular sources are concerned, see my article in *Fund og Forskning* (Discovery and Research), Vol. XXVII.

The archives of institutions, including the Carlsberg Laboratory and the Museum of National History at Frederiksborg, contain a number of letters and other documents from the hand of J.C. Jacobsen. The business records, which are fundamental to the history of the firm, are to be found in the main archives at Carlsberg A/S. The Carlsberg Research Centre contains a modern library which is rich in brewery history. Finally, the Carlsberg Museum, of which the oldest brewery plant forms a part, is indispensable as regards interiors, effects and objects.

Most of the literature on J.C. Jacobsen is fixated on anniversaries, and the true biographies are few in number. The most detailed is the commemorative volume of 1911 by the industrial historian Camillus Nyrup, a diligent piece of work containing much historical detail including the personal element. In the following year the orientalist Johannes Østrup published his short biography of Jacobsen, which is coloured by his strong national sentiment. The historian Johannes Steenstrup's book of 1921 dealing with the relationship between father and son was written from letters and recollections by a close friend of the family, and it bears the marks of this. Arnold Fraenkel's commemorative work of 1897 on Old Carlsberg also contains a biography. Fraenkel was inspector at the Alliance bottling firm from 1877 to 1882, and he founded the Aktiv bottling factory for Carl Jacobsen in 1883. His knowledge of the techno-industrial complex is great. In the absence of any modern presentation of the brewery's history, Fraenkel's book is still a major work, but its weight of 4.5 kg makes it one of the „heavy brigade" in the ranks of business literature, which has found few readers because of its unwieldiness. Fraenkel's is the least successful portrait of Jacobsen, being coloured by his own socio-political ideas. The same author gives a more rounded picture in his biography of 1937 in the Danish Biographical Dictionary, where Jacobsen is presented as a transitional figure straddling the divide between the guild era and the age of industrialism. In the new edition (1983) of the same Dictionary, the archivist Birgit Nüchel Thomsen has given her view of Jacobsen, inspired by the model of an entrepreneur presented by the economist and sociologist Joseph A. Schumpeter. In this article and in her great edition of Philip W. Heymann's papers from Tuborg she presents new findings concerning J.C. and Carl's divergent business principles in the 1880s. Among the modern works are the small popular account of Jacobsen's life and works by the author and historian Palle Lauring, commissioned by the Carlsberg Foundation and published on the 150th anniversary of the Brewer's birth.

Beyond the circle of historians there have been several writers who have felt attracted by the figure of Jacobsen and have approached him from various angles. The basic work on the architecture is by the German art historian Dorothea Zanker von Meyer, who published *Die Bauten von J.C. und Carl Jacobsen* (The Buildings of J.C. and Carl Jacobsen) in 1982. The literary scholar J. Bonde Jensen attempted an analysis in 1976 of the contributions of J.C. and Carl to science and art, especially building art, as a framework in which to discuss the social significance of the aesthetic dimension. The topic is interesting, but the study founders on the reefs of error and misinterpretation. More entertaining is the author Ole Wivel's bitter-sweet essay *Guder i foraarslys* (Gods in the Spring Light) of 1983, in which the epoch between the Golden Age and Modernism – termed the Age of the Lion – is analysed by reference to the two chief figures who as patrons stood behind the painting of history and led the conquest of the Copenhagen parks by the Greek gods and fauns. The list of selected literature below includes inter alia the works to which reference is made in the notes under the title's list number, possibly followed by the page number.

Finally, my sincere thanks are due for the support and goodwill shown to me in many quarters. These thanks are addressed to the archives, museums and libraries mentioned, and also to Mrs Grethe Stig Iuul for the loan of the correspondence between Nanna Rygaard and Jens Brask, and to the late Flemming Vøgg, engineer by profession, great-grandson of brewer J.C. Jacobsen, and faithful guardian of the family tradition. I am especially indebted to the Carlsberg Foundation and its secretariat and bursar's office, which have helped me in practical matters and thereby facilitated the progress of my work.

Literature

1. Bligaard, Mette, Frederiksborg Slot. Kongeborg og Museum (Herning 1987)

2. Colding, Torben Holck, „Carl Jacobsen", Dansk Biografisk Leksikon, 1983

3. Fode, Henrik, „Liberalisme og frihandel 1814-1914", Dansk Toldhistorie III (Copenhagen 1989)

4. Fraenkel, A., Gamle Carlsberg 1847-97 (Copenhagen 1897)

5. Fraenkel, A., „J.C. Jacobsen", Dansk Biografisk Leksikon, 1937

6. Glamann, Kristof, Bryggeriets historie i Danmark indtil slutningen af det 19. århundrede (Copenhagen 1962)

7. Glamann, Kristof, Carlsbergfondet (Copenhagen 1976)

8. Glamann, Kristof, „The Scientific Brewer. Founders and Successors during the Rise of the Modern Brewing Industry", Enterprise and History. Essays in honour of Charles Wilson. Ed. by D.C. Coleman and Peter Mathias. (Cambridge 1984)

9. Glamann, Kristof, „Videnskabsmanden og Bryggeren. Emil Chr. Hansen og J.C. Jacobsen", Fund og Forskning XXVII (Copenhagen 1984-85)

10. Holmen, Grete, „Laura Jacobsen og Ottilia Jacobsen", Frederiksberg gennem Tiderne vol. XVI (Copenhagen 1985)

11. Hude, Elisabeth, „Johanne Luise Heiberg og J.C. Jacobsen", Studier fra Sprog- og Oldtidsforskning vol. 74 (Copenhagen 1964)

12. Hyldtoft, Ole, Københavns Industrialisering 1840-1914 (Copenhagen 1984)

13. Jacobsen, J.C. og Rothe, Tyge, Beskrivelse af Væxthusene i Universitetets Botaniske Have i Kjøbenhavn med Oplysninger om Havens Anlæg og Ordning i 1871-74 (Copenhagen 1879)

14. Jacobsen, J.C., „Bryggeriindustriens Fremskridt i de sidste 50 år", Den tekniske Forenings Tidsskrift (1884)

15. Jacobsen, J.C., Autobiographi in Levnedsbeskrivelse af de ved Københavns Universitets 400-års FEST promoverede Doktorer (Copenhagen 1879)

16. Jarnhus, K.L., „Gamle Kongens Bryghus 1771-1960", Brygmesteren No. 12 (Copenhagen 1960)

17. Jensen, Jørgen Bonde, Carlsberg. Et Københavnsk drømmebillede (Copenhagen 1976)

18. Kristensen, Johs. E. Tang, Jyllandsrejsen. Dagbogsoptegnelser af Sophus Møller om Laura Jacobsens, Carls og Sophus' rejse til Jylland 1855 (Vendsyssel Historiske Museum 1986)

19. Lauring, Palle, J.C. Jacobsen, Hans liv og gerning (Copenhagen 1961)

20. Lettres Échangées entre J.C. Jacobsen et Louis Pasteur au cours des années 1878-82 Publiées par La Fondation Carlsberg propriétaire des Brasseries Carlsberg (Copenhague 1964)

21. Lopdrup, Hanne, De sammensvorne ...et maleri af Otto Bache (Det nationalhistoriske Museum 1989)

22. Madsen, Hans Helge, Meldahls Rædselsprogram (Copenhagen 1983)

23. Mathias, Peter, The Brewing Industry in England 1700-1830 (Cambridge 1959)

24. Nielsen, Rolf et.al., Gamle Carlsberg 1847-97. Fra Håndværk til Stordrift. Udg. af Carlsberg Bryggerierne (Copenhagen 1984) (stencil)

25. Nordhagen, Per Jonas, Henrik Ibsen i Rom 1864-1868 (Oslo 1981)

26. Nyrop, C., J.C. Jacobsen 1811-1911. Et Mindeskrift (Copenhagen 1911)

27. Nyrop, C. og Jacobsen, Carl, Ny Carlsberg. Et Jubilæumsskrift (København 1896). Included: Jacobsen, Carl, „Carlsberg. Erindringer om J.C. Jacobsens Virksomhed som Brygger".

28. Nørregaard, Georg, „Københavns Vandforsyning i ældre Tid", Københavns Vandforsynings Historie (Copenhagen 1959)

29. Pedersen, Jesper, Træk af udviklingen på Carlsberg Bryggerierne og J.G.A. Eickhoffs Maskinfabrik og Jernstøberi 1851-1914 specielt med henblik på ufaglærte arbejdere (unprinted ext.essay from The University of Copenhagen 1985)

30. Rahbek, Just (ed.), Breve fra og til Johanne Luise Heiberg II vol.1867-1890 (Copenhagen 1955)

31. Rerup, Lorenz, „Hvordan fandt Brygger Jacobsen frem til A.D. Jørgensen?" Sønderjyske Årbøger 1983

32. Ritzau, Tue og Ascani, Karen (ed.), Rom er et fortryllet Bur. Den gyldne epoke for skandinaviske Kunstnere i Rom (Copenhagen 1982)

33. Scharling, E.A., „Om Ølbrygning i Baiern", Industriforeningens Kvartalsberetning (Copenhagen 1848)

34. Schepelern, H.C., og Eller, Povl, Omkring Frederiksborg Slots Brand, 17. December 1859 (Hillerød 1964)

35. Schmidt, Ingeborg, Blade af Carlsbergs Historie (Copenhagen 1956)

36. Sestoft, Jørgen, Arbejdets Bygninger in Danmarks Arkitektur (Copenhagen 1979)

37. Sibbern, Fr. Chr., „Nogle Betragtninger over Stat og Kirke", Indbydelsesskrift til Kjøbenhavns Universitets Fest i Anledning af Hans Majestæt Kongens Fødselsdag den 6te October 1849 (Copenhagen 1849)

38. Steenstrup, Johannes, Carl Jacobsens Liv og Gerning, udg. af Ny Carlsberg Fondet (Copenhagen 1922)

39. Steenstrup, Johannes, Carl Jacobsen og hans fader (Copenhagen 1921)

40. Stemann, Helga, F. Meldahl og hans venner I-VI (Copenhagen 1926-32)

41. Strømstad, Poul, J.C. Jacobsens Bryggergård i Brolæggerstræde (Copenhagen 1977)

42. Thomsen, Birgit Nüchel, Industrielle foretagere på Tuborg 1873-1885. Kilder og Studier (Copenhagen 1980)

43. Thomsen, Birgit Nüchel, „J.C. Jacobsen", Dansk Biografisk Leksikon 1983

44. Thomsen, Birgit Nüchel, Tuborg 1873 – 13. Maj – 1973. Tuborg og bryggeriindustrien under skiftende markedsvilkår 1873-1973 (Tuborgs Bryggerier A/S 1973)

45. Troels-Lund, Troels, Et Liv (Copenhagen 1924)

46. Vogelius, August, „Bryggeriet Carlsberg og den bayerske ølbrygningsmetode", Industriforeningens Kvartalsberetning (Copenhagen 1854)

47. Wamberg, Bodil, Johanne Luise Heiberg (Copenhagen 1987)

48. Wivel, Ole, Guder i forårslys, (Copenhagen 1983)

49. Worsøe, Hans H. og Colding, Torben Holck, Familien Jacobsen (Copenhagen 1985)

50. Worsøe, Hans H., „På sporet af det første bayerskølbryggeri i Danmark: Thomas Charles Grut og hans virksomhed i Odense 1834-1842", Brygmesteren No. 3 (Copenhagen 1975)

51. Zanker-v. Mayer, Dorothea, „Die Bauten von J.C. und Carl Jacobsen zur Bautätigkeit einer industriellen Familie in Dänemark" in Kunstwissenschaftliche Studien vol. 52 (Berlin 1982)

52. Østrup, I., Brygger, Kaptajn J.C. Jacobsen in Mennesker vol. VIII (Copenhagen 1912)

List of illustrations

CM   = Carlsberg Museum
CF   = Carlsbergfondets arkiv (Carlsberg Foundation archives)
UB   = Universitetsbiblioteket, avissamlingen (University library, newspaper archives)
KB   = Det Kongelige Bibliotek (The Royal Library)
FRB   = Det nationalhistoriske Museum på Frederiksborg (The Museum of National History, Frederiksborg)
Ill.T.   = Illustreret Tidende (Illustrated News)
CL   = Carlsberg Laboratorium (Carlsberg Laboratory)
G   = Glyptoteket (Glyptothèque)
SMK   = Statens Museum for Kunst (National Museum of Art)

INDEX